BEING GEORGE

The Indispensable Man,

WRITERS
David Pietrusza, Chris Stewart, David Harsanyi, James D. Best

CONTRIBUTORS & RESEARCHERS
Sharon Ambrose, Andrew Allison, Hannah Beck, Allison Coyle,
Christine Dietzel, Peter Lillback, Mary M. Parker, Jay Parry, Ashley Reaves,
Matthew Scafidi, Benjamin Weingarten, Martha Weeks, Angela Wiltz

WRITTEN & EDITED BY

GLENN BECK

& KEVIN BALFE

WASHINGTON

as You've Never Seen Him

Threshold Editions

Mercury Radio Arts

New York London Toronto Sydney New Delhi

Threshold Editions / Mercury Radio Arts

A Division of Simon & Schuster, Inc.
1230 Avenue of the Americas
New York, NY 10020

First Threshold Editions / Mercury Radio Arts paperback edition July 2012

THRESHOLD EDITIONS and colophon are trademarks of Simon & Schuster, Inc.

GLENN BECK is a trademark of Mercury Radio Arts, Inc.

For information about special discounts for bulk purchases,
please contact Simon & Schuster Special Sales at 1-866-506-1949
or business@simonandschuster.com.

The Simon & Schuster Speakers Bureau can bring authors to your live event.
For more information or to book an event, contact the Simon & Schuster
Speakers Bureau at 866-248-3049 or visit our website at www.simonspeakers.com.

Designed by Ruth Lee-Mui

Manufactured in the United States of America

10 9 8 7 6 5 4 3 2 1

ISBN 978-1-4516-5926-9
ISBN 978-1-4516-5927-6 (pbk)
ISBN 978-1-4516-5931-3 (ebook)

Dedication

To my son, Raphe, whom I fear we are leaving with an overwhelming amount of work to do to make things right. I hope you always remember that one man can make a difference. That *you* can make a difference.

George Washington struggled to become a better man every single day of his life. But, through those struggles, he ultimately gave mankind its first real taste of freedom since the Garden of Eden. Now it's up to you and your generation to ensure that we don't lose it. But you have one great advantage over me: you can start now. It wasn't until after you were born that I found the man who I really want to be and finally got down to work.

Raphe, there will be many struggles ahead; many years of sacrifice and hard work. The only advice I can offer is that if you spend your life in pursuit of becoming the man you read about in this book, you will never go wrong.

Contents

About the Writing of This Book

It would be nice if Twitter and Facebook had been around during the Revolutionary War. We'd have minute-by-minute accounts of every battle and historic decision that Washington ever made along with photos of the Delaware crossing, the trenches outside Yorktown, and the misery at Valley Forge. Instead, we have to rely on history books to tell us what really happened and our own minds to visualize how things really looked.

In crafting these chapters we tried our best to rely on published historical accounts and other reference material, taking dramatic license when necessary, so long as it did not change any of the major facts. Generally speaking, we simply added plausible details that have been lost to history in an effort to turn extraordinary events into readable stories.

There are, of course, disagreements among reasonable people over many of the events of this era. Like a two-century-long game of telephone tag, rumors become fact and facts become rumor. Whenever we encountered one of these disputed stories we attempted to make note of it so that you can do your own homework and make your own determination.

I also want to offer special thanks to the experts who helped with research and accuracy, including Mary V. Thompson, Research Historian at Mount Vernon. And I am grateful to the National Center for Constitutional Studies (NCCS) for its permission to use portions of *The Real George Washington* in the creation of this book.

Finally, it should go without saying that any errors or omissions outside of dramatic license are mine alone.

Author's Note

My name is Glenn Beck, and I am George Washington.

I am the leader of men. I am fearless. I am the person others will aspire to be for generations. I am the indispensable man.

I am also . . . nothing special. I am average. I am flawed. I am fallible. I am emotional. I am awkward. And I am way too fond of ice cream.

Right now, in a café that a corporation has designed specifically to look independent of corporate influence, a blogger is typing furiously. He or she is sipping briskly from an eight-ounce can of lightly carbonated energy drink in an effort to stay awake for just a few more minutes to complete work on their newly discovered but soon-to-be mega-controversy-of-the-day.

Glenn Beck thinks he's George Washington! He has a Washington complex! He's actually named his book "Being George Washington." His ego is out of control! He must be threatening to start a revolution? I knew the Tea Party was dangerous!

The news of my self-elevation to national fatherhood will likely spread from blog to blog, then to news sources and pundits, all of whom will be more than happy to spread the news that Glenn Beck's messianic complex can no longer be contained.

None of them, of course, will take the time to realize the irony of the situation: they are literally judging a book by its cover.

So, what's the truth?

Simple, *I do* believe I am George Washington.

But I believe that you are, too.

I don't believe this because I have an extraordinarily high opinion of myself. I believe it because I have a real understanding of who George Washington was.

Contrary to popular belief, George Washington was not born as a 555-foot, 5-inch monument. He was never a painting or a statue or a city. He was just a man, albeit one who happened to see his principles as immovable objects rather than minor inconveniences.

That's what is truly inspiring about George Washington: He was human, a capeless superhero. He faced many of the same challenges in life that we all face. Yes, he was given the responsibility to deal with historic challenges on a scope that is difficult for us to imagine today, but the reason he was given enormous responsibilities is that people admired how he handled the small ones. He lived his life in a way that impressed and inspired others, so when the most trying times arrived, they all looked to him. Over and over again, he was willing to sacrifice his own happiness for the good of others.

George Washington wound up at the top of every insurmountable mountain he came to because he never acknowledged that there was an insurmountable mountain in front of him. Sure, he knew the enormity of what he was facing, but he saw each decision as just another step and he used his principles and faith (yes, sorry, critics: the man clearly believed that God's hand was guiding America) to constantly maintain sure footing.

The Washington Monument tells this story, albeit unintentionally, as it towers above Washington, D.C. From a distance, it is a perfect structure. It owns the skyline. It is bigger than life itself in a city filled with people who think *they're* bigger than life itself. But as you walk up to the structure and view it up close—you can't help but notice all of its imperfections.

In 1854, six years into its construction, work on the project ground to a halt. There was simply no more money left for the monument. (Yes, amazing as it seems, the government used to actually stop projects when they couldn't fund them.) When construction began again, the quarry that provided the stone for the first half could no longer be used because it had been exhausted building bunkers for the war.

Today, when you stand close to the monument you will notice that it is two-toned. The marble, granite and stone used for the lower half is clearly a lighter shade than those used on top. It is the monument that life and war got in the way of. But those imperfections serve as a perfect tribute to Washington. He *was* that monument. From the distance of hundreds of years, he appears superhuman, able to soar to heights that you and I cannot. In reality, however, his life was a series of challenges, handled with honor, firmness, and faith, brick by brick.

Many times he succeeded in facing those challenges, but sometimes he did not. Slavery is one frequently cited example. Yes, it's true: George Washington owned slaves. You can make all kinds of excuses for it (it was the norm of the time, he strongly advocated for the practice to be abolished, he treated his slaves well, he freed them upon his wife's death, etc.), but you cannot ignore it. It is a flaw, an imperfection, a part of his life that, were he around today, I am sure he would regret. But it's also proof that this man really was *just a man*.

Throughout the coming pages, we will not fall into the trap of exclusively gazing at the final monument from a distance. Instead we will get up close and examine some of the most important stones—how they were laid into place, and what quarry they came from. And, most important, we will use these events to help sketch a blueprint of how to inspire the *next* George Washington, and millions more like him.

This book's title will serve as our guide through that journey in two different ways. First, you will experience some of Washington's major exploits in a way that perhaps you never have before. Too often, the stories of our founding are told in a way that makes you feel like you are reading boring anecdotes about old men in powdered wigs. But, for those of us who aren't academics, that kind of historical accounting simply doesn't work.

I don't want you to just read about Valley Forge or Yorktown, I want you to *live* it. I don't want you to just read about George Washington, I want you to *know* him. I want you to *be him*.

Second, this book will attempt to show that *all of us can be the next George Washington*. We all have a role to play. No one, not Washington, Lincoln, or anyone else could do it alone. America will only change for the better when more of us believe this to be true instead of simply dismissing it as meaningless self-help pseudo-psychology.

George Washington was just a guy. Before that, he was, like many of us, a young man who navigated personal relationships like an awkward teenager in an after-school special. He asked a young woman named Betsey Fauntleroy to marry him. She said no. He asked again. She said no again. He wrote poems to her. He became the old-timey version of John Cusack standing outside of the bedroom window of the girl he loved holding a boom box playing Peter Gabriel over his head—except, in this movie, there was no happy ending. Betsey's parents saw the man who would eventually be the father of the greatest country to ever grace the earth as too low-class for their daughter.

While he was president, Washington's mother accused him of abandoning her. She claimed she was starving while he was spending tons of money on ice cream, which was one of his vices. She claimed he neglected her and tried to get a law passed mandating that presidents not neglect their mothers.

Imagine how that would play on cable news today?

None of the accusations of neglect were true (although Washington did spend the equivalent of $5,000 in today's money on ice cream during the hot summer of 1790), but Washington dealt with the same crushing and ridiculous family drama that everyone does at one time or another.

Yet the way most people remember him flies in the face of the lessons we should learn from his life.

We remember a normal-sized man with a giant monument in his honor. We remember a man who was too poor to impress the parents of the girl he loved because he didn't have much money by putting his face on our currency. We remember a man known for his honesty with a fabricated story about a cherry tree.

That must stop. We must instead remember that while Washington was a fearless leader who truly was indispensable, he was also average, emotional, awkward, and way too fond of ice cream.

For America to achieve the greatness that George Washington achieved, we first have to remember that it is achievable. We have to remember that any difficult journey always begins with a first small step. We have to look up at the insurmountable mountain and pretend that it doesn't exist. You won't be George Washington next week or next year, and you may, in fact, not ever cross the finish line . . . and that's okay. The simple act of reaching for a standard that so many others will dismiss as unattainable is enough to make a real difference.

I can tell you unequivocally that being George Washington will be the hardest thing you ever attempt to do in your life. It will also be the most fulfilling and rewarding. Living a life of honor, integrity, and humility may not make you millions of dollars or result in your name being splashed across movie posters—but it will earn you something far more enduring: the lasting respect of those you care about most. And if that doesn't happen? Well, you can always eat ice cream.

Glenn Beck
New York City, 2011

Introduction

Had I Not Been Witness

Our rifles were leveled (at Washington), rifles which, but for him, knew not how to miss—'twas all in vain, a power mightier far than we shielded him from harm. He cannot die in battle. . . . Listen! The Great Spirit protects that man, and guides his destinies—he will become the chief of nations, and a people yet unborn will hail him as the founder of a mighty empire!

—UNNAMED INDIAN CHIEF
ON THE OHIO FRONTIER, FALL OF 1770

July 9, 1755
Banks of the Monongahela River
Ten miles upstream of Fort Duquesne
(Current location of Pittsburgh, Pennsylvania)

10:45 A.M.

The colonel's horse was terrified. And how could she not be. There was no way to have prepared her for the chaos, no way to inoculate her from the frantic movements and the smoke, the sound of gunfire spinning over her head or the hysterical cries of battle.

The air was thick with smoke, billows of gray and white that made it nearly impossible to see. The horse pinned her ears back; her eyes were wild, her shoulders quivering underneath the leather saddle.

How similar her reaction is to that of these men! the colonel thought.

He had no way of knowing, but it wasn't the chaos that terrified the mare, it was the smell. Human bowels spilt upon the ground, exposed muscle and bone. The mud bloodied beneath her hooves. These were the things that caused her to want to run.

She was a good horse, but she was not his, and so she was nervous beneath his unfamiliar hand. Still, he had no choice but to take her. His original horse, a hulking mare capable of carrying a large man such as he, had already been shot out from underneath him, her chest blown away in a hail of fire. Then his second horse had been taken, again shot out from underneath him. Two horses! In the same battle! It was the kind of thing he would ordinarily consider deeply. But not now. Any contemplation about why he was spared would have to wait.

He spurred his new mare, which he'd taken from a dead soldier, toward the tree line where there was a little cover. Even there, the acidic smoke was so thick that it burned his eyes, causing a trail of tears down his dirty cheeks. The shots from the trees kept coming like a constant crack of thunder that seemed to have no end.

His army was falling all around him now, their bodies scattering among the trees. The afternoon sun pressed against him like a blanket, humid and wet and oppressive with stench. Leaving the cover of the trees, he spurred the horse again, riding up and down the battlefield, trying desperately to rally his men. He shouted at them. Some who were running, he cut off, sending them back into the battle. Riding before them, he waved his gun, lifting it high into the air while crying out directions to reposition the troops. He pointed as he shouted, giving his commands. But it was too late. Far too late! It pained him as much as any ball to the chest, but there was no more denying what he was watching take place: an awful, demoralizing battlefield defeat.

1:15 P.M.

The colonel could see that General Edward Braddock's soldiers were in complete panic, their gold-trimmed red coats and oversized hats flashing all around him. These English men were trained for regimented battle on Europe's open fields: straight lines of soldiers set in a solid block formation, a measured march toward the enemy, fire, move aside, let the next man step forward to fire, reload, take position, aim and fire once again. It was a thing of beauty and precision.

European armies had been fighting like that for generations, the procedures ingrained as strongly as the urge to breathe. But, having been so conditioned, the British regulars were not prepared for what they were now facing. The enemy concealed behind deep cover. They had been pre-positioned on all sides. Fighting from the brush *without revealing themselves*! Half-naked Indians slithered like frightening ghosts among them. It was terrifying. *And uncivilized!* They would never survive against these kinds of tactics!

The colonel shook his head in shame. He should have pressed General Braddock more than he had. He should have been more urgent in his warnings about how they would fight. He could have made a difference.

But it was too late now. If they didn't hold their line, if only temporarily, even a respectable retreat would soon be impossible.

The colonel turned his horse toward the enemy. Sitting high atop the saddle, his legs much too long for the short stirrups, his officer's emblems in plain sight, he willingly drew the enemy's fire. White-hot balls zipped around him like horizontal rain, a sound that was so surreal it was impossible to forget. Other soldiers seemed to scatter from him, realizing the danger of standing near—but the colonel didn't hesitate. He called out encouragement, shouting instructions left and right. He felt a violent tug at his jacket but there was no time to stop; he kept yelling, directing, pleading.

After some time the battlefield was filled with smoke. The enemy was no longer visible and the British retreated to the cover of the tree line. From the edge of the battlefield, he watched a scene of carnage such as he had never seen before slowly unfold. He watched the army crumble. He watched his pride, his future, his entire world fall apart.

3:00 P.M.

Surrounded by thick trees and brush, the British soldiers and Virginia militia fired without aiming, then quickly reloaded and fired again. Occasionally they hit the enemy. More often they shot their own men. Some soldiers, in fact, were completely turned around now, *firing toward their own lines*! The terrifying cries of Indians cut through the trees, the sun catching an occasional reflection of the knives they were using to scalp the dead or dying, adding more terror to the scene.

The colonel moved his horse forward and she stomped atop a dead man's chest, forcing a final puff of air from his lungs, his neat British uniform stained with blood and dirt. The colonel tried to guide the horse, but the ground was so thick with bodies now that it was getting hard to ride without desecrating those who had fallen. It made his stomach churn.

Turning a final time, he held his horse in place and stared upon the scene. He felt her shiver through the saddle and he reached down to pat her neck. She moved left and right, ready to bolt, her hooves dancing in anticipation, begging her master to let her go.

He watched in shame as the British soldiers turned and ran, their red coats flashing against the green foliage, making them easy targets as they went. Many held their muskets pressed against their chest, but some didn't carry anything at all, having lost or abandoned their weapons in the pandemonium that had taken over the battlefield.

He frantically looked around, searching for General Braddock's bright officer uniform. He found the general lying in a heap atop the bloody ground. The colonel spurred his horse toward him and dismounted feebly. He was so weak that he almost fell, every movement coming with great pain, the result of the bloody flux and fever that had been racking him for weeks.

Seeing that the general was badly wounded, he called out to the closest man. "See that small cart there!" he shouted, bullets whizzing over both of their heads.

The regular ducked before he turned to look. "Aye, I see it, sir!"

"Go to it! Bring it to me! Now!" He shoved the enlisted man toward the cart. Turning to some fellow officers who had taken cover behind a stand of fallen trees, he shouted to them. "Come here and help me! Our commander lies wounded!"

The officers looked at him in desperation, and then ran forward, ducking behind the nearest tree. Under fierce fire, the officers loaded the general into the small cart, being as careful as they could. The colonel looked at their fallen leader, seeing the floor of the cart grow bloody underneath his uniform. The general tried to whisper orders and the colonel leaned toward him so that he could hear. "Yes, sir. I will see to it!" he promised before he motioned to the regulars who had taken the handrails of the cart. "Take it away!" he cried.

Returning to his horse, he moved out of the line of fire. A few brave men stood their ground, fighting to protect the others, but most of the British troops were quickly retreating. He watched in growing disgust. This was no last stand. No orderly retreat! They were running like sheep pursued by dogs. Their cowardice was inconceivable. He cursed them all in rage as he knew they were condemning their brave comrades to certain death, leaving them with no one to cover their own retreat.

These were the best soldiers the kingdom had to offer?

No, these were weak and frightened cowards! What he saw before him, the chaos and disrepair, the weakness and confusion in the midst of battle, this couldn't represent the greatest army in the world! This couldn't be the best of the royal regulars. This had to be . . . what? He did not know.

Before leaving the scene of the battle, the colonel and his fellow soldiers made a final effort to sort through all the fallen, gathering up the wounded to take back home. They moved the dead into horrible piles, throwing leaves and branches over them as best as they could. General Braddock still lay in the cart, sometimes speaking, sometimes unconscious, always in great pain. The colonel knew the general would not make it.

7:45 P.M.

Late that evening, when the sun was nearly set, what remained of the British and Virginian army collected the few provisions and munitions they had left. Turning south, they headed downstream on the Monongahela River, back in the direction from which they'd come, back toward Virginia, leaving the French and Indians behind.

The colonel now stared mournfully into the evening fire. A few officers sat beside him, but none of them spoke. All around him he heard the moans of the wounded, many of whom were doing nothing but the hard work it took to die. The army doctors, such as they were, and few as they were in number, were doing everything that they could to help the wounded, but it proved to be precious little, as the cries of the anguished made very clear.

That morning, nearly 1,500 British and Virginian soldiers had marched proudly toward the French position at Fort Duquesne, intent on planting the British flag there once again. But in the early afternoon, they walked straight into the jaws of disaster. They encountered the enemy just a few miles from the fort.

Some of his fellow officers now claimed the French and Indians numbered in the thousands. The colonel knew that was absurd. His army outnumbered the French and Indians by a great number, he was sure of it. That was what filled him with anxiety. They had been massacred—and by a much smaller force. The British had fought shamefully, then panicked, then finally turned around and ran. Evidence showed that many of his soldiers had died from British muskets, not the French arms, which were smaller.

Had I not been witness, he thought, *I would not have believed it.*

As he stared into the fire, the colonel took off his coat. Shaking it out, he found two holes, the shells having passed right through the fabric. He stared at them in disbelief, pushing a finger through each hole as if to convince himself that they were real. He slowly shook his head in disbelief.

A small group of officers was watching. One of them, a scrawny Virginian with jet-black hair, leaned forward on his knees, his face a pale yellow in the firelight. "There's another one in your hat, sir."

The colonel took his hat off and examined it. Yes, there was another hole.

Two shells through his clothes. Another through his hat. Two horses shot out from underneath him. He shook his head again.

A fellow Virginian officer watched him carefully. "Who are you?" the man wondered aloud, a deep hesitation in his voice.

The colonel turned to look at him, pushing the tattered officer coat aside. It almost seemed he tried to hide it, and he didn't answer the other man.

"Who are you?" the officer repeated.

The colonel looked his fellow Virginian in the eyes. "I am George Washington," he said.

There was a quiet pause and a hint of a smile, then the officer spoke again. "Pardon me, sir, I know your name, but that was not what I meant."

Washington looked at him, snapped his officer's jacket a final time to shake the dirt out, and put it on again. The officer watched him carefully, seeming to take him in. Washington was only twenty-three, but tall enough that he towered over most other men: wide shoulders, strong arms, large hands, a handsome face, blue-gray eyes, a firm mouth. He was broad, but also graceful, and there was something else about him. Something majestic, maybe? Or was it something else? Whatever it was, every man around the fire seemed to sense it.

The officer pushed on. "Those who saw you, those who watched and fought beside you, they say that you cannot be killed in battle."

Washington scoffed at the notion. "I assure you, sir, I can."

"Yet, you were not, sir. Hundreds were killed in battle on this day. We have the tally, colonel: nine hundred and seventy-seven casualties out of a little less than fifteen hundred men. More than sixty officers. Most of our leadership fell today. General Braddock fell, as did many others. Yet here you are before us, sir." He nodded to the tattered colonel's uniform. "How many holes did you find there?"

Washington turned his head away.

"Is the hand of God upon you, sir?"

Washington was growing angry. "What is your name?" he demanded.

"Lieutenant Colonel Charles Lee," the soldier answered.

"Well Lieutenant, I assure you, good sirs, if Providence holds anything in store for me, it is nothing but indignity and shame. Look at the results of what we did here! How many of our brothers lie here dead or in agony! We were their leaders—we *are* their leaders—yet we are now the officers of an army of corpses. We have failed them. I have failed them. From General Braddock on down the line. We marched our men straight into the jaws of hell, then let them panic, throwing more lives into the wind. There is nothing here that God is pleased about. Nothing here to bring us honor. We were sent to defend the Crown . . . and we have failed.

"So, I can assure you, good sirs, that if God has anything in store for me, it is to make me suffer a lifetime of regret for the failure we have seen here, upon this battlefield of shame."

The other man shook his head with great emotion. "You did everything you could, Washington. Everyone who lives as a witness to this battle knows the bravery that you displayed. You rode with greater courage than I have ever witnessed, the only valor upon display. So please, sir, say not that you were shamed here. We met the enemy, and he bettered us. We live to fight another day.

"And you, sir, you *will* fight another day. There is no stitch about that. God has saved you for a purpose. We who fought with you here today know not what that purpose may be, sir, but you must know that we will follow you until God makes your purpose clear."

Washington stared into the fire, then shrugged an unspoken No. Never again would he stand among the officers who would lead men into battle. He'd done so on two occasions and both times he had failed. He had not just been defeated, but humiliated. The prospect of doing it again was too painful to even consider.

"I am unequal to the task," the colonel muttered to the other men. And turning from the fire, he walked into the darkness.

9:50 P.M.

George Washington lay in a makeshift cot beneath the stars. The sky was bright and clear, the day's humidity having taken its own slumber. A million thoughts were going through his mind. He was anxious and angry, humiliated and humbled. But something else also kept at him. It had been rolling around in his head for a few hours but, distracted by the day's brutality, he'd not yet been able to dissect it.

Now, as his head cleared, the thought began to take shape. It came to him slowly at first, but the more he thought about it, the more obvious it became.

Could the entire world really have been mistaken?

The British army was the best-trained, best-equipped, and most disciplined army in the world. There was absolutely no doubt about that.

But, as George Washington had seen with his own eyes earlier that day, it was not invincible.

The revelation impressed upon him with enough force that it bore deep into his soul.

The British could be defeated. What an absolutely terrifying thought.

He pondered it for a few seconds, then pushed it aside, back into the deepest recesses of his brain, and slowly drifted off to sleep.

August 2, 1755
Mount Vernon, Virginia

George Washington had been back at his Mount Vernon estate for a week now, the defeat in Pennsylvania still weighing heavily on his mind.

After his morning chores and a breakfast of porridge and tea, he retired to his office to write a letter to a friend who had nervously inquired about his health after hearing the reports from Pennsylvania.

> *It is true we have been beaten—shamefully beaten by a handful of men who only intended to molest and disturb our march. Victory was their smallest expectation. But see the wondrous works of Providence and the uncertainty of human things! Contrary to all expectation and human probability, and even to the common course of things, we were totally defeated and sustained the loss of everything.*
>
> *I join very heartily with you in believing, that when this story comes to be related in future annals, it will meet with unbelief and indignation, for had I not been witness to the fact on that fatal day, I should scarce have given credit to it even now.*

Washington signed the letter and sealed it shut.

He could not have known it then, but the Battle of Monongahela had planted an idea. It was an idea that, over the next four decades, would steadily grow. And then, one day, that idea would blossom into something greater than Colonel Washington or anyone else who fought alongside the river on that hot July day could have ever expected.

I

Victory or Death

Friday, December 13, 1776
The Widow White's Tavern
Basking Ridge, New Jersey

It required a very special manner of general to have a tranquil breakfast in the middle of a war in which his own side confronted massive peril.

But Charles Lee was that sort of general—and man.

The torch of freedom, shining so brightly following General William Howe's evacuation of Boston, was now threatened with darkness. New York City had, in battle after battle, been ingloriously lost. Even the outpost named for Lee himself—New Jersey's "Fort Lee"—had been abandoned. Philadelphia seemed next. Thousands of rebel soldiers had been lost, either slain in battle or now bound in heavy iron chains. Thousands more had simply vanished and gone home.

It was mid-morning, nearing ten o'clock, yet General Lee sat quietly in his soiled, rumpled cap and dressing gown, here at the widow Mary White's two-storied, two-chimneyed tavern in Basking Ridge, New Jersey. The slovenly Lee cheerfully munched upon his eggs and hard bread and plentiful portions of bacon and ham, occasionally pausing to fling a scrap or two of what had recently been ambulatory swine to the ravenous pack of faithful hounds who seemingly accompanied this strange man wherever he traveled. Between munches and flings, Lee took quill pen in hand to inscribe a letter to General Horatio Gates furiously raging against their mutual superior, George Washington. "A certain man," Lee scribbled hurriedly, "is damnably deficient."

Lee wrote rapidly for a very good reason: All hell was breaking loose. To enjoy this breakfast (and perhaps more of the company of the tavern's comely ladies), Lee had foolishly separated himself from his troops—troops he had long delayed bringing southward from New York state to reinforce Washington's woefully depleted forces. Troops that were now busily heading for a semblance of safety across the ice-choked Delaware River in Pennsylvania. Only a handful of guards had accompanied Lee and his aide to the widow White's tavern.

"You're surrounded, you traitor, Lee!" came a shout from outside. "Surrender or forfeit your worthless life!" The startled Lee finished writing his last sentence, breaking his quill point as he did, and sprang from his seat. Falling to his knees, he peered out from the bottom of a nearby sill to view a squad of green-jacketed British dragoons, their muskets at the ready.

Lee could not be sure which one had shouted, but that was the least of his problems.

It was, in fact, twenty-two-year-old Cornet Banastre Tarleton, among the most capable and vicious men fighting under the Union Jack. Lee bolted from his table and scurried for safety just as the hard-faced Tarleton's men unleashed a cascade of fire. Smoke and deafening thunder—and lead shot—filled the air. Several of Lee's guards fell dead or wounded.

"Hide here!" screamed a barmaid. "Hide in my bed!"

"I'd die first!" shouted Lee, as his hounds growled and barked and ran about the house in panic. "I will fight to the last!"

"I'll burn the house down! To the ground!" shouted Tarleton. "You have five minutes to surrender!"

Charles Lee's last came very soon. But it ended with neither death nor victory. Now attired in his old blue coat and battered cock hat, his breeches spattered with grease, he merely shuffled out the tavern's front door. His captors hustled him upon a horse and sounded a bugle as Charles Lee was led away to a British camp at Brunswick.

December 1776
Trenton, New Jersey

"What's going on?" Colonel Johann Gottlieb Rall questioned. The gruff, fifty-year-old "Hessian Lion" spoke no English. He spoke only war—and contempt for his *Amerikanischen* adversaries. Before him, he saw a body carried forward. Another Hessian soldier hobbled past him, assisted by two more grenadiers, blood still seeping freely from the bandages wrapped tightly just above his left knee.

"Another ambush, Colonel Rall. Corporal Schmidt killed. Shot straight through the heart. Private Keller wounded," answered Lieutenant Andreas von Wiederholdt, who had recently begun to appear much older than his forty-four years. His soldiers could not venture a step outside this miserable village of Trenton without being fired upon by these rebel madmen. Even being within its limits offered little safety. A shot from the woods—*blam!*—might be fired into the back of an unsuspecting sentry patrolling Trenton's outskirts. And what could anyone hope to do about it?

Wiederholdt and his men could no longer rest decently at night. They remained on constant alert, fitfully sleeping in their blue-and-black uniforms, ready to spring into action at a moment's notice and confront a patriot's musket. The darkening bags under Wiederholdt's eyes and the disheveled nature of his own once invariably neat, brass-buttoned uniform revealed that.

A column of men appeared on the horizon, on the road leading northward out of the town, but they were too far away to clearly identify. Was it the Americans? Daring to attack us directly? Wiederholdt's bony face froze in fear. But now he noticed something—shafts of reflected sunlight danced about the head of each figure advancing toward him, emanating from the tall, pointed, polished brass helmet that each Hessian grenadier so proudly wore. It was, Wiederholdt now saw, merely Lieutenant Jakob Piel's company trudging home from a fourteen-mile march to the British outpost at Princeton. A small, very relieved smile played across his thin lips.

Rall could not but help notice Wiederholdt's cascading emotions.

"Ha!" he joked to his subordinate. "You see Americans everywhere! Are you a soldier or an old woman?"

Wiederholdt silently accepted the insult. Who is Rall bluffing? he thought. He knows what's going on; that it's unsafe for messengers—or *anyone*—out there. These Americans hate us. They see us as invaders—oppressors. That's why we have to send a hundred troops to guard a single messenger to Princeton!

But Wiederholdt was not about to maintain his silence about everything. "Colonel Rall," he said deferentially, hoping not to agitate his commandant too much, "perhaps we should now move to fortify Trenton. I know Colonel von Donop has recommended erecting redoubts on both the upper end of town and along the river."

"Donop!" snapped Rall. "*Dummkopf!* Let the Americans come! So much the better! If they dare to come we will have at them with our bayonets—and *that* will be the end of George Washington!"

December 1776
(George Washington's headquarters)
Outside the farmhouse of Robert Merrick
Ten miles north of Trenton Falls
Bucks County, Pennsylvania

Perhaps it *would* be the end of George Washington—and of his revolution.

Colonel Rall certainly thought Washington was on the ropes.

General Lee had thought so as well.

And so, though he hated to admit it, did Thomas Paine.

It was no comfortable Philadelphia print shop in which Paine now sat. Patriotism meant more than words to the English-born pamphleteer. At forty, he now wore the short brown jacket and feathered hat of his unit of the Philadelphia Associators militia, "The Flying Camp."

Since August, Washington had done nothing but retreat. But while so many others had fled (only two days earlier he had been among those ordered to evacuate Fort Lee), Paine had remained and now, by flickering campfire light, employing the taut calfskin of a Continental Army drumhead as his desk, he scratched out the words of a new pamphlet. Hard circumstances demanded hard truths. Events mandated a call to action worthy of a sounding trumpet.

Normally, Tom Paine wrote slowly and painfully—but that was a luxury he could no longer afford. He paused—but only for his smallish hand to dip a sharpened quill once more into the blackness of his pewter inkpot. His piercing blue eyes ablaze, he rapidly composed word after word in the fine penmanship he had learned as a boy in England. Before long he'd completed his task.

"My good man! Come here!" Paine demanded of an army courier, a rough-hewn frontiersman from the Pennsylvania backwoods who was mounted atop a horse that looked like it had served with its rider in the French and Indian War. "I'm Thomas Paine. I hear you are bound for Philadelphia, to the Continental Congress."

The courier stared blankly at Paine, who seemed a tad too excited for his tastes. He said nothing, but his horse flicked its tail—more out of habit than anything else. It was now too cold for flies—or any other sort of insect.

"Well, man? What is it?" Paine demanded, drawing out each syllable so this dimwit before him might better understand his simple question.

"Aye," came the answer in a harsh Scotch-Irish brogue, "Philadel-phia."

"I mean to ride with you, soldier. I need to return to my print shop. To have something printed of importance to our cause. How fast can you ride?"

The messenger eyed Paine with contempt. "Fast enough for General Washington, sir," he answered. He was clearly annoyed by this Paine fellow, whoever he was.

But Tom Paine didn't care whom he offended. He wanted his words printed—while there was still an army to read them to.

December 1776
Merrick farmhouse

"Any word yet from General Gates?" General Washington asked.

Washington had entreated Horatio Gates to join his forces, but Gates pled that he was simply too ill to travel. Like Charles Lee, he seemed strangely reluctant to meet with his commander—or to follow simple orders.

"No, General," came a voice from the back of the room. It belonged to another general. "But, enough of Gates. We have plenty of business before us, and I must repeat what I said yesterday: we must retreat to Philadelphia to safeguard our capital and our Congress. The very existence of our government is at stake. And besides that, we have suffered the capture of so many—not to mention the thousands more whose enlistments have expired and have simply gone home. Two thousand from Maryland and New Jersey alone! And who knows how many more have simply deserted our cause? We must safeguard Philadelphia at all costs."

Silence filled the room, which was crowded with the Continental Army's senior staff.

George Washington was often slow to speak. Now, in this very crucial moment, he again paused before answering. Was he simply composing his thoughts? About to agree, or disagree with this unpalatable proposition? Or was he waiting, as he often did, for as many officers who so wanted to speak freely?

No one said a word.

Nathanael Greene might have been one to speak up, but his recent counsel to hold Fort Washington in upper Manhattan had proven so disastrous that he hesitated to offer any advice at that moment. It would take a while for the marvelously capable Rhode Islander to regain his confidence, so on this morning Greene merely shifted his feet and kept his gaze downward.

A young artillery officer, Alexander Hamilton, as slight and delicate as a fifteen-year-old regimental fifer, but as hardened as any grizzled veteran of Fort Necessity, stood, arms folded, his back stiffening in barely controlled rage. But it was not for twenty-two-year-old captains to publicly upbraid generals. So he, too, kept his silence.

The normally jovial Henry Knox's puffy eyes narrowed in anger. If Knox could have marshaled his 280-pound frame to crush this defeatist, he would have gladly done so right then and there. But, as even his many friends would have conceded, General Knox's ample body contained nary an ounce of actual muscle. Nay, if Henry Knox were to dispatch him, it would have to be by sitting upon the old faker and suffocating him.

Knox gave the idea of retreating to Philadelphia some thought. He was about to set off his booming voice when Washington instead began to speak.

"General," Washington said, his tone measured but firm, his words addressed to his questioner, "our soldiers take their leave because we retreat. Men enlist for victory, not humiliation. We must, even in this hour of peril—no, *particularly* in this hour of gravest peril—provide our men with the taste of victory to feed their hungry souls. And I speak not merely about the men under arms but of an entire continent of patriots.

"The enemy has spread his forces thin. They should be pursuing us—building boats and bridges and moving to crush us in our weakness. But, no, instead they rest. *We* must not rest. *We* must strike. We have the boats to move back victoriously across the Delaware, just as we once ingloriously fled the other way.

"We must strike! Now!"

"Yes, General," came the response of yet another general, another senior officer skilled in the art of disguising inaction in the more fashionable garments of logic and reason. "But where would we strike? How? When? Against what units of the enemy? And what do we really know of their encampments and habits? Grand strategies must be grounded in hard intelligence—or they are no procession toward triumphal monuments and arches, but rather to our gravestones."

Washington began to ponder that point, when suddenly a hard rapping noise at the door broke the silence. A guard announced that a visitor was demanding to see General Washington at once. He could not wait, he said—and he had to see the general *alone*.

It was all highly irregular, of course, but something told Washington that he should indeed confer with this mysterious visitor.

He abruptly broke off his council of war, letting his critics, all puffed up with fine excuses for retreat, own the last word. When all had departed, Washington sat alone, awaiting this stranger and whatever it was that he might have to convey.

A man, rough-hewn but stout, gingerly dared to enter.

"You demand my time," Washington instantly challenged him, catching him off guard. "State your name and purpose."

"I, sir, am John Honeyman," the man answered in the burr of his

native Scotland. "I am a farmer from near to Trenton, and I sell my vegetables to the Hessians stationed in the town. They pay good money—"

"We pay in continental scrip, if you are here to peddle us your
wares," Washington cut him off.

"They pay good money," Honeyman continued, "but they work for
our British oppressors, and I hate them. Neither gold guineas nor Spanish dollars can buy my love for them!"

The glint in Washington's eyes conveyed the pleasure he felt in those
words, a secret satisfaction his ever-guarded lips dared not betray.

Honeyman now reached his point.

"I sell my wares. I take my oxcart to Trenton. I see everything—and
I remember everything, sir. I can draw you a fine map. I can tell you
where each man is stationed. The very position of each cannon. The
hour at which their guards are changed—that there are no fortifications.
I can even tell you when their Colonel Rall arises. He is quite the late
riser, you know—or you may not know that. Such is what I have to sell
to you today, General Washington."

"Mr. Honeyman," Washington replied, as he extended a chair to this
burly gift from the gods of war and fortune, "please, take a seat. We have
much to discuss . . ."

December 1776
Peter Cochrane House
Brunswick, New Jersey

Charles Lee was not alone. Held captive in a room as disheveled as himself, he was in a long, low house where, just months before, patriots had
proudly proclaimed the Declaration of Independence. He was continu-
ously guarded by two unsmiling and silent Hessian sentries. They were
silent, however, for good reason—neither spoke a word of English.

Lee was down, but he was hardly out. He still had cards to play, and
as long as the British didn't first hang him as a deserter and a traitor to
the Crown, he intended to play every single one of them.

"Captain!" He bolted from his chair, bellowing to a man who stood
just outside the door. "Captain Münchhausen, how many times must

I ask you? I need to speak to General Howe. I demand to speak with General Howe—*I wish to tell him how the rebels can be beaten. I know Washington! I know his tricks.*"

Captain Friedrich von Münchhausen, General Howe's reserved Hessian adjutant, merely turned away in disgust, bounding over a snowbank and onto Brunswick's Queen Street.

"Is he at it again?" The voice belonged to Cornet Banastre Tarleton, the dragoon who had captured Lee not long before.

Münchhausen nodded in disgust.

"Lee is as perfect in treachery as if he were American born," Tarleton marveled. "They swallow their allegiance to both king and Congress alternately with as much ease as you swallow poached eggs!" With that he roared back in high-pitched laughter. Of all spoken and written humor, Tarleton valued his own the most.

Münchhausen, however, valued it less. He was not particularly amused at Tarleton's current jest. Besides, if he were to expend any energy laughing at an Englishman's jokes, it would be at General William Howe's.

"Is it too late," Münchhausen turned the question on Tarleton, "to send this *schwein* back to the rebels? A man of his character will do much more harm to them when he is on their side than he can on ours."

Unlike Cornet Tarleton, Captain Münchhausen wasn't joking.

December 24, 1776
Merrick farmhouse

George Washington had no time for rest, not even on Christmas—particularly not on this Christmas Eve.

He sat at his table. On a small scrap of paper, he scribbled the briefest of notes to a staff member. He repeated the process, again and again.

Dr. Benjamin Rush eyed this scene contemptuously. Rush, now a surgeon with Washington's army, was a member of the Continental Congress. Only a few months before he had boldly signed the Declaration of Independence, but now he feared that George Washington was squandering any chance that America's fragile independence had to survive. One retreat followed another. *If only Horatio Gates were in charge,* the doctor thought, *if only Charles Lee were still a free man and in command—we would have the soldiers of the Crown on the run.*

Washington arose. He nodded to Dr. Rush before leaving the room to summon a guard to deliver the brief messages he had just composed. But as Washington departed, he left one document behind. It floated to the wooden plank floor below where he had just sat.

Rush hurried to retrieve it. He might now learn a little more of what ill-conceived plans ran through this wretched Washington's mind.

To his great disappointment, there were no detailed battle plans or grand outlines of strategy on the piece of paper that Rush now held in his hands. It contained just three words:

Victory or death.

2

The Harder the Conflict,
the More Glorious the Triumph

Twilight, December 25, 1776
Western bank of the Delaware River
Near McConkey's Ferry, Knowles Cove
Bucks County, Pennsylvania

Officers barked terse orders to their drummers. Hard wooden drumsticks beat furiously in every corner of George Washington's encampment. In the low hills surrounding McConkey's Ferry, 2,400 infantry shouldered their muskets and crammed their knapsacks full of sixty rounds of ammunition, a blanket, and three days' worth of rations. Cavalrymen loaded their pistols and tightly cinched their horses' saddles. Henry Knox's gunners checked and then checked once more to ensure that they would be transporting sufficient shot and powder and fuses in their cannon's side boxes and trail boxes for whatever hell awaited them on this grand expedition.

These men's faces betrayed not fear—but anticipation, even eagerness. Many soldiers had already left the army, but those who remained had grown hard and fiercely loyal, devoted not only to the causes of independence and liberty, but also to their commander: George Washington. To these men, Washington had become more than just a general. He had become a father.

Still, their enlistments would soon expire. They had families and businesses and farms to worry about. They were not Hessians a thousand miles from home, with no way of returning there. They were ill-paid and ill-equipped and had done their duty. They could go home honorably and most of them probably would. And once they did, the long odds against this revolution would grow only longer.

But while they remained, they were still in the fight. If Washington desired them to brave this ice-choked river and then tramp eight miles in utter darkness cross-country in sleet and snow to strike before the winter sun rose again—to strike at William Howe's fearsome Hessians, the very cream of Europe's fighting men—then, by God, they would do it. They would, to a man, die for George Washington.

The men's faces, stung and reddened by winter's blasts, shone brightly with their fidelity. Standing as tall and straight as amateur soldiers might, these New Englanders and southerners, Pennsylvanians and New Yorkers, and Jersey men longing to liberate their homes were eager to go. Waiting for action wore upon their nerves. Marching forward filled them with energy—and courage.

They scrambled to board the slapdash armada that Washington—aided by the Marblehead, Massachusetts, fisherman General John Glover—had assembled to ferry them toward the enemy. It was a flotilla of diverse vessels, none of which might be found in any real navy: the sturdy flat-bottomed "Durham boats," made originally to transport iron ore; a handful of scows; all manner of fishermen's craft; and the two ferryboats that had regularly plied this Delaware crossing in times of peace. All of them would be needed.

The men would cross the Delaware first, mostly aboard the fairly spacious Durham boats. Then would come skittish horses, and, finally, all eighteen pieces of Henry Knox's cumbersome and heavy, yet crucial and powerful, artillery: three-pounders, four-pounders, five-and-a-half-pounders, and six-pounders. Despite its name, a six-pounder's barrel and carriage alone could weigh as much as 1,750 pounds.

A journey of a mere eight hundred feet would take hours. But everything had to proceed on the tightest of schedules. The Continental Army needed to invade Trenton before daylight to maintain any hope of surprise.

Every minute lost could cost a life. Every hour lost could lose the battle. The battle lost could forfeit the revolution.

Yet, despite the obvious pressure, Washington paused to complete one last task. Two days earlier he had read from a pamphlet. Its words rang like a siren. They roared like a cannonade. His men needed to hear those words, and they needed to hear them now.

In the freezing air at Knowles Cove, Washington distributed a dozen bound copies of this little work to his officers. "Read this—or have it read to your men. They are better words than I am capable of. Read them now, before we depart."

General Knox chose to read the words himself. Famous for his booming voice, Knox calculated that he could best bellow out whatever his commander thought so necessary for his men to hear. Never send out a man to do a job you could better do yourself, thought Knox.

General Henry Knox cleared his throat and began to proclaim the words that Tom Paine had scribbled out upon a drumhead not long ago and then galloped so quickly back to Philadelphia to print:

> *These are the times that try men's souls. The summer soldier and the sunshine patriot will, in this crisis, shrink from the service of their country; but he that stands it now, deserves the love and thanks of man and woman. Tyranny, like hell, is not easily conquered; yet we have this consolation with us, that the harder the conflict, the more glorious the triumph.*

When Knox had finished, his final words echoing across the land, only silence remained. The icy breath of the soldiers filled the air.

Finally, Washington broke the silence. "All right, men," he bellowed, his voice firm with resolve. "It's time to go."

December 25, 1776
Mount Holly, New Jersey

Colonel Carl Emilius von Donop savored his Christmas dinner—the finest meats and vegetables, served upon a modest lace tablecloth, eaten not with pewter, but with sterling silver utensils. Across the Delaware River, American recruits had no time for feasting. Drums were beating, and men assembling, for a march toward the unknown.

But there was none of that at Mount Holly, only Colonel von Donop and his very gracious and beautiful—and *so very accommodating*—hostess. Von Donop, a man known for his appreciation of the fairer sex, could not believe his own luck. While every other female in the community had fled the approach of his troops, this incredible beauty, this young widow, had chosen to remain.

Ah! thought von Donop. The fortunes of war!

"*Colonel* von Donop," asked his adjutant, a large but nervous young man named Captain Johann Ewald, "might we be leaving soon for Bordentown? We have been here since Monday."

Bordentown, where they'd be close enough to support Colonel Rall's troops in Trenton should any difficulties arise, was their ultimate destination. But Colonel von Donop wasn't ready to get going just yet.

"Don't worry, *Captain*!" von Donop barked. Then he softened his tone as he eyed his newfound companion, who was ever so slyly glancing back at him. "*Colonel* Rall isn't going anywhere. Besides, just look at that weather out there—and it will only be worse when set upon the road. Remember, it's eighteen miles to Trenton!"

Once more von Donop cast his glance toward his comely hostess. "Don't you agree, my dear?"

"I could not agree more," she answered. "Would you care for some brandy?"

The name of the woman who entertained von Donop that Christmas night is not really known. Nor are her reasons for remaining in Mount Holly when all other women had fled. But among the locals there is a story still told: that her name was Betsy Ross—and that not all patriots shouldered muskets on that Christmas night.

December 25–26, 1776
Delaware River

Great, hard slabs of jagged ice, as big and thick as coffins, slammed with incredible force into the sides of George Washington's Durham boat.

There was no place to sit in these immense, canoe-like vessels. So Washington and all the other men in the black boat with bright yellow trim wrestled to steady themselves, fearing they would be tossed into the dark, rushing, ice-choked waters. Four sailors, snug as they could hope to be in their short seaman's coats and tight woolen caps, struggled to steer Washington's boat, to keep it from being swept downstream. Slush and ice lapped over the craft's low sides and onto their feet, making a dangerous and miserable voyage still more wretched. Hard, cold winds stung everyone's faces.

Washington peered through the darkness and struggled vainly to catch sight of solid Jersey ground. It was nearly impossible. A bright moon had arisen early that evening, but great black clouds had then rolled in, causing the December sky and everything under it to disappear into cold, inky blackness.

And as Washington struggled to look forward, words began to roll through his mind. They were words that he'd recited from his earliest childhood, but they had never possessed greater meaning than they now did on this faithful night, the birthday of the One who had first offered these sacred words to the whole world.

". . . and deliver us from evil," George Washington's silent, but fervent, prayer concluded. "Amen."

Morning of December 26, 1776
Western bank of the Delaware River
Opposite Beatty's Ferry

On the Pennsylvania side of the Trenton ferry, eight miles downriver from George Washington and McConkey's Ferry, General James Ewing, a tough Scotch-Irishman hailing from the Pennsylvania frontier, stood not in a boat, but on the snow-covered shore, swearing mightily. He was near Trenton Falls, and the rushing mass of water hurtling upon the jagged rocks below it had created a massive ice jam nearly five feet deep. Pockets of water flowed only sporadically, and those pockets, where they existed, were just thirty to forty feet wide.

It was the worst of circumstances. The Delaware was too frozen for boats to sail, yet not frozen enough for Ewing's seven hundred soldiers to trudge across.

Washington had ordered Ewing's troops to join him as he battled the Hessians at Trenton. But there was no way to do that. His boats and men were being held up by a barrier more powerful than what any Britisher or Hessian might have constructed. He had tried as hard as possible, given it everything he could—yet he had failed.

If George Washington were to secure victory, it would be without General James Ewing's reinforcements.

Early morning, December 26, 1776
Eastern Bank of the Delaware River
Opposite McConkey's Ferry

Campfires blazed along the Jersey side of the Delaware.

Despite Henry Knox's bellowing commands and tireless enthusiasm, the crossing had proved far more harrowing than anyone had imagined. The tide had been swifter, the ice thicker, the wind colder. Horses bucked and resisted boarding the ferryboats that had been designated for their transport. They wanted no part of this voyage.

Perhaps they were smarter than their commanders.

And moving cannon . . . well, that was the most impossible task of all. It was hard enough to transport Henry Knox's guns on rutted roads and through rolling fields and hillsides. Shoving them on—and off—these boats, and over these rough waters was harder and slower still. "Put your shoulder to it, men!" Knox shouted. "Put your shoulder to it!"

George Washington waited for the last of the cannon to complete the crossing. Only then could they begin the march to Trenton. He had loitered on this shore for so long that he had made a little seat for himself, a broken wooden box that had once contained a beehive.

As he sat there, dressed in his great blue cloak, in the cold and dark, he pondered whether he had already lost his chance. Could he still reach Trenton before daybreak? Would General Ewing—and General Cadwalader, who was launching his own force from Dunk's Ferry—be there to meet him?

So much had to go right. So much had already gone wrong. The Continental Army had lost the great majority of its men since its first losses on Long Island. Its back was against the wall. There could be no more defeats, no more retreats. Today it was all or nothing—"Victory or Death," as he had once written.

Suddenly, Henry Knox, puffing mightily and clapping his pudgy gloved hands together for warmth, approached.

"General," he said, "we are all across."

Washington arose quickly, his little seat toppling over.

"To Trenton, men! Before the sun rises."

Morning, December 26, 1776
Western bank of the Delaware River
Near Dunk's Ferry

General John Cadwalader was a cultivated Philadelphia merchant. He was not a ferryman.

Yes, he had men from his city's waterfront to assist him in making his crossing of the Delaware, but he was still getting absolutely nowhere. The same ice floes that stymied General Ewing to the north hamstrung Cadwalader. He had been assigned to cross at Dunk's Ferry, across the river from Burlington, New Jersey, but his boats could barely be put in the water there, let alone be rowed or poled toward the opposite shore. Changing plans, he moved north along the river, but it was the same story there. Slabs of ice the size of mattresses and as hard and sharp as bayonets filled the river. An advance party had made it across earlier, but that was it. No one else could.

The British might yet somehow be defeated, but this wretched river could not.

Cadwalader just stood there, forlorn and staring, his hands jammed hard into his pockets, a scarf covering his face. He was too much the gentleman to swear as General Ewing did. All he could do was order his men—tired from lack of sleep and disheartened from failure—to march home to camp and pray for General Washington.

Morning, December 26, 1776
Bear Tavern Road, beyond Jacob's Creek
Western bank of the Delaware River

Now it was sleeting.

Not just squalls of heavy snow, but the worst and wettest sleet anyone in the Continental Army had ever seen. Freezing and stinging, it made moving forward even more difficult.

Washington's march to Trenton had commenced a full four hours late. Shoeless men, their feet swaddled in rags, deposited an ominous trail of blood along their path. Washington saw a drummer lad, a red-headed boy from nearby Delaware, so weary that he lay down in the snow to rest, perhaps even to sleep.

"Rouse him! Shake that boy!" George Washington shouted from horseback, through gales of sleet. "To sleep this night is death!"

The road had run upward from the river, a good two-hundred-foot change in elevation, with portions of that incline extremely pitched. That made the hard work of Henry Knox's burly gunners into something that was more akin to impossible. Then came even more trouble, this time in the form of Jacob's Creek—which, despite its name, was no ordinary stream, no bucolic brook in sunlit meadows. Lying in a steep ravine, it required Knox's men to lash their longest drag ropes to trees to winch their guns down—and then up—its perilous slopes, placing at risk their guns' often fragile wooden carriages and high wheels.

Washington rode alongside his men. Watching, yes, for others who might fall sleep, but all the while encouraging them onward—faster, faster, and, yet, faster still. "Press on, boys, press on!" he shouted. Time and weather had already allied themselves against his cause. He could not risk any more delay.

Galloping on sloping, icy ground, his horse skidded to a stop. Bucking and panicking, the beast started tumbling downward, threatening to crush the general under its weight. Washington panicked not for a second. Dropping his reins, he extended his arms and grabbed the horse's mane with his powerful hands. Miraculously, he pulled the mane—and the animal itself—upward, steadying it enough to keep it, and him, from falling to earth.

"Was I dreaming?" exclaimed the drummer boy whom Washington had only just roused. "Was that real?"

"No, lad," said the soldier standing next to him. "I saw it, too. We all did. And this I know: *nothing* can stop George Washington from reaching Trenton this day. I just hope we make it with him."

• • •

Perhaps that anonymous soldier was wrong. Perhaps there was something that could stop Washington from reaching Trenton: his own men.

Along he rode. In the snow-whitened distance, men marched toward him. Hessians in their fine brass helmets? The British, venturing from snug winter quarters?

"Hello!" came the call. "Don't shoot! We're Virginians!"

"What are you doing here?" Washington demanded. He knew they could not be Ewing or Cadwalader's troops. They were, to a man, Pennsylvanians and Rhode Islanders.

"Those damnable Hessians snuck like the skunks they are across the river and killed one of our boys. So we had to even the score. We just came from Trenton. Gave them a little taste of their own medicine! I reckon we got one or two of 'em."

Washington's heart sank. The element of surprise he had plotted so carefully had vanished, simply flung away like a chicken bone by a few dozen buckskin-wearing squirrel shooters.

"What now, General?" asked a voice barely heard above the general's own seething breath.

"We have come this far, Hamilton," Washington answered, "if we go forward we may very well lose our lives. The element of surprise is gone. The chance of arriving before the sun rises is evaporating by the second. But if we march these men back to the river after all this, we will surely lose our army.

"Captain Hamilton—we have no choice: we go forward!"

Morning, December 26, 1776
Outskirts of Trenton

At 7:20 the sun had risen in the morning skies over Trenton.

George Washington was not there. He had failed yet again.

He stared toward the town in the distance, or at least where the town should have been. He could see nothing. Another storm had commenced, and it was historic. The sleet and snow that filled the air was completely blinding and deadened all sound.

And that was exactly the break Washington needed.

A horizontal avalanche of white may not have allowed the rebels to see the town, but at least they knew where it was. The Hessians inside that town, on the other hand, had no idea that American muskets and bayonets and cannon now advanced upon them.

George Washington's prayers had not failed him; they'd just been answered in an unexpected way.

The storm also had another benefit: any enemy advance sentries had been forced inside. But while Washington might have guessed that, there was something he could not: the British had spies—and they were much better paid than the ones working for the rebels.

One of those spies had infiltrated Washington's headquarters and scurried back to bring word of Washington's plans to his masters. Washington had no way to know it, but the Hessians *expected* to be attacked this holy season. When those foolish Virginians had shot up their town and hightailed it back upon the Bear Tavern Road, Colonel Rall and his men had made the only reasonable conclusion that they could: the rebel attack, such that it was, had been easily turned away. What wretched soldiers these fools were! Rall thought. It was hardly an attack even worthy of his attention.

And so Rall and his lieutenant Wiederholdt let down their guard and got back to the important task of recovering from the holiday festivities of the previous night.

"Gentlemen, your watches, please," Washington commanded General Greene and General John Sullivan, who would lead separate wings of the attack. "We will synchronize them all so that we will all strike at once."

"This damnable snow," Sullivan whined, "causes our gunpowder to grow wetter by the minute. We won't be able to fire a shot upon the enemy!"

"Then use your bayonets!" Washington retorted.

By some small miracle, all segments of the army that had reached Trenton were advancing at once.

Inside Trenton's barrel maker's shop, Lieutenant Wiederholdt huddled with his seventeen men. No use keeping them outside on such a morning—especially not with the Americans on the run, their pathetic attack having been easily turned away. It was stuffy, though, with so many men cooped up within the small space. He stepped outside and thought he saw some men advancing toward him. Probably Captain Brubach's detachment. But then there were more of them—and then still more.

"Der feind! Heraus!" Wiederholdt exclaimed—"The enemy! Turn out!"

The fight, Wiederholdt knew in that moment, was far from over. It was just beginning.

Colonel Rall, still in his nightclothes, stood dumbly at his window. All Hades was exploding round him. Washington's units advancing. Knox's batteries bombarding the town. Yet Rall, having spent a very late evening playing chess and drinking brandy, barely understood what was happening.

His adjutant, Lieutenant Jakob Piel, burst into the room.

"What is happening?" Rall demanded. The reality of his situation was now sinking all too painfully into his sleepy Hessian brain.

"Do you not hear the firing, Colonel?"

Rall threw on his uniform, dashed into the street, and mounted his horse, ready for battle.

Gunfire erupted from all sides. The Hessians should have remained inside their stations, picking off Greene's and Sullivan's columns as they advanced. Instead they rushed out to counterattack, making themselves easy targets for American fire—and turning their own gunpowder into sodden mush so that it might not fire. Their regimental band, Colonel Rall's great pride and joy, took up its accustomed station, blaring out its traditional Teutonic martial music, but this time it made it even harder for his men to comprehend their own officers' commands.

It was complete chaos.

But these Hessians would not be taken easily. They rolled out two cannon onto King Street, ready to cut the Americans to ribbons. Undeterred, the rebels rushed forward and captured the two cannon before they could be used.

Rall, however, rallied his men, spurring them into capturing the cannon back. As this seesaw battle continued, George Washington's second cousin, Captain William Washington, along with Lieutenant James Monroe led a charge to once again seize the Hessian cannon. Musket fire hit Captain Washington in the wrist and Monroe in the chest, severing an artery. He crumpled, his blood spurting out onto the ground, melting the snow and forming a wide, dark red pool round his body. A surgeon struggled to clamp Monroe's wound and save his life.

Colonel Rall saw his men fleeing the village. The sight enraged him. They would not be driven from Trenton by this *Amerikanischen* rabble! Atop his horse in a nearby orchard, he once again rallied his men, ordering them back into battle. They would once again recapture those cannon that Captain Washington and Lieutenant Monroe had seized. "My brave soldiers, advance!" he cried, waving his sword in the air.

History will never know if he might have triumphed because as he turned to look at a wounded fellow officer—

Blam!!

A musket ball ripped into his side.

Blam!!

And then another.

Rall tumbled from his mount. His men retrieved his body and gently carried it into a nearby church.

When pressed to choose between victory and death, the rebels had chosen the former. But while they had clearly won an important battle, they still had a very long way to go to win the war.

December 31, 1776
Trenton, New Jersey

General Washington pleaded with his troops. Today was the expiration of their enlistments and most of them had every right to leave. Not just the right, in fact, but the yearning. Worn down with fatigue, and bloodied in battle, most had their hearts fixed on the comforts of home.

Washington, mounted high on his horse, alluded to their recent victory at Trenton; he told them that their services were greatly needed, and that they could now do more for our country than they ever could at any future period. The drums beat for volunteers, but not a man turned out.

The general wheeled his horse about, rode in front of the regiment, and addressed the troops again. "My brave fellows," he said, "you have done all I asked you to do, and more than could be reasonably expected; but your country is at stake, your wives, your houses, and all that you hold dear. You have worn yourselves out with fatigue and hardships, but we know not how to spare you. If you will consent to stay only one month longer, you will render that service to the cause of liberty, and to your country, which you probably never can do under any other circumstances. The present is emphatically the crisis, which is to decide our destiny."

The drums beat a second time. The soldiers felt the force of the appeal. One soldier said to another, "I will remain if you will." Another remarked, "We cannot go home under such circumstances." A few stepped forth, and their example was immediately followed by nearly all who were fit for duty in the regiment, amounting to about two hundred volunteers.

An officer inquired of General Washington if these men should be enrolled. "No!" he replied. "Men who will volunteer in such a case as this, need no enrollment to keep them to their duty."

The Aftermath

At Mount Holly, Colonel von Donop was so panicked by the news from Trenton that he abandoned his wounded men and fled—though he first managed to cart away a hundred and fifty wagons chocked full of booty.

In New York, General Howe, who had thought George Washington's army beneath contempt, was stunned.

In London, the British politicians blamed the Hessians for their own downfall. Perhaps, they thought, these Germans were not worth the precious gold that Parliament and the Crown had expended to pay them.

But the inhabitants of the thirteen former colonies thought differently. Their hungry, cold, ragtag army had beaten the best soldiers that any money could buy. When all had seemed lost, their revolution had been saved.

At least, the rebel soldiers thought, he had saved it *for now*.

They did not, *could* not, know precisely what struggles might lie ahead—and that in itself was a miracle. For if they'd seen the future then they would've seen that the winter they were currently enduring by a river in New Jersey would be nothing compared to the one that lay ahead not far outside Philadelphia.

3

When None Expected Much,
He Did the Unexpected

Circumstances do not make a man, they reveal him.

—JAMES LANE ALLEN

Let's talk about soldiers and shoes.

It had been only a few months since the United States declared its independence from Great Britain, but the rebels were already facing serious challenges. George Washington's army suffered stinging defeats on Long Island, at Kips Bay in Manhattan, at Fort Lee in New Jersey, and at Fort Washington in northern Manhattan. Retreating south through New Jersey with the British forces at his heels, Washington and his battered men ended their perilous trek in Pennsylvania.

His troops were hungry, sick, and cold—many lacked basic clothing. One of Washington's officers described the march to Trenton this way: "It is fearfully cold and raw and a snowstorm setting in. The wind . . . beats in the faces of the men. It will be a terrible night for the soldiers who have no shoes."

Seriously, no shoes? I'm the first to admit that I wouldn't be able to make that march even if the world's greatest outfitter of warm-weather clothing custom designed a wardrobe for me—but still, no shoes? Barefoot? In winter? How many of us can really even fathom that level of sacrifice?

Common Shoes

I know I'm harping quite a bit on this shoe thing, but it's just so incredible. Think about how much time and effort we put into our footwear today: length, width, material, arch support—the list goes on and on. But back then, when our soldiers were lucky enough to actually have shoes they often had "common" shoes, meaning they weren't specifically designed to fit your left or right foot. They "fit" either foot—which really meant they fit neither.

But shoes weren't the only essential missing from the army: so was morale. It was abysmal, and understandably so. How many losses were these soldiers supposed to endure with no end in sight? It's one thing to march through the bitter cold and freezing snow when you feel like you're winning—it's another thing to do it loss after loss after humiliating loss.

Even though it was still early in the revolution, many of the men had already had enough. Nearly all of those who fought (and lost) with Washington in New York had deserted or disappeared. Anyone else who was still hanging on was mainly doing so because their enlistments would be up in short order. They'd be home soon and, unless Washington was crazy, there wouldn't be more fighting before then.

But low morale and the ever-growing number of British troops weren't Washington's only enemies. One of the main reasons he was forced to march farther south in the first place was the incredibly reckless actions of his second in command, General Charles Lee.

Washington had ordered Lee to march his men south and provide him with much needed reinforcements. Instead Lee brazenly ignored the order and stayed put in northern New Jersey. No one knows exactly why he did it—but this much is known: the British-born Lee thought Washington was beneath him and didn't deserve to be calling the shots.

Washington wrote to Lee several times during his retreat, the situation becoming so dire that he practically begged for help. The only correspondence that Washington received back was the kind a boss gets from a lazy employee: excuses, delays, and still no progress. One particularly damning letter Lee wrote was never intended for Washington's eyes, but rather the sympathetic ear of another high-ranking officer. He excoriated Washington for his "fatal indecision of mind," which, he declared, is in war a "much greater disqualification than stupidity."

The strangest part is that this hatred of all things Washington was quite a flip-flop for Lee. In July of that same year, he'd written that "no man loves, respects and reverences another more than I do General Washington. I esteem his virtues, private and public. I know him to be a man of sense, courage and firmness."

What caused the waffling? Well, perhaps Lee was bitter that Washington had lost Fort Lee (named after him) in a hasty retreat. If that was really the reason, then—pardon my candor—he was a moron. The entire war could have been lost if it weren't for Washington's quick actions to move the doomed troops at Fort Lee before they were surrounded and forced to surrender—which is exactly what happened at Fort *Washington*, right across the Hudson River.

A Bridge to Nowhere?

Modern-day Fort Lee is located at the west end of . . . the GEORGE WASHINGTON Bridge. It's actually kind of a fitting commentary on history: without Washington, Lee is pretty irrelevant.

Whatever the reason, things were not going well at all. The British had all the momentum, and their soldiers were already receiving a hero's welcome in the streets of New York after their victory. Washington's men, meanwhile, were demoralized, unorganized, disappearing, and dying. Enlistments for many of the remaining men were rapidly ending. The weather was getting brutal. The fate of an entire fledgling nation hung in the balance. And now, much like arsenic icing on a cake of rat poison, some of Washington's top commanders were not only ignoring his orders, they were actually plotting *against* him.

These were the perilous circumstances confronting George Washington in the winter of 1776—circumstances so difficult that they inspired

Thomas Paine to urgently write *The Crisis* and begin with the immortal line *"These are the times that try men's souls."*

The character beneath George Washington's steely surface was not about to be formed—it was about to be revealed . . . and then put to the ultimate test.

CULTIVATING CHARACTER

> No People can be bound to acknowledge and adore the Invisible Hand, which conducts the Affairs of men more than the People of the United States.
> —GEORGE WASHINGTON, FIRST INAUGURAL ADDRESS

It goes without saying that George Washington was not a dumb man. He knew that the odds were stacked so high against him that it defied all logic to push forward and attack. Any general worth his salt would retreat all the way to Philadelphia and try to protect the capital. An attack on the notorious Hessian army in Trenton would be suicidal—especially in the unforgiving cold. This was an easy call. Or, at least it should've been.

Who Were the Hessians?

Most people know the Hessians were mercenaries. But they weren't *volunteer* mercenaries. They weren't like Christopher Walken in *The Dogs of War* hiring out on his own. These Hessian guys were basically draftees who were hired out by their ruler for cash on the barrelhead. The landgrave of Hesse-Kassel got the bucks; these poor slobs got shot at.

Now, don't get me wrong, the Hessians didn't make a lot of friends in America. They played rough. They looted and murdered with the worst of them.

But here's the takeaway: freedom is contagious—even to eighteenth-century storm-trooper dudes.

While they were here, killing us, they saw what freedom was like for the very first time. They saw how decently Washington treated them when they were captured. They got the message. Some of them—a lot of them—bought into the American Dream.

At war's end, 17,313 Hessians returned to Germany. No surprise there. But 4,972, more than one in five, remained to settle here among their old enemies.

They chose America. They chose *freedom*.

Washington's decision-making process during this extremely tumultuous time gives us an inside look at his character. Ever since his childhood days he had respectfully listened to the opinions of others. "Let your conversation be without malice or envy," he had copied out to his notebook as a teenager. "Always submit your judgment to others with modesty." In 1776, that meant listening to other military brass—even if he disagreed with every single one of them. He probably never imagined that practicing such seemingly obvious and mundane virtues as a boy would play such a large role in arguably the most important war in all human history (we'll see this same virtue play itself out in the critical battle at Yorktown).

But what if instead of being modest, Washington had been an arrogant mess like Charles Lee? What if he had been unable to win the trust of the men he'd led into battle? How would things have been different? Would those men have followed him through hell on earth?

Probably not. It's far more likely that if Washington had not been modest and humble then we'd all have English accents, bad teeth, and one of those annoying royal families to contend with.

Washington spent his childhood—and the rest of this life—focused (arguably obsessed) on etiquette, values, ethics, and morals. For a boy so young such determination to work on his character and reputation was highly unusual. A lot of times a kid like that grows up to be a nerd, or, if not a nerd, a goody-two-shoes or a stick-in-the-mud whom most people can barely stand to be around; a guy who's so hung up on *looking* right that he forgets to *do* right; an empty three-cornered hat.

But Washington combined his overwhelming sense of rectitude (he's the guy who willingly gives up his seat on the subway) with genuine humility and incredible physical courage. He was, to put it bluntly, a man's man, the real deal—the total package.

I know what you may be thinking: But I'll never be the whole package.

Fair enough. But you'll probably never be asked to lead a revolution, either. You might just be asked to help with a food pantry. Or help clean up the mess on the local school board. Or make sure that your children know our real history. If you haven't been George Washington *before*— well, start being George Washington *now*. Yesterday can be an easy excuse on the way to missing out on tomorrow.

Washington's unyielding emphasis on character and reputation helped make him one of the most trusted leaders in all history. How do I know? Well, consider that in 1776 he wrote Congress asking for unprecedented power to execute maneuvers without waiting for approval. This was all he wrote:

> *It may be said that this is an application for powers that are too dangerous to be entrusted; I can only add that desperate diseases require desperate remedies, and with truth declare that I have no lust after power, but wish with as much fervency as any man upon this wide, extended continent for an opportunity of turning the sword into a plowshare. But my feelings as an officer and a man have been such as to force me to say that no person ever had a greater choice of difficulties to contend with than I have.*

Is there *anyone* on the planet today who could just say, "I swear I'm telling the truth—I don't really want power, but please give it to me anyway," and actually be believable? Of course not—but Congress not only gave Washington unprecedented control of the army, it also gave him this:

> *[The power] to take, wherever he may be, whatever he may want for the use of the army, if the inhabitants will not sell it, allowing a reasonable price for the same; to arrest and confine persons who refuse to take the continental currency, or are otherwise disaffected to the American cause; and return to the states of which they are citizens, their names, and the nature of their offences, together with the witnesses to prove them....*

In other words, they gave him the power to basically imprison anyone he wanted to.

George Washington's name was synonymous with trust (the Congress said it had "perfect reliance on [his] wisdom, vigour, and uprightness"). His word was his bond. Congress granted him six months of emergency power and, if they had any reservations about doing so, those fears likely vanished once they saw Washington's response:

Instead of thinking myself freed from all civil obligations by this mark of... confidence, I shall constantly bear in mind that as the sword was the last resort for the preservation of our liberties, so it ought to be the first to be laid aside when those liberties are firmly established.

The Great Author, Revealed

Revisionist historians have tried to diminish Washington's faith in God, but it is clearly evident in his writings. Washington learned very much from his father, who (as the legend goes) once taught young George a lesson using cabbage seeds. He arranged them in such a way that they spelled "George." When they began to grow, he showed them to his son and explained to him that they just grew that way by happenstance. When George correctly rejected that premise, suspecting it was his Dad who arranged them, he told George to look around at how perfectly everything else was placed. The trees. The grass. The water. The hills. The sky.

Was it all mere coincidence, or was it part of a grand plan?

Washington immediately knew the answer.

PROVIDENCE'S PROTECTION

Anyone who walked a single day in Washington's shoes would likely suspect the involvement of a greater power in his life.

He was a surveyor (of all things) as a youth and his knowledge of the lay of the land would later be crucial to winning the war.

He was minutes away from becoming a British sailor, until the last minute, when his mom persuaded him to stay home.

During a humiliating defeat in the French and Indian War, Washington should have been killed when his unit was ambushed.

Washington wrote that the English "regulars" displayed "more cowardice than it is possible to conceive." Meanwhile, Washington's horse was shot out from under him multiple times and he miraculously escaped four bullets that pierced his hat and clothing.

The Great Protector

A thousand enemy soldiers were captured, killed, or wounded in battle. But the toll on the rebels' side was not nearly as dramatic. Washington lost two soldiers, and five others were injured. That's it. It's no wonder he believed so fervently in the Invisible Hand.

The list goes on and on, and while many say all of it was simply coincidence or luck, Washington himself did not believe that, writing to his brother: "I now exist and appear in the land of the living by the miraculous care of Providence, that protected me beyond all human expectation; I had 4 Bullets through my Coat and two horses shot under me, and yet escaped unhurt."

With those experiences running through his mind as he stood before an icy Delaware River and contemplated taking his beaten-down army across it to face a powerful enemy, Washington prayed that God would once again defend the fight for liberty.

So, given his reliance on the great Author, no one should have been surprised when Washington took the unconventional route and decided to go ahead and attack the Hessians at Trenton, even though no one, including Washington and his officers, had any idea how they were going to pull it off.

Washington's CIA: "The Continental Intelligence Agency"

Because of the American army's smaller numbers and lack of firepower, Washington knew that an essential element of effective defensive warfare would have to be superior intelligence. The Americans needed to know at all times not only where the British were and what they were doing, but also what they *planned* to do. When the British were weak, Washington could strike suddenly and powerfully (as he did at Trenton and Monmouth). When the British were strong, the Americans could safely keep their distance (as he did in retreating across New Jersey).

But gathering the kind of solid intelligence that would allow for these sorts of decisions to be made could only be accomplished in one way: with a web of reliable spies.

When British forces occupied New York early in the war the patriots realized they had quickly lost one of their most strategically important cities and naval centers. So, by 1778, Washington appointed an unsung hero, an officer named Benjamin Tallmadge, to establish one of the war's most potent, vital, and successful spy rings. The group—known as the Culper Spy Ring—did more damage than any espionage ring from either side.

In addition to the gradual establishment of other elaborate spy networks (Nathan Hale was Washington's most famous and valiant—if least successful—spy), Washington created a smooth counterintelligence system through which he fed a stream of false information to British agents. Some fabrications reached the enemy through three or four different—all seemingly reliable—sources, and some of the misinformation actually bore the ultimate mark of authenticity: Washington's own handwriting.

ABOVE-AVERAGE INTELLIGENCE

Was it a leap of faith? Sure—but he wasn't about to leave it *all* up to Him. Washington is more than just a Founding Father of our country—he's also considered by many to be one of the founding fathers of American espionage. "There is nothing more necessary," he wrote of his experiences in the French and Indian War, "than good intelligence to frustrate a designing enemy, and nothing that requires greater pains to obtain."

It was a lesson that he applied throughout his military career (especially at Yorktown), but perhaps nowhere did it matter more than at the Battle of Trenton.

By April 1776 Washington had spent $5,232 (a fairly large sum) on intelligence gathering. Documents also show that, as late as December 1776, Washington wrote letters focused on acquiring intelligence on British troop locations, numbers, plans, and more—and senior officer Colonel Joseph Reed was also busy gathering intelligence for the Trenton invasion.

But gathering intel was one thing—*applying* it was what really mattered, and at that Washington excelled. When he conspired with Trenton-area spy John Honeyman, he instructed Honeyman to continue trading with Americans and the enemy alike. The plan worked a little *too* well—Honeyman was the subject of attacks from patriots upset at his dealing with the Brits. That all but erased any doubts the British and Hessians might have had about Honeyman's loyalties.

The Spy Who Never Was?

The story of double agent John Honeyman is legendary—but no one really knows if it's true.

Honeyman, it is said, offered Washington detailed information about the Hessian positions and conditions of their troops in and around Trenton. Perhaps more important, he fed the Hessian commander *disinformation* about the Americans, claiming that the colonial army was too weak to launch an attack.

When a mob of colonialists almost lynched him in his home in New Jersey in 1776, Honeyman and his family were only saved because they had a letter of safe passage from Washington.

If the story is accurate, then Honeyman is undoubtedly a hero of the American Revolution—but that accuracy is very much in doubt. The first written record of his involvement as Washington's spy appears in an 1873 magazine article written by Honeyman's own grandson. Given that this was nearly a hundred years after the event, the account has been met with a lot of skepticism. Since then the legend has only grown and has been integrated into historical accounts.

In his Pulitzer Prize–winning book, *Washington's Crossing*, historian

David Hackett Fischer writes that stories of Honeyman's double-crossing the British are "unsupported by evidence" and he treats the entire story as legend. The CIA's *Studies in Intelligence* published a paper titled "The Spy Who Never Was: The Strange Case of John Honeyman and Revolutionary War Espionage." You can guess from the title what the agency believes.

Honeyman used his credibility to gather as much information as possible and, eventually, Washington staged an elaborate capture-and-escape sequence to get briefed. He received all of Honeyman's intelligence on military—but more important, after his "escape," Honeyman is said to have reported to Hessian commander Colonel Johann Rall that morale among Washington's men was so low that there was no chance they could ever attack Trenton. This was all very plausible to Rall, especially with Christmas right around the corner, and it gave the colonel a false sense of security.

Honeyman's point on morale was partially true. It *had* been low. But that was only before Thomas Paine's immortal, inspiring words were read to Washington's men before they crossed the Delaware.

Paine sold 120,000 copies of the pamphlet that contained those words in just three months. He sold 500,000 by the end of the war—meaning that almost 13% of the entire population had received a copy.

His stirring words, combined with Washington's determination to push forward, reenergized the Continental Army. But on their march to Trenton, the freezing soldiers must have been asking where their commander's "Invisible Hand" was. Not only were they woefully behind schedule, but they also left behind a nine-mile trail of blood from frostbitten feet wrapped in rags. Two men perished during this intolerable trek. It was a miracle that more did not die.

While raging storms caused Washington's army to miss its scheduled arrival time, the Invisible Hand still remained hard at work. Colonel Rall was overconfident and understaffed (he only had about 1,500 troops on site; Washington had 2,500 and would have had several thousand more if his other regiments weren't stymied by the raging river). Rall might have been reinforced except for the mysterious young widow who busily "entertained" Colonel Carl von Donop nearby. Von Donop's dallying kept his troops from perhaps tipping the balance against Washington.

A Mystery Woman

While it's not at all certain that Betsy Ross was the widow who stayed with von Donop, she is a likely candidate. Her husband, John Ross—to whom she'd been married for just two years—had recently been killed while guarding munitions for the war effort. The Rosses went to church in Philadelphia and sat in the pew next to George and Martha Washington's. She was passionate about the revolution, working with upholstery to repair uniforms and stuffing paper tube cartridges with musket balls. And, while it's not confirmed, she reportedly stitched the first American flag and presented it to George Washington in person in the spring of 1776.

Whether or not it was actually Betsy Ross who made the first Stars and Stripes or "entertained" the enemy doesn't really matter—what matters is that *someone did* do those things. Someone used their skills to create a symbol of freedom that would help to rally demoralized troops and remind them what they were fighting for. A widow *did* actually pretend to be interested in some pompous British colonel for the cause of liberty. Troops *did* march barefoot in the freezing cold and driving snow—lead by a man of honor. And, of course, someone *did* watch over it all.

It's easy to get lost in the grandeur of Washington's accomplishments: commander, war hero, president, Founding Father—he was almost mythical, larger than life. But his accomplishments are not what make him great: it was his small, nearly unnoticed acts that did. His simple faith in God, his desire to be a man of virtue in everything he said and did, his focus on the tiniest of character traits all accumulated over time and formed an unshakable, virtuous character built on solid rock. He could not be bought off, tricked, or beaten into submission by the world around him.

You may not lead an army of men onto the battlefield. You may not ever help to found a country or serve as president, but you can *absolutely* be every bit as great as George Washington. Be great in your own city, your own neighborhood, and, most important, your own family. Be someone who relies on character and honor to lead and there will be no bounds to what you can accomplish.

4

A Valley Forged of Despair

December 21, 1777
Valley Forge, Pennsylvania

It was, by the calendar, four days before Christmas and, by the map, eighteen miles northwest of Philadelphia—though nothing about this forlorn place and time suggested anything resembling Christmas festivities or the traditional urban comforts, like taverns, well-stocked shops, or a busy harbor ushering in fine wines and silks.

There was no luxury at all upon this barren, windswept countryside.

General Washington, his breath billowing into little clouds of steam against the late December air, tugged at his great chestnut steed's reins, bringing the animal to a halt. Washington's officers recognized his cue and instantly barked commands to their ragged troops, their mismatched uniforms threadbare, their once spit-shined boots and shoes long reduced to filthy leather tatters. One by one, eleven thousand cold, tired men, trudging in a column that seemed to stretch from one defeat to the next, stopped in place.

Washington surveyed the woodlots and farmsteads that surrounded him. It was good, solid farm country, but, at that moment, farming was the furthest thing from his mind.

They called this place they had come upon a valley, but it was not. And that was good. A valley would merely act as a trap for an army trying to settle into its winter quarters while its enemy, General William Howe, lurked dangerously within striking distance. This place, this "Valley

Forge," as they called it, was instead a high ground bounded by a brace of creeks and the Schuylkill River. If Howe was determined to attack, Washington thought, his own ragged Continental Army might at least enjoy some advantage of terrain.

But terrain, Washington realized, might be his sole advantage. His magnificent triumphs at Trenton and Princeton, though less than a single year ago and but a few dozen miles away, now seemed like victories from the worn history books that he had read as a child—books of battles won by ancient Greece and Rome, of ancient republics that had long since fallen to ruin and despotism.

Washington's army had recently faced its own ruins. General Howe, not satisfied with merely holding New York, had set sail southward, to seize Philadelphia, capital of the upstart colonists. Washington resolved to stop him, but it was not to be. At Brandywine, south of Philadelphia, Howe and his assistant, General Charles Cornwallis, along with their British and Hessian troops, had dealt Washington a stinging defeat. The armies of the Crown marched into cobblestoned Philadelphia, causing the Continental Congress to pack up and flee west to Lancaster, and then even farther westward, to York. It seemed the Congress could not run far enough.

Washington leaned forward in his saddle. He saw a snowflake fall upon his heavy blue woolen sleeve and he felt the cold wind upon his cheeks. This Valley Forge contained little of value to shelter an army with a Pennsylvania winter fast approaching. Not only was it not a valley, but it no longer even contained a forge. Beyond that, the British had already moved through the area, stripping it bare of what little provisions it may have once contained. Its inhabitants were largely Quakers and, being pacifistic, had little urge to aid any armed rebellion. There was no appreciable lodging nearby—only a few scattered farmhouses—so enough shelter to quarter eleven thousand men would have to be built quickly.

Eleven thousand men, thought Washington. That would make this isolated encampment the fourth-largest city in the colonies. He caught himself: No, not the "colonies"—the states. Washington pondered all this as he caught a glimpse of the area's lone sawmill. The Valley Creek upon which it stood was already frozen solid. It would be of no help to Washington or his men in building their city of wretched little huts.

He looked to the west of Valley Creek, through the gray wintry clouds already buffeting the midday sky and saw one of the two peaks that bounded the area. Its name alone should have foretold what this winter would bring for Washington and his thousands of men.

It was called Mount Misery.

This encampment, Washington saw, would need everything. And it needed it fast.

He swung down from his horse. "Pitch our tents here," he ordered. "This is where we will stay." Then came another command. "Summon my general staff, if you would. We cannot survive long protected by mere canvas!"

Quickly a wagon rolled toward General Washington. Soldiers scrambled to pull a great white linen tent down from it, to hoist sturdy ropes skyward and to hammer iron stakes into the rocky ground. Orderlies rustled to set up Washington's folding wooden camp table and low stools.

"Roll out that map of the area, Colonel Hamilton, if you would," Washington said matter-of-factly. "Now, look, there," he continued, drawing imaginary lines on the document before him. "We will erect roads, here, here—and there. Here will be a line of barracks. As well as here—and here. General Knox's artillery brigade will be here. A guardhouse there. And the outer defenses, trenches and forts, will form lines there—and there. Our parade ground shall be in the center." Again there was a sharp jabbing of his index finger to indicate the location of his plans. "And let us not forget hospitals. Two hospitals for each brigade."

Some of the junior officers marveled at how Washington had so quickly absorbed the lay of the land to reach such logical conclusions. But Lieutenant Colonel Alexander Hamilton, Washington's brilliant young chief of staff, knew better. He knew that his commander had unrolled his maps before ever arriving at Valley Forge. He knew that he had consulted with his officers and sought advice from the locals as he rode to this destination. George Washington's genius, Hamilton knew, rested not only on good judgment, but on good listening and detailed preparation.

But Hamilton also knew something else: they would all need a lot more than listening and preparation to survive a winter in Valley Forge.

•   •   •

A cart that seemed to be from hell itself rolled and lurched down the heavily rutted mud- and rock-strewn path that passed for a road, leading south out of the portion of Valley Forge that sheltered the Marquis de Lafayette's encampment.

Instead of being piled high with provisions or armaments, it was stocked with corpses—rotting, vermin-infested, stinking corpses. Some with their eyes wide open, staring heavenward, others with their mouths agape, their gums blackened from sickness and malnutrition. This cart—and the one that closely followed it—reeked of death. Not of heroic battlefield death, but rather of the stench of death from gnawing, ever-present hunger and horrible sickness.

A shoeless body, dressed in blue rags, tumbled from the cart down into the mud. With this sorry remainder of what had once been a farmer, a husband, a father—a soldier—came a rat. And when both corpse and rat landed upon the winter's ground, the rat, as ravenous as Washington's surviving troops, flew right back toward the dead man—Private Joseph Hawthorn of the First Massachusetts Infantry—and sunk his teeth once more into what had recently been the deceased's right hand.

December 31, 1777
Philadelphia

"Another glass of claret, my dear?" asked General William Howe, the fifth Viscount Howe.

"No, thank you, Your Excellency," coyly replied the woman before him. Her name was Betsy Loring and she was the beautiful, blond wife of the stocky Loyalist commissary of prisoners, Joshua Loring. Even without another glass of claret, however, the twenty-five-year-old Mrs. Elizabeth Loring was really enjoying this wonderful masked ball. Gossips whispered—and they were probably for once correct—that this splendid affair had cost at least three thousand guineas.

If it did, Mrs. Loring thought, it was well worth it.

A chamber orchestra played the latest music from England—no rustic colonial tunes would annoy the patience of this crowd. Officers in silks and ladies in satins and high white wigs curtsied and danced. The finest foods and liquors were served. If this was what occupations were like, then the current occupation of Philadelphia was going very well indeed for the half-German General Howe and his three thousand redcoats.

For his part, General Howe was enjoying not only Philadelphia, but Mrs. Loring, as well. After all, Betsy had been his mistress—and rather openly so—since his occupation of Boston. The genial but corrupt Mr. Loring's official duties kept him in New York for long stretches of time. General Howe saw to that.

"Excuse me, General, but may I have a word with you?"

The voice belonged to the local superintendent-general of police and head of Philadelphia's civil government, Joseph Galloway. Galloway was no ordinary Loyalist. He had served with Washington in the First Continental Congress and had been Speaker of the Pennsylvania House. But Galloway had drawn back from independence and cast his lot with London.

Howe, clearly resenting this interruption of his conversation with Mrs. Loring, gruffly nodded for Galloway to begin.

"Your Excellency," Galloway said, becoming more and more excited as he spoke, "my spies have returned from Valley Forge. They have seen everything, and they all report the same: The rebels have no supplies. They are naked, dressed in rags. They are shoeless. Their enlisted men pack up and leave as their enlistments expire." His voice was now rising to fever pitch and speed. "Thousands—yes, thousands!—of their men lay sick at hospitals. This is an army on the verge of extinction. If we move against them now, not only will they be in no position to resist, they may very well not even possess the strength to flee. We might sweep up the whole lot of them—once and for all! Even Washington himself!"

"Even Washington?" responded Howe, his eyes widening, his eyebrows arching. Galloway had finally piqued his interest.

"Yes," said Galloway. *"Even Washington."*

The ground beneath George Washington's high boots was white and brown and red.

It was white for the drifts of snow and ice that remained upon it.

It was brown for the sodden mud born of wildly fluctuating weather, from warm spells that had punctuated freezing cold, melting snow and ice and creating the mire that clogged the primitive roads in Valley Forge. It would have been better had the snow remained, since one might then drive sleighs upon the hard-packed snow. But the mud ensured that nothing could pass upon these wretched thoroughfares, these lattice works of impenetrable ruts that snapped axles and shattered wheels and hobbled horses. These excuses for roads brought no clothing, no food, no medicine, no muskets or ammunition—only carts of corpses; corpses that were responsible for the final color beneath Washington's boots: blood red.

Crimson streaks marred Valley Forge's patches of whitened ground— the red painted by bleeding, shoeless, frozen feet, frostbitten extremities soon to feel the agony of a surgeon's sharpened blade.

Yes, white and brown and red were the colors of Valley Forge. White and brown and red were, this season, the very colors of hell.

January 5, 1778
Valley Forge

George Washington silently dismounted and walked steadily away from the crowd of ragged militiamen who eyed his arrival, past a gently sloping wooded hillside and into a small clearing, where, at this hour of day, a shaft of light might illuminate his view—and his soul. He was alone. No one accompanied him in these moments.

Washington looked skyward. Despite the winter's cold he removed his woolen tricornered hat and held it before him as he pondered the terrible nature of the burden he had placed upon himself. In more ways than one, he held in his hands the life and fortunes of every soldier in his command. But that wasn't his only burden, for he also knew that the fate of this great experiment in human freedom and dignity depended on their success. If it—*if he*—failed, it might never be repeated.

Mankind's history had, after all, revealed its remarkable tolerance for tyranny. But maybe, he thought, these men here today might prove different. Perhaps this place, this Valley Forge, might now forge not iron but a world made anew. But if a new order of the cosmos were to be forged, George Washington knew he could not do it alone.

And so, in the solitude of a snow-covered Pennsylvania clearing, George Washington knelt—and he prayed.

In nearby Reading, General James Wilkinson was downright drunk.

Good and drunk.

Wilkinson did his drinking at the headquarters of the wounded general Lord Stirling. Stirling had originally been a New Yorker with the far more modest name of William Alexander but had gotten it into his head that he was Scottish nobility and so, not long before the revolution erupted, he'd assumed the vacant title of "Lord Stirling." Whether Stirling was nobility or not wasn't of much concern to the shifty and pudgy Wilkinson. He was far more concerned with pouring his guts out to his aide-de-camp, Major William McWilliams. And those guts, it seemed, contained equal quotients of admiration for his superior, General Horatio Gates, the recent hero of Saratoga, and contempt for General George Washington.

Wilkinson was hardly alone in his opinions. In Congress, similar sniping circulated. The Continental Congress's president, South Carolinian planter Henry Laurens, had even found an anonymous anti-Washington pamphlet, *Thoughts of a Freeman*, openly circulating among its members. The knives were out for George Washington. He had not won a battle since Princeton and now he was refusing calls from Congress's armchair generals hiding in York to attack Howe in Philadelphia.

"No, by Jove!" General Wilkinson thundered to Major McWilliams, pounding his fat fist upon the heavy oak table before them for emphasis, "Washington is not the man for the job! And the officers who surround him—this Quaker general Nathanael Greene, for example, or these boys Hamilton and Lafayette—well, they make him look like a genius, a veritable Alexander the Great or Cromwell!"

Wilkinson wasn't done. "You know General Conway, don't you?" he shook a finger at McWilliams, referring to yet another ambitious general who fancied himself superior in experience and judgment to Washington. "Well, Conway might be an Irishman, but he was one of the best generals the French had before he came over here, and he thinks the way I do—the way we *all* do! Conway wrote right to Gates himself, I can quote it direct to you: 'Heaven has determined to save your country, or otherwise a weak general and bad counselors would have ruined it.' "

Wilkinson paused from his tirade long enough to loudly demand another portion of rum from the innkeeper. The hour was late. And the more alcohol that entered General Wilkinson the more of what he considered truth burst forth.

"What do you think of *that*, McWilliams? I'll tell you what *I* think: truer words were never spoken—and heaven will soon deal further with the master of Mount Vernon, unless, that is"—and here Wilkinson chuckled wildly—"hell takes him first!"

January 12, 1778
Valley Forge

"Fire cakes again?" stormed Corporal Amos Barnett of New York's Westchester County militia. A deep, long scar that had turned a hideous purple in the Valley Forge cold ran down Barnett's right cheek. It had been bestowed upon him courtesy of a dragoon's slashing blow during the Battle of Long Island.

Barnett's eyes fixed ominously on the concoction stewing in the fireplace before him. The men called it a "fire cake." They took what little flour meal they had left, mixed it with water and a little salt (if they were lucky to have any), and ladled it onto a griddle—or in this case, on a flat rock—in their hut's fireplace. And there was their "fire cake."

"Damn it all!" the scarred New Yorker thundered even louder now. "Are we never to have meat again? Never?"

The flour-and-water mixture turned a brownish hue upon the flat, heated rock.

"Are you through, Corporal?" answered the recruit cooking the fire cakes, a slight lad—growing slighter every day—who was barely into his teens.

"No, I am not!" Barnett sputtered. "What manner of army is this? What kind of war when men die more in camp than in battle? Who bears responsibility for this?"

"I do," came a voice from the doorway.

A dozen pairs of eyes turned toward the powerful figure standing before them, his left arm tucked beneath his great red-lined cape, his hand taut upon the gold handle of his sword.

"I apologize to every man here for every hardship," Washington said, his black manservant Billy Lee, along with Colonel Hamilton and General Lafayette, standing just behind him. "I thank you all for the service you have rendered to the causes of liberty and independence."

But responsibility was not truly his. Congress had taken the issue of supplies out of his hands. It had placed its trust in men who were thieves, incompetent, or who simply did not care.

But George Washington took responsibility anyway.

The soldiers before him remained quiet, so Washington continued. "I have sent parties out to forage for grain and cattle and horses and clothing and boots. General Greene will assume overall command of supplies. We are even sending our men to New England to secure cattle. We will bring them back on the hoof, Providence willing.

"Meat, gentlemen, meat."

His audience remained silent. Too dumbstruck to speak. A now-forgotten fire cake blackened and burned in the fireplace. It charred and smoked. No one noticed.

"Do you take me at my word, fellow patriots?" their commanding officer asked softly.

Finally, Corporal Barnett spoke: "You have not lied to me yet, General, nor to any of us here. So yes, we take you at your word."

"Will you join us for dinner, General? We have not much, but what we have is yours."

"Yes," said General Washington, thinking not only of the men before him but of the West Indies–born Hamilton and the highborn French nobleman Lafayette and the slave Billy Lee behind him. "I would be honored to dine with you tonight—*to dine among Americans.*"

Yet another foreign-born officer now stood at attention before Washington.

Hamilton spoke excellent English, and the brave young Lafayette spoke enough so that he could be *mis*understood—but this chap, this pudgy man with the great sunburst medal, the Star of Fidelity of Baden, pinned over his heart, a bulbous nose and a twinkling smile, spoke nary a word of the King's English.

The officer standing before Washington spoke German, along with a touch of French that he had acquired along the way from one European battlefield to another. He called himself Baron Friedrich Wilhelm August Heinrich Ferdinand von Steuben and informed one and all—or at least the one and all who could understand him—that he had been a close associate of Europe's greatest warrior, King Frederick the Great of Prussia.

Washington placed his reading spectacles upon his nose and pored over the letter of introduction from the Congress that Steuben presented to him. Benjamin Franklin, representing the rebels in Paris, and the Congress residing in York had dispatched this foreigner here to Valley Forge—but what had they dispatched him to do exactly, make schnitzel of the enemy?

Washington read the portion of Franklin's letter concerning Frederick the Great and it impressed him. Frederick was the most noted warrior in all of Europe. Washington solemnly nodded his head in appreciation, and, as Steuben noticed Washington nodding, the German too began to nod, adopting the general's somber manner. Steuben had no idea why Washington—or he—was nodding. But he kept nodding anyway, and as Washington kept reading and nodding, Steuben kept nodding—faster and faster and faster.

He figured it wouldn't hurt.

Even had he noticed it, Washington would never have been able or willing to keep pace with Steuben's nodding, but he really began to nod when he read that von Steuben proposed to serve without salary. He would take only necessary expenses, and he would only receive a salary if the rebels ultimately triumphed.

George Washington was a betting man. He would bet on fox hunts, on horse races, on lotteries, on just about anything. If the Virginian had one vice, it was gambling. Now, in Steuben and the deal he had cut with Congress, Washington saw a kindred spirit. The baron had bet the table on American independence—and Washington, who had bet his very life on it, really liked that.

And, if that were not enough for Washington, there was even more to like about von Steuben. In a Continental Army flooded by European officers grabbing for every rank, promotion, and command that they might, this von Steuben fellow requested nothing but to serve.

Washington liked him right away. Here was a chap he might already possess plans for. Washington stopped nodding, looked the shorter man in the eye—and delivered a rare smile.

Steuben burst into a great grin. "Ja!" he exclaimed, "Ja! Vashington! Ja!"

"Ja!" said Washington. "Steuben!"

"Major General Thomas Conway to see you, General Washington."

Conway, his epaulets of golden braid glistening in the midday sun, kicked the dust off his boots as he entered Washington's headquarters, located at the very rear of Isaac Potts's modest two-story, six-room gray stone farmhouse. The egotistical Conway might have tidied himself *before* entering his commander in chief's private office, but that would have indicated his respect for Washington.

Conway was feeling his oats, and his smug expression only further betrayed his confidence. And why, after all, should Conway not display unbounded swagger? The noose was now tightening around Washington—not a British noose, but an American one. Congress had snubbed Washington by appointing a "Board of War" to oversee the army. Washington wasn't on it, but Horatio Gates was—and his drunken henchman General James Wilkinson served as its secretary.

Now Conway had even more salt to rub in George Washington's wounds.

"You know why I am here, General. Congress has promoted me to major general and made me inspector general of all continental armies."

Conway could barely contain himself in pronouncing those words.

Washington, invariably gracious, had no welcome for this man. "Major General Conway, I will treat and provide you with every ounce of respect and cooperation that *your rank and appointments* entitle the bearer of that rank and assignment. When official business demands that I consult with you, I will. No such business exists at present. You are dismissed."

Conway stood there stunned. The world suddenly seemed enveloped in silence. Even the sparrows outside in their nests seemed to have ceased their songs. A minute previously, Conway had felt himself at the top of the world. Now he had absorbed an icy blast worthy of the North Pole. George Washington had cut him dead. George Washington, he had just discovered, was afraid neither of British bullets nor of strutting, scheming backstabbers.

Conway exited the Potts farmhouse. He tried to provide the impression that all had gone well inside, but he noticed a semicircle of Washington's officers had gathered around him. They followed him to his horse in an oddly menacing manner, speaking not a word. Their silent, icy glances were nearly as frosty as the reception Conway had endured inside and conveyed one unmistakable impression: George Washington had the undying loyalty of every one of the troops who served with him.

If Conway and his ally Horatio Gates were to triumph it would not be with the support of the men who had suffered alongside George Washington at Valley Forge. They'd need to look elsewhere.

January 21, 1778
Philadelphia

General William Howe drummed his finely manicured fingers upon his fine Chippendale mahogany desk. Behind him, in an elaborately carved and gilded frame, was a portrait of his monarch, King George III. The frame had not always contained the monarch's portrait. Until Howe's arrival it had held a family portrait of John and Elizabeth Cadwalader and their daughter, Anne. But now Cadwalader served in Washington's army and William Howe—along with Betsy Loring, a woman half his age—slept in Cadwalader's bed.

Superintendent-General of Police Galloway once again stood before him. "Your Excellency," Galloway began, "you know that we have word that the worst may have passed for Washington's army—"

"Yes! I know that," Howe impatiently interrupted. This Galloway was more than he could bear. "He has more recruits," Howe continued. "He is now receiving supplies. French and German and even Polish officers join his ranks. Yes. Yes. Yes. I know all of it!"

Galloway tugged nervously upon his fine lace cuff. He knew that

Howe did not want to hear what he was about to suggest—but he was bold enough to make the suggestion anyway. He had to, so much depended upon it! General Howe might be able to return to his estates in Britain if Washington succeeded, but, if, heaven forbid, Washington and his rebels triumphed, Galloway would have to abandon his own fortune and board a sailing ship for Canada—assuming the British still held Canada—or for London, or, maybe even for India. No, Joseph Galloway had to make his case whether William Howe liked it or not.

"We still have time, General," Galloway continued. "A force of sufficient strength could still wreak havoc on the rebels at Valley Forge."

Howe thought otherwise. Washington had supply problems, yes, but he had chosen Valley Forge wisely. It would be a difficult place to attack, even in perfect weather. But an attack in wintertime? What was Galloway thinking? *Real* armies would never so much as contemplate that!

Galloway saw the look upon Howe's face that he had seen many times before. But as Galloway continued making his case, he looked beyond Howe, through the leaded-glass window onto Second Street, where a gleaming black sleigh, brightly upholstered in green fabric, had pulled up. Assisted by her footman, the beautiful Betsy Loring stepped daintily down onto the cobblestones. Almost simultaneously, and without any willful thought on his part, bits of doggerel began to play in Galloway's brain.

The rhymes now invading his head had torn their way through Philadelphia like wildfire. Superintendent-General Galloway wasn't the only individual frustrated by Howe's abysmal lack of military initiative. Many blamed Howe's lethargy upon his reluctance to leave the City of Brotherly Love—not simply because of its brotherly love in the form of urban comforts, but also because of its sisterly love provided by the beautiful Mrs. Loring. And so, in rough waterfront taverns, behind General Howe's red-coated back, an increasing number of critics hoisted their pewter flagons of ale to chant a poem first penned by a rebel:

> *Awake, arouse Sir Billy,*
> *There's forage in the plain,*
> *Ah, leave your little Filly,*
> *And open the campaign.*

and . . .

> *Sir William Howe, he, snug as a flea,*
> *Lay all this time a-snoring;*
> *Nor dreamed of harm, as he lay warm*
> *In bed with Mrs. Loring*

There was much truth in those words, but even if Mrs. Loring had chosen to remain as faithful to Mr. Loring as Martha Washington had remained to George, General Howe had little interest in pursuing Washington's rebels through bramble bushes or across frozen streams. In fact, he seemed to have little interest in pursuing any rebels *anywhere*.

General Howe, disgusted with the war and how Parliament's politicians ran it, had already submitted his resignation to the king. He now waited only for Betsy Loring—and for his orders to return to London.

He'd be damned if he took a rebel musket ball through the neck before he got there.

February 2, 1778
York, Pennsylvania

Inside the brick and log Golden Plough Tavern, the Continental Congress's president, Henry Laurens, was having a hard time. "Laurens," the angriest of his adversaries said, jabbing his finger at him, "when will you stop defending your friend Washington? The game is over. Gates is the general we want—the general the revolution needs! He wins! He *fights*!"

"Yes, Henry," pronounced another congressman, a balding man barely over five feet, who busied himself tapping the remains of burnt tobacco from a white clay pipe that measured a full half yard long. "The revolution," he continued, "is bigger than any one man—even if he *is* as tall as General Washington!"

Even Henry Laurens had to chuckle at that one.

At that moment, a weary traveler entered through the Golden Plough's heavy red wooden front door. Garbed in white buckskin, he could not help but catch every patron's eye, and before he had reached the bar, excited shouts erupted.

"It's Daniel Morgan!"

For they knew Morgan had fought at the recent Battle of Saratoga. They clamored for firsthand news of it and how General Horatio Gates had vanquished Britain's General Burgoyne—and demanded to know what Morgan thought of the remarkable Gates. Morgan extended a calloused hand above his head as a crowd gathered around him.

"I'll talk, if you buy!" he shouted and the crowd laughed. "And when I talk I'll tell you the truth about Saratoga—and that cowering old woman Horatio Gates. If it were left up to him, Gentleman Johnny Burgoyne would be drinking here with you instead of me.

At that the crowd began to quiet down.

"It was Benedict Arnold who led the charge and saved the day! Horatio Gates is not half the general George Washington—or even Johnny Burgoyne—is and that's the truth, too! If you replace Washington, you can replace me! Half my army would march home to Virginia if you did that! The other half would join the British—and hang the lot of *you*!

"Now, who's buying?"

The crowd had been stunned into silence. Morgan's broad smile was met only by a host of blank stares.

"I'm buying!" exclaimed Henry Laurens, "for you and for the house!" Surveying his suddenly sheepish fellow congressmen, Laurens softly said, "Now, can we finally have the end of this foolish talk?"

"Yes," said the small congressman with the big clay pipe, "but only if we drink a toast."

"A toast?"

"Yes, Mr. President," he answered, with a laugh, knowing he was beaten, "a toast, to Daniel Morgan—and to our commander in chief, George Washington!"

With that, the Congress spoke no more of Horatio Gates.

February 28, 1778
Valley Forge

"Eins!"
  "Zwei!"
  "Drei!"

"What the deuce is going on out there, General?" General Charles Lee asked Horatio Gates, who had recently arrived from New York, as the two Washington critics stood watching the unlikely scenario unfolding before them, "Are we the last officers in this Valley Forge to speak English? Lafayette! DeKalb! Pulaski! Now, this fellow! And he calls himself a baron, a general—and he is out there drilling troops like a sergeant! They can't even understand him! He has to have his commands translated. This encampment is a bedlam, and I know not whether our so-called commander is its warden or a mere inmate!"

The object of Lee's ire was Baron von Steuben, who, on George Washington's orders, had assembled a squad of a hundred men to learn the latest in modern European military techniques. Steuben strode before his command, barking orders in German, pantomiming what he wanted them to do, and either beaming with pride when they followed his orders—or throwing up his hands and sputtering a long list of Teutonic imprecations better left untranslated when they didn't. That such a high-ranking officer would deign to directly train enlisted men was unheard-of—in either the aristocratic old world or in the republican new. But Steuben was doing whatever he was doing enthusiastically—and, perhaps more important, with General Washington's blessing.

As Steuben swore and sputtered and harrumphed up and down the line, his chosen squad could barely contain their smiles. This was something new, they thought, and while they may not have known what to make of this mad Prussian, they knew that they liked him. Whatever they thought of what he was teaching them, they were at least learning *something*. It was almost like a game. But in the process they learned to shoulder arms, march in formation, and use a bayonet for more than roasting rabbits over an open fire.

Whether they knew it or not, they were learning how to be more than rebels. They were learning how to be soldiers.

General Lee continued glaring at Steuben. He spat at the ground in contempt. Horatio Gates glanced downward to see if Lee had somehow hit his boots. He was relieved to see his comrade had missed.

"So, General Gates, what think you of our Prussian drillmaster with his great 'Star of Fidelity of Baden' upon his chest?"

Lee had pronounced each word of "Star of Fidelity of Baden" slowly and with the utmost contempt.

"I think," answered General Gates, in a low voice so none but Charles Lee might hear him, that 'Baden' bears far too close a similarity to 'bedlam.' "

Wednesday, May 6, 1778
Valley Forge

A lone six-pound cannon roared fire and smoke and shattered the Valley's mid-morning silence. It thundered not in violence, nor in attack nor in defense.

It thundered instead in sheer joy.

The previous evening General Washington had received correspondence from Benjamin Franklin in Paris containing the news that all Americans had long awaited: France had entered the war against Britain. The colonists no longer faced the world's mightiest empire outgunned and alone. Franklin—along with a victory at Saratoga—had finally convinced France's King Louis XVI to declare war upon George III. It would now be a fair fight and perhaps only a matter of time until London grew tired of war, of expending its blood and treasure in a fruitless struggle against men who no longer wished to be called English subjects but rather free Americans.

Washington summoned his officers. By flickering tallow candlelight he read to them the wondrous news. Tears streamed down Marquis de Lafayette's cheeks. He rushed toward Washington and embraced him.

Washington knew a celebration was in order, but it was Steuben who knew what to do—and how to do it.

Somehow, this ruddy-faced Prussian had done more than simply train these rough and ready and—not long ago starving—Americans how to shoulder arms and respectably march around Valley Forge's vast parade ground. He had achieved a miracle. In a matter of weeks, he had transformed a horde of patriots into a cadre of professional soldiers—capable, confident, and, hopefully, deadly effective.

Now Steuben would stage a grand show for Washington, for the men themselves—and for an entire world still wondering whether a revolution of free men might succeed.

Two great lines of Continental troops faced each other on Valley Forge's parade grounds: the first line was half under the command of Major General Lord Stirling's command and half under Lafayette's. The second line was entirely under the command of yet another foreign-born volunteer: the German-born French general Baron Johann DeKalb.

Three thirteen-gun salutes punctuated the morning air, but the most heartening portion of the program was the great show the enlisted men staged—a *feu de joie*, a "fire of joy"—a spectacular running of musket fire from the seven brigades that marked the two lines of men. As each musketeer fired a blank shot into the air, the soldier next to him instantly discharged his own weapon. On and on, the men fired in precision, without a hitch, up one line and down the next. The thunder they sent skyward was long and loud, continuous and resounding. General Horatio Gates covered his ears from the noise. General Charles Lee's faithful dogs cowered under their master.

Baron von Steuben had indeed transformed an ill-trained, half-starved rabble into professionals. And Valley Forge had toughened the men it had not killed or frightened away. Those who remained were hardened patriots, not frightened by battle or adversity, willing to follow George Washington anywhere.

And so, on this fine spring morning, Frederick the Great's grenadiers could not have performed better than these freemen who fired their muskets faster and faster, as the fire of joy splendidly unfolded. This morning's muskets rang as loudly for freedom as Philadelphia's great bronze Liberty Bell or Thomas Jefferson's words in the Declaration of Independence.

And these men—Washington and Steuben's men—would soon be granted a chance to see if their ability to march in line and fire into the air would match their ability to fight. Because if General William Howe wouldn't take the fight to the rebels, General Charles Cornwallis certainly would.

5

A Good General, a Great Author

I am sick, discontented, and out of humor. Poor food, hard lodging, cold weather, fatigue, nasty clothes, nasty cookery, vomit half my time, smoked out of my senses—the devil's in it; I can't endure it. Why are we sent here to starve and freeze? What sweet felicities have I left at home: A charming wife, pretty children, good beds, good food, good cooking—all agreeable, all harmonious! Here all confusion, smoke and cold, hunger and filthiness. . . .

—SURGEON ALBIGENCE WALDO,
VALLEY FORGE, DECEMBER 14, 1777

Around ten thousand men arrived at Valley Forge in December 1777, surviving in drafty, makeshift tents before they built small, freezing huts—fourteen feet wide by sixteen feet long—that would go on to house twelve soldiers each.

At some point during their stay, around 30 percent of these soldiers would suffer from one disease or another; 2,500 of them would die. When they first got to the camp, about 4,000 men were without blankets; 2,000 would never have one during their entire stay at Valley Forge.

Washington must have noticed the streaking blood coming from lacerated feet on the icy paths that led to the camp. Thousands of his men were without shoes and, soon enough, army surgeons were amputating frostbitten and gangrened legs and feet in astonishing numbers.

And shoes weren't the only thing missing. Eventually some of the soldiers' clothing grew so ragged that it fell off their gaunt bodies, leaving them with only blankets to cover their nakedness. With no clothes to wear, the men were too embarrassed to even leave their quarters.

To make matters even worse, the British, the world's largest and most powerful fighting force, were amassed only eighteen miles away in Philadelphia, ready to pounce. They'd already taken New York and had just handed Washington a bruising defeat in Brandywine.

Morale was low. Not a single shot had been fired to defend the City of Brotherly Love—the capital of revolutionary America. In fact, it's possible that Washington heard about the cheering crowds that awaited the British's arrival in Philadelphia.

Have Government—Will Travel

With the loss of Philadelphia, the colonists were quickly running out of cities to call their capital. Or, perhaps more accurately, you could say that America seemed to be running out of people who believed the patriots would ever need a capital to begin with.

So, how many official capitals did the United States actually inhabit? It's hard to keep track, but the answer is nine. The First Continental Congress met in Philadelphia in 1774. The Second Continental Congress, though, seemed to be on the run quite a bit during the war, meeting at Philadelphia's State House, in Baltimore, in Lancaster and in York, Pennsylvania, and then back again to College Hall in Philadelphia.

Under the Articles of Confederation, Congress met again in Philadelphia, and then in Princeton, New Jersey; Annapolis, Maryland; Trenton, New Jersey; and then New York City. After the U.S. Congress was instituted by the U.S. Constitution in 1789, it was housed in New York and Philadelphia, before finally settling down (for good?) in Washington, D.C.

Despite the apparent hopelessness of the situation, Washington maintained his resolve. He may not have been the greatest tactical general of all time, but he knew how to lead. And he knew that real leadership required bravery—especially when all hope seemed to be lost.

The American Job

Washington was living the story of Job.

Like Washington, Job was a prosperous and respected man of his time. He led a charmed life and had seven sons and three daughters. One day God asked Satan what he made of such a righteous man. Satan retorted that Job was only decent because he had been shielded from crisis and suffering by God. If Job were to live without divine protection, if he were to experience loss and catastrophe, Job would surely turn to the dark side.

God tested Job's resolve by taking everything from him. Despite the hardships, Job remained humble and true and was soon rewarded again for his trust.

If God was indeed watching over Washington and the rebels, then Valley Forge was likely their Job moment. Faced with the loss of everything, they very easily could have given up, or worse, turned against their own cause.

But, led by Washington, they did the opposite. And, just like Job, they were eventually rewarded.

THE STRUGGLE TO KEEP IT ALL TOGETHER

"Naked and starving as [our troops] are," Washington wrote, "we cannot enough admire the incomparable patience and fidelity of the solider."

It was that admiration that made the unfathomable suffering and death he saw every day even harder to take. But that wasn't Washington's only problem—many men had also decided to return to their families or farms once their conscriptions to the army had ended. Of those who stayed, many complained endlessly about the dreadful conditions and were dragging down morale of everyone. "This is not an army, this is a mob," one general noted after a visit to the camp.

And some soldiers had more nefarious intentions in mind. There were two thousand colonial deserters during that winter. The British, after all, could pay them in the sound currency of pounds sterling, while the Continentals offered only depreciated, nearly worthless money. (Boy, does that sound uncomfortably familiar.) It's estimated that around eighty colonists joined the English as spies that season. Consequently, scores of rebel spy rings in and around Philadelphia were exposed, decimating the important intelligence operations that Washington so desperately needed.

Right Man, Right Place, Right Time

There are many great lessons to take away from Valley Forge, but one of the best is that you are only as good as your preparation. We see this so many times in Washington's life—what seems to be luck or coincidence is really the result of preparation and skill, all guided by the hand of the great Author. And we see it in our lives as well. People who seem to be "overnight successes" are generally those who've spent years preparing for the one moment that might decide the rest of their life.

Valley Forge was not the first time Washington had commanded ill-equipped and sickened troops. If it had been, he very likely would've failed. Starting as a Virginia regiment militia commander who was charged with defending colonists from vicious frontier Indian attacks, Washington had learned to survive with insufficient supplies in conditions so harsh that even most of his fellow colonists would have found them completely unbearable.

And then there was his experience with suffering. Washington had spent nearly his whole life battling sicknesses (diphtheria, malaria, smallpox, dysentery, quinsy) and fighting against the cruelty of nature— something that had steeled him for this critical winter of the revolution. During the French and Indian War, Washington battled a vicious bout of dysentery. It hit him so hard that rumors of his death began circulating throughout Williamsburg. Though he bounced back from this illness with renewed strength, his familiarity with suffering from disease allowed him to be both empathetic toward the pain of soldiers and strong-willed about their chances of survival.

As a young man, Washington also suffered from numerous bouts of high fever, and "pleurisy." That was just part of life on the frontier. He'd visited Barbados with his half brother (who would die from tuberculosis) and contracted the often-fatal smallpox. During a widespread epidemic, Washington remained bedridden for at least a month in tremendous pain and with dangerously high fever. The episode left him scarred for life, but it gave him important immunity to the disease; immunity that allowed him to walk with confidence among the sick in Valley Forge.

Without these experiences, he may not have been able to be the rock of strength in Valley Forge. And if he were not personally strong during that awful winter, then how could he ever expect his troops to be?

Not only was Washington assailed by every imaginable obstacle that nature and war could offer, but he was also undermined by his own impotent government. Despite his continual protests, the army was constantly undersupplied and on the verge of dissolution. If it wasn't the British who were disrupting supply shipments to the troops it was politics, internal strife, and the duplicity of fellow Americans, like army quartermaster general Thomas Mifflin, George Washington's former aide-de-camp, who had been accused of embezzlement and of ignoring his duties by failing to procure and distribute the food, clothing, and supplies so urgently needed by the army.

Washington was not one to exaggerate the dangers of his situation, yet a few days before the army had even arrived at the winter encampment, Washington was imploring Henry Laurens, president of Congress, to take the situation more seriously. He wrote:

I do not know from what cause this alarming deficiency or rather total failure of Supplies arises; But unless more Vigorous exertions and better regulations take place in that line, and immediately, this Army must dissolve. I have done all in my power by remonstrating, by writing to, by ordering the Commissaries on this Head . . . but without any good effect, or obtaining more than a present scanty relief.

But, whether because of incompetence or a simple lack of ability to effect real change, it doesn't seem like Congress was taking the dire warnings of the general very seriously. Before Washington had even taken shelter in Valley Forge, the Pennsylvania legislature had criticized him for pulling his army back to such "luxurious" winter quarters. After a string of military losses, prominent members of the independence movement (even John Adams) and Congress were beginning to question his fitness to command the army. There was even a contingent openly calling for his removal. All of these engineered distractions undermined Washington and his army and put the entire cause of the revolution in serious jeopardy.

Washington did his best to avoid the ugly and divisive world of political intrigue because, as we see throughout his life, he found it beneath the dignity of an honorable man. Not to mention that getting involved in that kind of political back-and-forth would mean revealing top-secret military information that would undermine the larger cause, even though doing so might have helped his position. "My enemies take an ungenerous advantage of me," he wrote to Henry Laurens. "They know I cannot combat their insinuations . . . without disclosing secrets it is of the utmost moment to conceal."

There's a great lesson in that quote for us (especially our politicians) today: put your country above yourself. Always. Washington sat there and took the insults from his critics without responding because he knew that to prove them wrong, he'd have to put out confidential information. Even in the most important of times, like the Constitutional Convention, Washington primarily stayed above the fray, leading by example but never lowering himself to participate in the debate or lob insults at others. Too many times we see our political leaders engaging in petty arguments or hurling insults at others simply to protect their own reputations when they should instead be rising above the noise and doing what is right for the country.

NO BIGOTS NEED APPLY

Despite winter's hardships, George Washington was still very much focused on victory. He began to welcome new volunteers into camp—and his depleted forces obviously needed the help. Incredibly, and as a testament to his leadership, his army marched out of Valley Forge with more men than it had first set up camp with.

He accomplished that, in part, by being creative—and very open-minded. It was in Valley Forge, for example, that Washington allowed Rhode Island to augment its troop strength by enlisting black soldiers for the first time. Soon after, the state promised to free any slaves willing to join the fight. Other states soon followed Rhode Island's lead and soon there were, according to some eyewitnesses, more than seven hundred African-American soldiers in the fight. It's nearly inconceivable to think that a prominent southerner—maybe the most prominent—would not only accept black men into his army, but also assist in the freeing of slaves. It's a miracle that such a provocative move did not precipitate a mutiny against the commander.

Washington embraced those who embraced the ideals of liberty and were willing to fight for it, no matter their race, religion, profession, or nationality, and he continued to exemplify this quality throughout his life. In his famous 1790 letter as president to the Jews of Rhode Island, he wrote, "To Bigotry No Sanction, to Persecution No Assistance."

He lived by that motto.

Freedom Fighters

Americans still celebrate this tolerance today—and with very good reason. It's one reason why so many of us feel kinship with nations like Israel while having disdain for the world's dictators. Freedom is ingrained in us. If you want to be free, we want to be your friend. Washington was perhaps the first person of great consequence to look at the world in that way.

Washington's open-mindedness would soon be instrumental in helping the continental troops overcome a huge military disadvantage, turning them from a ragtag crew into a modern (well, as modern as you can get with muskets and three-cornered hats) fighting force to be reckoned with. It was, for example, at Valley Forge that Washington first warmed to the Marquis de Lafayette, a nineteen-year-old French nobleman who was soon to become one his most trusted aides and a hero of the revolution. There were others, like Tadeusz Kościuszko, a Polish engineer who was deeply moved by the Declaration of Independence and helped America achieve victory at Saratoga.

And then, of course, there was Lieutenant General Friedrich Wilhelm Ludolf Gerhard Augustin Baron von Steuben. Washington showed full faith in a flamboyant German who some claimed was as insane as his name was long. In reality he was neither a baron nor a lieutenant general, but he was an experienced drillmaster and, more important, a believer in the cause of liberty.

Baron von Steuben had served in the Prussian army under Frederick the Great, who in many ways was one of the most forward-thinking leaders in Europe at the time. Steuben had learned some of the newest and most innovative military tactics, and his guidance at Valley Forge was immeasurable. If Washington had simply judged him by his language or name, he would've never let him anywhere near his troops.

At Valley Forge, Von Steuben became a brilliant drillmaster who tested the adaptability and inner strength of the American forces. He taught the patriot troops how to maneuver in ranks, to use their bayonets effectively, and wheel in formation, rather than haphazardly as they were used to. He taught them how to move from column to column and become more nimble on the battlefield. He was a taskmaster and drilled the troops all day long by using profanities that Washington would surely have frowned upon had they ever been uttered in English.

In the end, Steuben's methods helped the Americans go toe-to-toe with the British. They were so innovative, in fact, that the instruction manual he authored, with the help of John Laurens (Henry Laurens's son) and Alexander Hamilton, was used by the United States Army all the way until the Civil War.

The Last Letter

While von Steuben is not a name at the tip of most Americans' tongues, his place in the revolution was not lost on Washington, who wrote him this gushing letter:

Annapolis, December 23, 1783

My Dear Baron:

Although I have taken frequent opportunities, both in public and private, of acknowledging your zeal, attention and abilities in performing the duties of your office, yet I wish to make use of this last moment of my public life to signify in the strongest terms my entire approbation of your conduct, and to express my sense of the obligations the public is under to you for your faithful and meritorious service.

I beg you will be convinced, my dear Sir, that I should rejoice if it could ever be in my power to serve you more essentially than by expressions of regard and affection. But in the meantime I am persuaded you will not be displeased with this farewell token of my sincere friendship and esteem for you.

This is the last letter I shall ever write while I continue in the service of my country. The hour of my resignation is fixed at twelve this day, after which I shall become a private citizen on the banks of the Potomac, where I shall be glad to embrace you, and testify the great esteem and consideration, with which I am, my dear Baron, your most obedient and affectionate servant.

—George Washington

Throughout the war, Washington employed tactics that had previously been unknown to his enemy: he used unreliable militia to harass the British foragers and local Tories; he attacked the main British army from every angle except head-on; and he trained and used sharpshooters to slow down British forces. Washington was not a great general in the European style, but he turned himself into a creative military leader who fought a uniquely American war and who understood that the melting pot of people and ideas was our greatest asset. It still is today.

Thinking Outside the Eighteenth-Century Box

Washington's embrace of foreigners and modern technology was hardly surprising. As a self-educated man, Washington was, in many ways, far more open to new ideas and methods than many of his contemporaries.

Washington stocked his Mount Vernon library with books and pamphlets on emerging agricultural science and up-to-date farm management systems. He regularly embraced cutting-edge procedures and had displayed an incredible ability to adapt to the times—another trait that Americans still embrace.

Washington experimented with crop rotations, and he replaced tobacco as his Potomac plantation's main crop with, at various times, corn, hemp, and wheat. He also experimented with various combinations of soil and fertilizers, treatment of seeds, grafting, and modern drainage systems, and had invented a resourceful drill plow that others would later copy. One historian called George Washington America's first "scientific farmer."

"HOWE" THE COLONIES WERE LOST

Washington knew that God works in mysterious ways—and nothing could be a better example of that than the incredible story of Elizabeth Loring's seductive hold on the British commander William Howe.

The beautiful and affable Loring was married to Loyalist Joshua Loring but was having an affair with General Howe, commander of the English forces. Howe had first led the British at the famous Battle of Bunker Hill and defeated Washington at the Battle of Long Island—though he was heavily criticized for missing an important opportunity to destroy the embryonic American army as it evacuated across the East River from Brooklyn to Manhattan. Things had been looking up since then, and after defeating Washington again at Brandywine, Howe had settled into cozy Philadelphia for the long winter.

The Lorings were with him.

Not only did Elizabeth benefit from this arrangement, but her husband did as well. Howe named him commissioner of prisoners of war—a position that would make him rich through the bribes he could procure from the would-be prisoners and their families. And while Howe tended to Elizabeth, Joshua oversaw rebel prisoners hellishly rotting away in ships in New York harbor and in a dank, converted sugar refinery in New York, simultaneously making plenty of cash shaking down their families and loved ones.

According to most historians, if General Howe had left the comfortable confines of Philadelphia that winter he could have crushed

Washington's depleted and ailing troops at Valley Forge, likely ending the revolution then and there. But, for a number of reasons, many of them still a mystery, he did not.

According to contemporary accounts, Howe very much enjoyed all the entertainment and indulgences that Philadelphia had to offer—but the one thing that grabbed his attention more than the theater, dancing, and gambling was Ms. Loring herself.

To be fair to Howe, there were plenty of reasons not to venture out of Philadelphia other than Elizabeth Loring. Howe, unlike Washington at Valley Forge, was not particularly interested in testing out newfangled military methods. Enjoying a position of strength, he remained loyal to many of the outdated conceptions of European warfare that had worked for him throughout the war. One of the most harmful of these tenets was a convenient resolve that gentlemen should never fight in inclement weather.

To what extent a crush on Loring prevented Howe from leaving Philadelphia is certainly up for debate, but there is no doubt Howe would have been able to inflict massive damage on the impaired Continental Army if he had. And while I'm certainly not saying that Loring was sent by, as Washington would say, the Author, to work in such miraculous ways, I'm not going to dispute it, either.

No Statues of Limitation

There are plenty of public statues of George Washington. There are seven in New York City alone. There are statues of him on horseback, of him with the Revolutionary War financiers Robert Morris and Haym Solomon, and even of him looking like Zeus. Oh yeah, and there's also that little one on Mount Rushmore.

But, as the famous English author G. K. Chesterton once said, "I've searched all the parks in all the cities and found no statues of committees."

Yet, in late 1777, the Continental Congress thought that it could replace Washington with exactly that: a committee. Congress, if you haven't noticed, is good at creating committees, and even better at stacking them with the wrong people.

To be fair to Congress, a lot of people were second-guessing Washington at that time. We'd just lost Philadelphia. Things weren't exactly looking up. So Congress, looking for a change in leadership, created a "Board of War" to run the war—and it wasn't a vote of confidence in Washington.

You might think, though, that Congress would have had the intelligence—or at least the decency—to include the commander in chief of its army on this committee. But I guess the collective intelligence of our politicians, or lack thereof, is the one thing that hasn't changed much over the centuries.

Congress stacked the Board of War with charter members of the "I'm-Jealous-of-George-Washington Club." General Horatio Gates (who thought he had won the Battle of Saratoga single-handedly) became chairman. General Thomas Conway (a leader of the anti-Washington "Conway Cabal"), and General Thomas Mifflin (the quartermaster who had done such a poor job with supplying Washington's troops with clothing and food) also were appointed. General James Wilkinson, a Gates staff member and one of the shiftiest characters in all of American history, was appointed as the board's secretary.

Nice going, Congress.

Congress granted the board all sorts of powers that rightfully belonged to Washington. The board even ordered Lafayette to lead a harebrained, never-launched invasion of Canada. Washington was clearly—in eighteenth-century terms—being "thrown under the stagecoach." A lesser man might have given in and stomped home in disgust, or even pulled an "Arnold" by using the personal slight as a reason to turn against the rebels—but Washington was not that man.

He had earned the trust and support of the great majority of his officer corps. He had stood with them during the most difficult of times, and now they stood behind him.

Congress eventually abandoned their idiotic idea and returned power to Washington. And today, the man who could not have cared less about statues being created in his honor has more of them than anyone.

FOREIGN AID: *FOR* AMERICA?

Though Washington might not have known it at the time, his brave and steady leadership at Valley Forge cleared the way for the most miraculous and important event up until that point. And it didn't happen in Philadelphia. In fact, it didn't even happen on this continent.

If Washington would have failed at Valley Forge, Benjamin Franklin, who had gone to Paris in 1776 to help enlist French support, would have failed. If the American army had not survived that winter, the British could have waited out the rebels and crushed their hopes of revolution. The Americans would not have been able to procure the money and supplies necessary to make a victory for liberty possible.

In very different surroundings than Washington, the wily old Franklin was busy impressing upon the opulent French court that the patriot uprising was for real and worthy of its support. Franklin also knew that the French despised Great Britain and the power they yielded and would be interested in undermining the British Empire if the American cause had any real chance of prevailing. Without the huge monetary and military help the French had to offer, however, independence would be only a dream.

Franklin emphasized the warm sentiments that the French felt for Washington in a letter. "You would, on this side of the sea," he wrote Washington, "enjoy the great reputation you have acquired. I frequently hear the old generals of this martial country, who study maps of America and mark upon them all your operations, speak with sincere approbation and great applause of your conduct, and join in giving you the character of one of the greatest captains of the age."

Without the high regard that the French had for Washington, would they ever have agreed to fund the effort? And, if they hadn't, what might have become of the revolution? It's hard to say, but it goes to show you just how much character matters. In the end, it might not have been Washington's leadership, intelligence, or military skills that actually won the war—it might have been his honor. It's something so simple, yet so many people today dismiss it as outmoded or unnecessary.

After news of the French alliance arrived, Washington wrote, "It having pleased the almighty ruler of the universe propitiously to defend the case of the united American states and finally raining us up a powerful friends among the princes of the earth . . ."

In the end, there's probably no event of the Revolutionary War that better exemplifies the faith that George Washington had in his fellow man and the cause of liberty than the winter spent at Valley Forge. There is certainly no event that better demonstrates his faith in God.

Some people claim to have witnessed Washington retiring to a grove in Valley Forge where he would sit alone in private reflection and prayer. We'll never know for sure whether that's true, and plenty of critics have tried their best to show that the whole "Washington-in-prayer" idea is nothing but a myth, but we do know that Washington thanked God for relieving him of struggles during his darkest days. "Humble and grateful thanks," he wrote in 1778, after finally leaving Valley Forge, are "due to the great Author of all the care and good that have been extended in relieving us in difficulties and distress."

One who believes in a great Author and Divine Providence must also believe in miracles—and, no matter what the critics want to say, Valley Forge had plenty of those.

6

Whom Can We Trust Now?

October 7, 1777
Bemis Heights, New York

Benedict Arnold could stomach no more.

In an alcohol-inspired fury, he ran to his horse, mounted it, and galloped off to face General John Burgoyne's army, which had sailed down Lake Champlain into upstate New York in an audacious bid to split the rebellious colonies in half.

"What are you doing here?" shouted General Daniel Morgan, who commanded the American left flank. "Has General Gates restored your command?

Arnold snorted. "Damn Horatio Gates to hell!" he roared. "I'm here to win this battle, not listen to that old fool!" Three weeks earlier, Arnold and General Gates had argued violently over tactics, and as a result, Gates had relieved Arnold of his field duties.

But now, as it seemed clear that Gates was failing and the battle would be lost, Arnold ignored the orders and roared into battle atop his horse. The tired rebels cheered when they saw him.

First Arnold drove against a German unit, where he saw a weakness in the line, and they collapsed. Then he saw British general Simon Fraser rallying the redcoats. Arnold turned to Morgan and ordered him to have one of his sharpshooters bring Fraser down. Tim Murphy received the assignment. He climbed a tree with his double-barreled rifle and, on the third shot, Fraser fell dead.

With the loss of their leader, the British pulled back to some nearby earthworks. Arnold and his men vigorously attacked, but they were repulsed. Arnold spurred his horse around to the other side, commandeered the troops of another general, and ordered them to attack the earthworks in force. "Come on boys!" Arnold shouted as he rode back and forth in a hail of enemy fire. Before long they had swept over the top and had driven the British from their stronghold.

"He's fearless," cried the Connecticut troops he led. "He's like a madman—but by all that's true, he's going to win this battle!"

The last holdout was a strong redoubt on the British right guarded by an elite group of Hessians. Arnold gathered two more regiments and drove his combined forces against this stronghold. Victory finally seemed within reach when suddenly—*Blam!!*—a musket ball ripped through the flesh of Arnold's left leg. He screamed in shock and pain. His sword tumbled from his hand. *Blam!! Blam!! Blam!! Blam!!* His great brown horse toppled over, pinning Arnold and crushing his already wounded and bleeding leg.

But he had done enough. While Arnold writhed in pain beneath his mare, the German in charge of the Hessians guarding the redoubt was shot dead by one of his own men.

With the battle virtually over, a messenger raced from the furious Horatio Gates to Arnold, ordering the disobedient Arnold back to camp. He had no choice but to obey; his blood-soaked body was carried off the battlefield on a stretcher.

"Do they know?" he moaned deliriously. "Do they know what I did?"

April 8, 1779
Shippen Mansion
South Fourth Street
Philadelphia

"I do," beamed Benedict Arnold, as he struggled to maintain his balance on his one good leg.

It was particularly important that Arnold not tumble over at this moment. For, in this ornate parlor room, crowded with friends and future relatives, Benedict Arnold—age thirty-eight—was about to marry the beautiful, brilliant, and blond eighteen-year-old Margaret "Peggy" Shippen.

Physical ailments were not Arnold's only problem. He was also a sensitive man—and with very good reason: Horatio Gates's official report of the battle gave Gates himself all the credit for the Saratoga victory—and completely omitted any mention of Arnold's heroic charge. But that wasn't all. As a result of Gates's lies, Congress had unfairly passed Arnold over for a promotion (and later for seniority), and he'd also been charged with corruption over a different matter. And, as if his professional insults were not enough, he'd suffered a personal one as well. Not long before this happy wedding day, another comely teenager, the vain Boston belle Betsy De Blois, had cruelly rejected his wooings—even refusing the four-diamond ring set in rose-colored gold that he had sent to her!

Benedict Arnold could not seem to catch a break. He was beaten both physically and mentally—but while he may have been down, he was far from out: George Washington had taken a personal interest in the cause of this wounded hero. "It is not to be presumed," he told his friend and fellow Virginian Richard Henry Lee, "that he will continue in service under such a slight." And so Washington sought out to ensure he would. He wanted this man, who had demonstrated his devoted loyalty to the rebels time and again, to be properly honored and so he appointed Arnold the military governor of recaptured Philadelphia—thereby at least restoring his ego, if not the sensation in his left leg.

Arnold now wobbled around in the parlor of Peggy's father's fine three-story black-and-red brick mansion. Every father-in-law carefully eyes the man daring to marry his daughter, but Philadelphia judge Edward Shippen IV grimaced particularly hard at Benedict Arnold. The Shippens were colonial aristocracy. Judge Shippen was even widely suspected of Loyalist sympathies, and Peggy Shippen had never been shy about keeping company with Philadelphia's British occupiers. It seemed that no royal officers' ball was complete without her dazzling presence. Arnold, on the other hand, was the son of a Connecticut town drunk and a former apothecary's apprentice. What fortune Arnold had accumulated had long since been lost in the revolution. Could this merchant-turned-crippled general, Shippen worried, possibly support his third-born daughter in a manner consistent with her heritage?

But his concerns were not necessary. A seed had been planted in Benedict Arnold that, nourished by all the right ingredients, would eventually grow into a plan to support Judge Shippen's gray-eyed daughter in just the manner in which she had always been accustomed.

And that plan was far bigger than Judge Shippen, or, for that matter, his admirer George Washington, could have ever imagined.

May 10, 1779
Kip's Mansion
Kip's Bay
New York, New York

"Why, Stansbury! It's grand to see you again! How have you been? What news do you bring from Philadelphia?"

Major John André, General Henry Clinton's cultured and finely featured young adjutant, stood in the foyer of the mansion. Good old—or, rather, *young*—André, everybody loved him. He was jovial, witty, educated, and charming. Yes, everyone loved John André—and that included Peggy Shippen Arnold.

That love, in fact, is why Peggy had dispatched Joseph Stansbury, a Philadelphia china merchant who catered to that city's elite, north to New York to meet with André. She had a very important message to convey to André, and Stansbury—a steadfast, intelligent Loyalist—was the best man to deliver it.

Stansbury responded with a laugh. "I haven't seen you since you were living in Benjamin Franklin's manse!" he said, referring to the days when André had been part of the British occupation—and busied himself looting Franklin's belongings.

"And when I used to dance the minuet with Peggy Shippen!" André slyly countered. He thought it best to leave out the part about any missing furnishings or paintings.

"Funny, you should mention her," said Stansbury, his face suddenly serious, his gaze lowered, his London-bred voice now barely above a whisper.

"What is it, Stansbury? Is she well?"

"Yes, very well. In fact, it was actually Peggy who sent me to you, Major André. She has a message for you from her husband.

"He has a proposition for you. I think you will find it most interesting."

July 31, 1780
Hudson River
Near Stony Point, New York

George Washington, under a sun high in the midsummer sky, pensively stood watching his troop of escorts—160 men strong—being ferried across the lower Hudson River's broad tidal expanse. Soon, he hoped, these men would be joined by French troops in marching against General Henry Clinton in New York City.

A march like that, Washington thought, might finally end this war—and, none too soon. His underpaid, undersupplied, underfed troops had mutinied in January. Charleston, South Carolina, had fallen to General Henry Clinton in May. And recruiting had flowed to a trickle.

The steam seemed to be running out of the revolution.

Mounted alongside the discouraged Washington was General Benedict Arnold.

"Your leg is better. Look at you, on that horse!" Washington said to Arnold. "And all that unpleasantness regarding you and the Congress should be over. So, now that we are alone, I have some news for you that I think might gladden your heart."

Arnold was surprised that Washington had more news for him—the military appointment he had given him in Philadelphia had already been more than he'd ever expected.

"There's no denying that you're one of the best combat generals on either side of the Atlantic," Washington continued. "So, as of this day, you are restored to active duty. You will command the left wing of my main army. I look forward to our moving forward together against the enemy! Congratulations, General—there is no one I would rather fight beside in our righteous pursuit than you."

Arnold's face reddened. Usually glib, he remained speechless, staring blankly across the Hudson, northward, toward the American garrison at West Point. His strange reaction alarmed Washington. It had to be the July heat, he thought.

"Let's get under that elm tree, General Arnold, then we can talk further."

The men guided their horses to the nearby tree, whose broad leaves cast a large shadow on the riverbank. "I can't do it, General, I just can't," Arnold pled as soon as they'd reached the base of the tree. He was now nearly frantic. Was this really the hero of Saratoga? Washington pondered. Perhaps he'd overestimated the man's determination.

"You must accept," Washington countered. "Even with your wound, you're twice the general of anyone else I have. You must do it—your country demands it!"

"I cannot," the stocky Arnold almost shouted at Washington, his deep-set blue eyes shifting wildly about.

"I . . . I . . . I cannot physically stand the strain . . . I . . . cannot move about. I attempt to show myself fit on the outside, but this leg is causing me tremendous agony. My days of battle, I fear, are long since gone. I appreciate your gesture more than you know, but I need a far more stationary command. Yes, I need to command a garrison . . .

"Perhaps"—Arnold turned from Washington and again looked northward—"say, at West Point."

September 18, 1780
Aboard Benedict Arnold's Barge
Hudson River
Between Stony Point and Verplanck's Point, New York

Eight oarsmen, their powerful arms straining with each stroke, rowed ever more forcefully toward the King's Ferry, on the Hudson's eastern shore. They needed to display particular efficiency this afternoon. George Washington was among the passengers on Major General Benedict Arnold's official barge.

"I am humbled by your visit and am so happy to see you again, general," said Arnold, the cool autumn breeze blowing into his face, the Hudson Highlands on either side of the river already assuming autumn's

yellow and crimson hues. But Arnold's voice failed to display the glad-
ness of his words. What was Washington really doing here? And why
now? Arnold thought. What damnable timing! What trap has this man
set for me?

Arnold had good reason to panic. The plan that had been merely a
seed not long ago was beginning to flourish. West Point was under his
command, and it was now for sale to the British for twenty thousand
pounds sterling; money that would help line the pockets of General and
Mrs. Benedict Arnold—a woman who very clearly knew how to spend it.

"How could I not visit you on my way to Hartford to see the French?"
Washington answered. "It's a shame my schedule is so tight. I can't wait
to see what you've done with West Point. But I guess I will have to. Yes,
I will definitely visit on my return."

Great, Arnold thought. That's all I need. Then he can witness for
himself the miserable shape I've purposefully reduced West Point into!
Perhaps Sir Henry and I can wrap everything up before he returns—
surrender the fort sooner rather than later; maybe even capture
Washington himself!

Hamilton and Billy Lee assisted Washington in stepping down onto
the Hudson's eastern shore from Arnold's barge and the Marquis de Lafayette was particularly solicitous in assisting Arnold. The aristocrat's
courtesy, however, merely annoyed Arnold all the more. He hated the
French.

Arnold's persistently peculiar manner continued to puzzle Washington. He prided himself on being a good judge of character—and now
something seemed off. Arnold was distracted and on edge, distant, and
yet too oddly friendly, all at once. Was it his physical pain that caused
him to act so strangely?

Washington requested Billy Lee to produce the great brass spyglass
that he always carried with him. Washington saw nothing of note up
ahead, but to the south he began to discern a billowing of great, white
sails—and, yes, the fluttering of the Union Jack! That the enemy had
dared to sail so far upriver, so near to West Point, struck Washington as
ominous. He asked Arnold what he knew of it.

"It's British all right—been there a while—a sloop," Arnold answered
nonchalantly, "with eighteen guns."

"Its name?"

"It's called . . . it's called . . . ," answered Benedict Arnold, trying to avoid seeming *too* familiar with the craft.

". . . the *Vulture*."

September 22–23, 1780
Hudson River
Teller's Point

Two oarsmen beached Major John André's craft upon the rocky Hudson River beach and hauled it farther up on the shore—completing their brief voyage from the *Vulture*. A shout—"Halloo!"—pierced the night's shadows. A shadowy figure, barely visible from the candlelight emanating from the swaying tin lantern he held in his hand, lurched toward them.

Benedict Arnold had business to conduct—but only with André. Tersely, he commanded André's oarsmen to keep their distance from the little knot of fir trees where he and André would hold their mysterious meeting.

Arnold began to rapidly relay information to André, forcing him to commit much of it to memory—countless details of weaknesses to exploit and strengths to avoid when he and Clinton would eventually storm West Point. Beyond that, Arnold provided André with maps and documents to aid the British in their assault—and nervously advised him to secret these documents inside his boot.

As if the meeting were not long enough already, André, bone-weary from lack of sleep, also had to endure listening to Arnold's continuing financial demands. The traitor not only wanted to be guaranteed his twenty thousand pounds sterling of blood money—his modern-day equivalent of Judas's thirty pieces of silver—on completion of his mission, but also that he would also soon wear the gold-fringed epaulets of a royal British brigadier general, receive a proper command—and, above all, receive proper respect. After months of sending and receiving conspiratorial encrypted messages, this was, after all, Benedict Arnold's first actual meeting with his new masters, and his delicate ego demanded assurance that he would never be slighted again.

It was now almost daylight. André's two oarsmen refused to row him back against a strong Hudson River tide to the safety of the *Vulture* so André instead rode back to a private home—the same home that had recently sheltered George Washington on his voyage to Hartford, Connecticut.

From its second-floor windows, André saw *Vulture* still anchored at low tide. Suddenly explosions roared from across the Hudson at Teller's Point. *BOOM!! BOOM!!* Two small American four-pounders belched smoke and shot at the enemy ship. *BOOM!! BOOM!!* Six shots in all hit *Vulture*, smashing into its hull and sails and rigging.

With no wind to fill her sails, the *Vulture* could not set sail. She was dead in the water.

Vulture's captain ordered its longboats lowered into the water. Sailors manned the oars; others strained at long, heavy ropes to slowly haul their mother ship beyond the reach of the roaring guns on Teller's Point.

Slowly, the wounded *Vulture*, John André's ticket home, passed beyond his heartsick sight. For no matter where the *Vulture* now anchored, and no matter how many American cannonballs had torn through its timbers and its masts, John André sorely wished he was aboard it, as far away as possible from the deadly dangers of being a spy behind enemy lines.

September 23, 1780
Tarrytown, New York

A rather scruffy man, barely twenty-two years old, jumped out from behind a clump of trees. He held a musket and looked like he knew how to use it.

His excited shouts roused two of his friends. They had been playing cards nearby, but suddenly they appeared at the ready—as did *their* two muskets.

Which meant that three muskets were now squarely pointed, with triggers nervously cocked, directly at Major John André.

That André found himself in this predicament was not entirely surprising, though he'd done all he could to prevent it. After the *Vulture* was attacked, André had set off on horseback south, toward New York City.

He had donned a suit of civilian clothes, a red coat with gold lace but-tonholes, yellow breeches and vest, and a round hat. Such a wardrobe, it seemed, would be far less noticeable and dangerous to wear behind American lines—where he had ended up that evening—than the British military uniform he typically wore.

The first musket pointed at André belonged to a tall and muscular young farmer named John Paulding. Four days earlier, Paulding had escaped from New York's Sugar House prison. After jumping from his prison window and finding the fall air to be chilly, he searched for a coat, eventually appropriating a Hessian uniform jacket. That bright green, though quite threadbare, coat caused André to jump to an immediate conclusion: Paulding fought for the British.

"Gentlemen, I see you belong to our party," he asked quite breezily and with real relief.

"What party?"

"The lower party," André answered, meaning the British.

The bumpkins at the other end of the muskets smiled. They were not as dumb as their manners and appearance made them out to be. "We do," Paulding solemnly responded.

That answer relieved the nervous André. True, he was a spymaster—but he was hardly a master spy. In fact, the last twenty-four hours had been his first actual day as a spy. He was painfully new at this game—and it showed.

"Ah, my good men," André continued, grinning broadly, "then you can be of assistance to me—and to your king. I am an officer of the Crown on a mission, a very special mission, and it is imperative I return as quickly as possible to General Clinton's headquarters in New York." André ostentatiously displayed his gold pocket watch to impress upon these rustics that he was, indeed, a man of some prominence.

"Do tell, your lordship!" Paulding answered. He paused a beat to allow André to properly absorb his sarcasm. "Well, we own no gold watches, but we know that the time is up for redcoats like you. We're pa-triot men—not Loyalist dogs." With that, the three scruffy rebels spread out to surround André, their muskets still pointed squarely at his head.

But if the rebels thought André would simply admit defeat, they were sorely mistaken. "But I was only pretending to be a damnable redcoat because I thought you were redcoats!" André stammered nervously. "You can understand that? Can't you?"

"... Can't you?!"

André nervously produced his Arnold-signed safe-conduct pass. But it was too late. Paulding and his friends stripped him and found Arnold's other papers—the incriminating maps and battle plans—stuffed into his boot. "A spy!" Paulding exclaimed.

André offered them a healthy bribe to transport him safely to the British lines. They could, he assured them, have whatever they wanted: gold, his horse and saddle, even dry goods from Manhattan.

"No," Paulding answered, "if you would give us ten thousand guineas, you should not stir a step."

Major John André was no longer dealing with Benedict Arnold. He was now dealing with Americans. And they were not for sale.

September 23, 1780
North Castle, New York

"What should we do with him, Colonel?" John Paulding asked Lieutenant Colonel John Jameson, commander of the nearest rebel post. Jameson looked like the very model of an officer of the Second Regiment of Light Dragoons that he was—a full six feet in height, blue-eyed, fair-complexioned, and with jet-black hair—but his demeanor was far different; he acted like a bureaucrat.

The documents from André's boot were highly suspicious—and worse, Jameson recognized that they were in Arnold's own handwriting. Yet Arnold was technically Jameson's superior. It was an impossible situation.

Jameson eventually decided to do what all good bureaucrats do: he hedged his bet. He sent a messenger, Lieutenant Joshua Allen, to Major General Arnold informing him of André's capture. But by separate messenger, Jameson also forwarded the sheaf of highly incriminating documents found in André's boot to a different general: George Washington.

September 25, 1780
Beverley Robinson House
Benedict Arnold's Headquarters
Garrison, New York

George Washington, a master surveyor in his youth, seemed lost.

"Mon Général!" the Marquis de Lafayette exclaimed, "This is not the road to the home of General Arnold." Washington clearly heard him but kept his horse pointed in the same direction.

Billy Lee suppressed a small smile. He understood that Washington knew exactly what he was doing. But now Alexander Hamilton also chimed in, reminding Washington that General and Mrs. Arnold were not only expecting their party, but also preparing a breakfast for them. They should not be late.

"Ah," Washington sighed, "you young men are all in love with Mrs. Arnold! I see you are eager to be with her as soon as possible. Go and breakfast with her then, and tell her not to wait for me; I must ride down and examine the redoubts on this side of the river, but I will be with her shortly."

Two hours later the breakfast was in full swing, but it did not include the gray-eyed Peggy Arnold, who was too busy feeding their new infant son upstairs to be bothered with entertaining guests.

The clattering of hooves interrupted their meal. The noise, however, did not foreshadow the arrival of Washington, Henry Knox, and Lafayette, but instead that of Lieutenant Joshua Allen, the courier dispatched from North Castle by Lieutenant Colonel Jameson.

Lieutenant Allen entered the home drenched and mud-splattered and handed Arnold a sealed packet, which the major general promptly ripped open. As he read the words that Jameson had written inside his eyes began to grow wide:

Sir:

I have sent Lieutenant Allen with a certain John Anderson from New York. He had a pass signed with your name. He had a parcel of papers

taken from under his stockings, which I think of a very dangerous tendency.
The papers I have sent to General Washington.

Arnold looked around for this "John Anderson." Had he really come with Lieutenant Allen? It made no sense—but Arnold was not about to interrogate Allen in front of his guests. His heart pounding, he excused himself and fled upstairs to Peggy.

"We're ruined, Peggy!" Arnold shouted mournfully. He really didn't have to say any more. She knew what their plot was and what he meant by being ruined: the hangman's noose for her husband and perhaps for her as well.

"What will we do, Benedict?"

"I must flee—now! There is no time. There's no way to talk my way out of this! They've got my papers. They've captured André."

Peggy Arnold blanched. Her knees wobbled.

"You play dumb!" Arnold ordered her. "Play more than dumb, play the madwoman! And play on Washington's sympathies! He has a great heart. I will do what I can for you!"

Arnold momentarily paused to reflect on the decency and honor of the man he had betrayed and manipulated. But that feeling passed in an instant. The only reflection he was seeing at that moment was his own—heading straight for the gallows.

Downstairs, Billy Lee rapped upon the front door to inform Arnold's aide-de-camp, Major David Franks, that George Washington would soon be approaching. It was now Franks's turn to hustle upstairs.

Arnold kissed his son, not knowing if he would ever see him again. He grabbed two guns for his safety and headed downstairs faster than anyone knew possible.

"I have to attend to some matters at West Point—to prepare for the general's inspection," he lied to his guests, jumping on his horse, whipping the steed furiously, and galloping down a steep, winding, and dangerous shortcut to reach his waiting barge.

He lied to Franks and Hamilton and Billy Lee, and he also lied to his barge's crew, grandly promising them two gallons of rum if they could row him downriver to Stony Point and back home so that he might be there in time to greet General Washington on his arrival. The crew, of course, had no idea that Arnold would not be coming back.

Standing on the barge's stern and waving his sword furiously, Benedict Arnold appeared for all the world like a hero heading toward battle instead of what he really was: the greatest traitor of his time.

September 25, 1780
West Point, New York

"It's all quite peculiar," George Washington said to himself, kicking at the rotted lumber he found at West Point and seeing it splinter and fall to the ground. Everything he saw seemed amiss: cannon in the wrong place, troops stationed at too great a distance to withstand an attack from Henry Clinton, construction so slapdash that a spray of grapeshot could topple it.

This was not the West Point he knew—this was no "Gibraltar of America."

Washington turned to address the superior officer present, Colonel John Lamb. At the Battle of Quebec, Lamb had been horribly wounded and a large green patch now covered his missing left eye. When Lamb became upset, it seemed that his scars assumed a particularly ugly hue.

"All quite peculiar, Colonel Lamb, don't you think?" he asked. "Are you sure General Arnold is not here? Are you *positive* he provided you with no word of my arrival today?"

"As I informed you previously, General Washington," replied Lamb impatiently. He was getting tired of being asked the same questions over and over again. "I received no word of anything. I have seen neither hide nor hair whatsoever of Major General Arnold!"

The scars upon Colonel Lamb's face were assuming a particularly reddish, purplish cast, revealing his agitation.

General Washington's face revealed nothing of the sort. In fact, it revealed nothing at all. But inside, he churned with the fear that something was horribly, horribly wrong.

September 25, 1780
Beverley Robinson House
Garrison, New York

George Washington stood bare-chested, alone in his room.

When he'd arrived at the house he'd been greeted with word that Benedict Arnold had left and not returned, and that, perhaps more ominously, Peggy Arnold had become hysterical since her husband's abrupt departure.

But if Washington were to untangle this maddening puzzle of vanished generals, frenzied women, and woefully deficient fortifications, he would first need to freshen up.

Alexander Hamilton wrapped on his door.

"General? I have a packet for you from Colonel Jameson downriver. I took the liberty of opening it to determine if it would require your personal attention. I can assure you that it does."

Can't I even be let alone to wash? Washington fumed to himself. Then, a flash of inspiration—or rather, fear—exploded within him. Hamilton's expression was strange, almost sickly. Might this message be connected to all that seemed so inexplicably wrong today?

He examined the documents Hamilton handed to him. He hastily unfolded the maps. They were official maps of West Point. He feverishly scanned the rest of the documents. Details of West Point's fortifications, strengths, weaknesses—and all of it in Benedict Arnold's handwriting!

All at once it finally came together: Benedict Arnold was a traitor.

Shaken, personally betrayed, barely able to compose himself, Washington threw on his shirt, waistcoat, and coat. He yelled for Knox and Lafayette. As they entered his room, they heard their commander, his heart and spirit broken, weep as they had never heard him before:

"I ask you men," he said through bleary eyes, "whom can we trust now?"

George Washington blamed himself.

Had he placed too much trust in Benedict Arnold? Had he ignored the warning signals provided by Arnold's increasingly suspicious behavior? Yes, in hindsight, he had—that was now easy to admit. He should have seen it, but Arnold had been a patriot, one of the boldest and bravest he had known.

Washington might have wallowed in self-doubt, perhaps, even in self-pity. He had been betrayed by Arnold. He had been wronged. It was a bitter pill for any man to swallow, but for Washington, so scrupulous concerning his reputation, so trusted by his nation, it was more than just bitter, it was nearly poison.

Even as he had cried out in pain, "Whom can we trust now?" he feared others would no longer trust *him*.

But his second-guessing vanished in the sound of that tortured cry. America faced a crisis. It needed sound judgment and instant action. It needed a leader. George Washington, reluctant as he was to fill that role, knew that he had no other choice. It was time to act.

"Hamilton!" he demanded. "We are going to West Point! It must be defended! The British may strike at any moment! I want every unit within a day's march to head there in short order. General St. Clair will take command of the post. No, wait—he's too far away. I still want him— but General MacDougall will command until St. Clair arrives! Greene must mass the troops in the Highlands. And, yes, sound the alarm! Scour the countryside for Arnold!"

September 25, 1780
Aboard *Vulture*
Hudson River

Benedict Arnold had a request.

Not for twenty thousand pounds sterling or a brigadier general's uniform—but for simple pen and paper.

He gathered his wits about him and sat down to write his first com-munication from the other side of the great divide he had just now so perilously crossed. And though he sailed down the Hudson, moving closer to Manhattan and Sir Henry Clinton and irretrievably farther from West Point and George Washington, it was to Washington that he now wrote the following words:

SIR:

The heart which is conscious of its own rectitude, cannot attempt to palliate a step which the world may censure as wrong. I have ever acted from a principle of love to my country, since the commencement of the present unhappy contest between Great Britain and the colonies; the same principle of love to my country actuates my present conduct, however it may appear inconsistent to the world, who very seldom judge right of any man's actions.

I have no favor to ask for myself; I have too often experienced the ingratitude of my country to attempt it; but from the known humanity of your excellency, I am induced to ask your protection for Mrs. Arnold, from every insult and injury that the mistaken vengeance of my country may expose her to. It ought to fall only on me: she is as good and as innocent as an angel, and is incapable of doing wrong. I beg she may be permitted to return to her friends in Philadelphia, or to come to me, as she may choose; from your excellency I have no fears on her account, but she may suffer from the mistaken fury of the country.

I have to request that the enclosed letter may be delivered to Mrs. Arnold, and she permitted to write to me.

I have also to ask that my clothes and baggage, which are of little consequence, may be sent to me. If required, their value shall be paid in money.

I have the honor to be, with great regard and esteem, Your Excellency's most obedient, humble servant.

B. ARNOLD.

The truth could no longer be found within Benedict Arnold—but an immense amount of sheer nerve had certainly remained.

September 28, 1780
Road to Washington's headquarters at Tappan, New York

John André thought he could talk his way out of it.

André rode toward Tappan, New York, alongside his newest captor,

George Washington's chief of intelligence, Colonel Benjamin Tallmadge. Surrounding him on every side was a troop of cavalry, ready to kill André without hesitation if he attempted to flee.

It hadn't taken long for the handsome Tallmadge to take a distinct liking to André. Then again, everyone had always taken a liking to Major André, so that was nothing new. As their carriage jostled along the rutted country road, André argued to Tallmadge that he had not actually landed behind enemy lines, he had landed on neutral ground. It was Arnold who had transported him to within the American lines. It wasn't his idea at all! He had not originally been out of uniform. It wasn't his idea that he don civilian garb! His original visit, André argued, had even been authorized by an American authority! Yes, of course, that man was Arnold, and he was a traitor, but still . . .

Tallmadge liked André, but André got nowhere. So he shifted his tactics. No longer pestering Tallmadge with his excuses, he now posed a question: what did Tallmadge think would be André's fate? Tallmadge hemmed. He hawed. But André nervously kept after him. He had played a dangerous game and lost, and now he desperately needed to be assured that he wasn't about to lose everything.

After it became apparent that André was not about to give up on this line of questioning, Colonel Tallmadge finally answered. "I had a much-loved classmate in Yale College by the name of Nathan Hale," he said, selecting each word with precision. "Immediately after the battle of Long Island, General Washington wanted information respecting the strength, position, and probable movements of the enemy. Captain Hale tendered his services, went over to Brooklyn, and was taken just as he was passing the outposts of the enemy on his return. Do you remember the end of this story?"

"Yes," André answered, his spirit sinking with each foot he advanced toward his judgment. "He was hanged as a spy. But surely you do not consider his case and mine alike."

"Yes, precisely similar, in fact," Colonel Tallmadge responded as bluntly and as truthfully as he could. "And similar will be your fate."

And it was. Just four days later, the handsome, dignified, twenty-nine-year-old André met his demise at the end of a hangman's rope. In the end, Benedict Arnold had lied his way out of the gallows. Nathan Hale and John André—died like men.

October 13, 1780
With the Continental Army
Passaic Falls, New Jersey

George Washington walked along the banks of rushing Passaic Falls, but the power and magnificence of its mighty waters failed to stir him. Disconsolately, he kicked at a pebble and absentmindedly watched it tumble down its banks.

Three weeks had passed since he'd first learned of Arnold's treachery, but it still felt to him like it had all happened yesterday. He was not sleeping well, not eating well, not able to focus on his duties the way he once had. His trust had been broken in the most visible and humiliating way possible—and he did not know how to recover from it.

The Marquis de Lafayette, seeing Washington's entire demeanor change for the worse, attempted to brighten his commander's spirits. He knew Washington wasn't thinking of waterfalls. "Sir, Benedict Arnold may have been a traitor, but his treachery has illuminated something far more important to our cause."

Lafayette had expected his provocative statement to prompt Washington into asking him what positive could possibly be taken from something so terrible. But, as it turned out, Washington did not need his aide's prompting; he was, in fact, already thinking along the exact same lines.

"Yes, Marquis, you are right," Washington replied, pulling his great blue cloak tightly round him to shield him from autumn wind. "In no instance since the commencement of the war has Providence appeared more conspicuous than in the rescue of West Point from Arnold's villainous perfidy."

Lafayette smiled. Washington had reached the same conclusion and now the word could be spread far and wide among the rebels: A turncoat may have been in their midst, but so was God.

March 3, 1781
Parade Ground
Winter Encampment of the Continental Army
Vails Gate, New York

George Washington's horse whinnied.

The animal seemed impatient, as if it had waited here too long, but its master seemed in no hurry to move along.

He was enjoying the view.

Before him, row after row of recruits marched forward on the muddy ground of late winter. Winters were never easy for the Continental Army—Valley Forge and Morristown had proven that—but this winter had somehow seemed easier than most. Perhaps it was because the shortages that had haunted Valley Forge were largely absent this year. Or perhaps it was because temperatures never approached those that had frozen Morristown solid.

Or, perhaps, it was something else entirely.

Recruitments had increased in the last few months. And the new men who arrived—along with those soldiers who had stayed—were tougher and more determined than any previous rebel force.

Yet there was another factor, too: In the fall the nation had shared George Washington's grim shock. *Arnold a traitor? If heroes like Arnold could desert, who was next? Was the revolution lost?* But shock soon turned to anger, anger to resolve, and resolve to belief—that the hand of Providence itself protected their Revolution.

Before, these men had marched against Parliament and George III. But now they also marched to teach Benedict Arnold a lesson in real patriotism.

George Washington turned to Henry Knox. "Do you remember last September at a certain house when I asked you and the marquis a question?"

To a stranger, Washington's question would have seemed oddly worded. *"At a certain house?"* But Henry Knox knew that his commander had vowed to never utter the name of Benedict Arnold again. And when Washington made a vow, he kept it.

Knox nodded. How could he ever erase the memory of Washington opening that package and seeing betrayal laid out so clearly before him? He had never seen the general so distressed.

"I know the answer to that question now," Washington continued, admiring the steady stream of new soldiers continuing to pass before him.

"Whom can we trust now?" Washington quietly repeated the question he had almost screamed only a few months earlier. Even now, the memory of that moment clearly caused him pain. His voice caught a little.

But then he looked once more at his troops.

"The Invisible Hand, General Knox . . ." He answered his own question. "We can always trust in the Invisible Hand."

7

A Tale of Two Founders

Judas sold only one man, Arnold three millions.

—BENJAMIN FRANKLIN

To me, the story of Benedict Arnold is about more than just betrayal. It's about choices. It's about how great challenges can test the character and strength of even the bravest of men. Some men pass, others don't.

Benedict Arnold turned his back on the revolution to enrich himself. George Washington embraced the revolution, and all of the sacrifice it required, without regard to his own circumstances.

Before Arnold's name became synonymous with *traitor*, he and Washington were two of the revolutionary era's greatest heroes. Both men respected and relied on each other. Both were admired throughout the colonies. Both had made immeasurable sacrifices for their cause.

Like Washington, Arnold's path to glory had not been easy. He had faced a great deal of challenges when he was younger: his brother passed away; his once very successful father descended into alcoholism; and his mother died. Instead of going to Yale, which he was scheduled to attend, he instead became a druggist's apprentice.

Arnold was a natural military leader, indeed in some ways perhaps an even more capable soldier than Washington. Leading one bold military adventure after the next, the fearless Arnold led by example—marching right into the heat of battle. He, like Washington, had numerous horses shot out from under him during combat.

In 1775, Arnold famously teamed up with Ethan Allen and the Green

Mountain Boys to launch a surprise attack on Fort Ticonderoga, capturing a number of the enemy's cannons, which were then transported back to Boston and used to drive out the British. He was so ferocious on the battlefield that he earned the nickname "America's Hannibal." Arnold had also taken up Washington's challenge and led a thousand starving men on a treacherous journey inland from the Maine coast in a frigid winter, attacking Quebec in a desperate battle during a snowstorm. He was shot in the leg in the process.

Arnold later turned back a British armada on his own initiative in Lake Champlain and put up a fierce fight against the British at Ridgefield, Connecticut. He beat them decisively in Saratoga—getting shot in the same leg for the second time. Doctors wanted to amputate the leg, but Arnold refused and instead lived with the pain for the rest of his life.

It was a pain that would serve as a constant reminder that he'd once been a patriot, that he'd fought valiantly for the rebel's cause. And it was a pain that, later in life, would also serve as a constant reminder of something else: that the country he sacrificed so much for had, at least in his own mind, turned its back on him.

Alternate History

According to one account, Arnold wished aloud that he'd been killed rather than wounded in Saratoga. Imagine if that had happened? The name Benedict Arnold would very likely now be associated with selfless heroism.

A FORK IN THE ROAD

Why is it that some people choose good while others choose evil? God and Satan; Jesus and Judas; Luke Skywalker and Darth Vader.

As I said early, it's all about choices. Benedict Arnold proved that some men fold under the pressure of history, while others use it as motivation to reach their highest potential.

After the Battle of Saratoga, Arnold lay wounded in a hospital while

Major General Horatio Gates took credit for the victory. As if that weren't enough of an insult, Congress had promoted five officers—all Arnold's juniors and most far less talented—over him. Even back then politics was part of the equation as Congress ignored Washington's consistent backing and praise for Arnold, whom he admired as a fierce soldier. Washington, ever loyal to Arnold, wrote to Congress that "surely a more active, a more spirited and sensible officer fills no department in your army." He went on to criticize Congress's action, saying "It is not to be presumed . . . that he will continue in service under such a slight."

Washington was almost proven to be right—Arnold nearly did quit the service, but he remained to help quash a British invasion of Congress. Only after that did Congress promote Arnold to major general, but even then it slighted him, refusing to restore his seniority over the five generals they had promoted earlier.

Arnold's rage grew.

Like most men of the revolutionary era, Benedict Arnold was not perfect—professionally or personally. Despite his many battlefield successes, he was also in debt (partly because he had personally funded much of the effort to attack Quebec—something that shows you just how much he cared for the cause). He also made some poor choices in marriage—his second wife being the daughter of a Loyalist sympathizer who . . . well, let's just say she had a wobbly moral compass.

Behind Every Great Man...

Sometimes I wonder how different my life would have been had I not met my wife, Tania, and had she not been the kind of woman she is. She saw the best in me. She certainly brought out the best in me. And rather than allowing me to slip back into the life I'd had before—one of selfishness and self-destructiveness—she instead built me up.

Peggy Shippen was most certainly *not* that kind of woman for Benedict Arnold.

Arnold is ultimately responsible for his choices; I'm not disputing that at all, but consider that one of those choices was his spouse. Many historians have wondered over the years just how influential Arnold's wife was in this whole affair. She, of course, vehemently denied any involvement in the event or even any knowledge about what was happening. But was that the whole truth?

While there is no consensus on the answer, here's what we do know: Shippen was considered one of the most beautiful women in Philadelphia. She was a demanding young lady and was thought to be quite the catch for the financially strapped Arnold. Her father was a judge and she was born into American aristocracy—or as close as you could get to it. She was well-known to the British and considered many Loyalists among her friends. She was also friendly with John André, the major in charge of British intelligence who secretly communicated with Benedict Arnold.

Arnold found himself in difficult financial circumstances and Peggy's high style of living demanded much more money than Arnold's modest officer's income could provide. Maybe she felt that her husband should have more? Maybe she stoked the fire of her husband's grievances by arguing for the British cause? Perhaps Arnold began to rationalize that maybe his wife was right?

It is without argument that Shippen acted weirdly—like a mental patient, actually—to distract Washington when the Americans finally caught on to the plot. Peggy is also said to have admitted her deception to Aaron Burr, who was also friendly with the Shippen family. Shippen had supposedly told the (somewhat unreliable) Burr that she was aware of the entire plot from the get-go and that she was the one who had convinced her husband to switch sides.

We will probably never know if that is true, but it seems pretty unlikely that she knew *nothing* about the plot. Either way, Shippen's actions tell us a lot about Arnold's integrity and his propensity for making bad choices.

In the same way, it says a lot about the man who picked a loyal and honorable woman to be his own wife. Not only was Martha Washington uninterested in social climbing and intrigue, but she was a selfless supporter of her husband and the American cause.

Shippen might have been a socialite comfortable cavorting with both sides, but Martha was the type of woman who visited her husband every winter, even in the bitter cold at Valley Forge. That winter she stocked her carriages with as much clothing, medicine, and blankets as she could and joined the men in the camp. She organized other women into groups and led an effort to stitch up torn clothing. She also played doctor, helping to relieve the suffering of soldiers whenever possible.

It may be a cliché to say that behind every great man is a great woman, but I'd like to see someone disprove the theory. And while it may be a pointless exercise, imagine for a moment if the roles had been reversed. What if George Washington had married Peggy Shippen and Benedict Arnold had married Martha Custis? Do you think both men would've turned out the same way?

All of the slights, and perceived slights, inconsequential or not, finally came to a boil. By 1779, Arnold had decided to change sides and opened secret negotiations with the British. "Having made every sacrifice of fortune and blood and become a cripple in the service of my country," he later wrote to Washington, "I little expected to see the ungrateful returns I have received from my countrymen."

It's kind of ironic to look at the language that Arnold used and compare it to Washington. Arnold says that he "became a cripple" in the service of his country while years later, at Newburgh, Washington tells his troops he has "grown gray and almost blind" in the service of his. Similar sentiments, obviously—but Arnold used his as an excuse. *You owe me! Look at all I've done for you!* Washington's utterance, meanwhile, was nothing of the sort. He was humbled and embarrassed at needing to put on glasses.

Two men, two choices, two destinies, and one invaluable lesson for today: always be on guard. It's easy to let seemingly mundane annoyances pile up until they boil over. It's easy to make the right decision ninety-nine straight times before greed finally gets the best of you. It's easy to let selfishness cloud your judgment or to surround yourself with people who have ulterior motives. Always be on guard. George Washington was; Benedict Arnold was not. One is now a national hero; one is now a national disgrace.

CRIME, PUNISHMENT—AND MERCY

Washington believed, for very good reason, that God—the Invisible Hand, as he often called Him—oversaw their mission, and that uncovering Arnold's plot was nothing less than providential. In a message to his troops after Arnold's treachery became known, Washington declared "the treason has been timely discovered to prevent the fatal misfortune. The providential train of circumstances which led to it affords the most convincing proof that the liberties of America are the object of divine protection."

Think about that sentiment: Here was a man who had just been personally and professionally embarrassed. A man whom he'd vouched for and supported had nearly helped the enemy to capture West Point. But instead of making excuses or trying to downplay the event, Washington instead turned it into a positive. Sure, this was terrible, he told his troops, but think about what it means: It means that God is with us! It's proof that He is on our side!

God may have saved the United States from the "villainous perfidy" of Arnold—it's difficult to see it any other way, actually—and the English might have saved Arnold from the American gallows, but John André did not fare as well.

André's fate caused Washington great heartache and put him in an unpopular position among his own countrymen. That was a pretty rare occurrence, but Washington never shied away from doing what he thought was best for his nation.

The question that caused such controversy was this: Should a "gentleman" like André be treated any differently than others? After all, André was a young and handsome officer who had conducted himself with great dignity throughout his captivity. Many thought he should be spared the usual fate met by spies. But Washington insisted that people were responsible for their own actions, no matter how "gentlemanly" they were, and that didn't sit well with a lot of people.

Most of the officer class did not believe that André's execution was moral or necessary. Some believed that Washington was being needlessly rigid and that he was perhaps attempting to exact personal revenge against Arnold, a man he could not catch, by executing André, a man he had.

Critics, including Alexander Hamilton, argued that André hadn't functioned as a true spy; he was just a messenger. Hanging him would be a needless act of aggression against the enemy. It wouldn't accomplish anything. Not to mention, they said, that being hanged was no way for a gentleman like André to meet his end. A much more honorable way was to be executed by a firing squad—a death that André would have far preferred to hanging.

Officers and gentlemen weren't hanged, after all. A noose was for blackguards and highwaymen, not military officers. A soldier should die in proper fashion.

Washington was in serious peril of losing the trust of his team at the very moment that he and America needed loyalty most of all. But failing to follow through and instead give André a pass would mean ignoring the dictate of both a court of law and of his own words and precedent. Allowing mercy at that moment could easily have been seen as a sign of weakness when strength was most needed.

André appealed directly to Washington:

Sir:

Buoyed above the terror of death by the consciousness of a life devoted to honorable pursuits, and stained with no action that can give me remorse, I trust that the request I make to your Excellency at this serious period, and which is to soften my last moments, will not be rejected.

Let me hope, sir, that if aught in my character impresses you with esteem towards me . . . I shall experience the operation of these feelings in your breast by being informed that I am not to die on a gibbet.

In other words, he wanted to substitute the gibbet (gallows) for a death by firing squad.

Washington, who so often allowed his trusted officers to help guide his decisions, was having none of it. Why not? Because spies were hanged. A message had to be sent. The decisions made by courts of law were to be honored. Discipline was essential. Besides, the British had hanged the American spy Nathan Hale, thereby setting a precedent that had to be followed. (Incidentally, the hangings of André and Hale also illustrate the difference between Washington and other leaders. Captain Hale was treated poorly by his captors, not even being allowed to read a Bible before his execution. And, in a story that would likely appall Washington, a letter that Hale had written to his mother was torn up right in front of him.)

But Washington did have feelings. He extended to André the only real mercy he could: he kept him in the dark about his ultimate fate.

He never answered André's letter—not out of anger or neglect, but because he hoped to provide André with some sense of peace.

Washington, it turned out, guessed right because André guessed wrong. The British major surmised incorrectly that he would not be hanged. It was only through that belief that his last twenty-four hours on earth contained some semblance of tranquility.

André only learned the truth when he walked out of the small stone house in which he was imprisoned and was led toward the gallows. The sight unnerved him. He jumped backward. Words caught in his throat. But he soon recovered his composure. "I pray you," he said from the gallows, "to bear me witness that I meet my fate like a brave man."

Though it would have been far easier for Washington to avoid the entire mess, John André was hanged on October 2, 1780.

Even in War, Honor

Washington did not take the issues of life and death lightly. From the beginning of his military career, he conducted his life honorably, contemplating every move and avoiding rash emotional decisions.

Revenge—especially when it involved the death of another—was not his style.

When Washington was first fighting in the French and Indian War, Half King, the Seneca chief, had called on the young lieutenant colonel to lead the attack against entrenched French troops on the frontier—calling him "Caunotaucarius" (Devourer of Villages). Washington and about forty of his men met Half King and other allied Indians. They had known for two days that a French scouting party of about fifty was nearby, ready to pounce on them.

Early the next morning, when two Seneca braves discovered the Frenchmen lurking in the woods, Washington and Half King ordered their men to silently surround the enemy camp and, upon Washington's signal, they attacked. The French soldiers desperately returned fire, but the French commander, Joseph Coulon de Jumonville, was quickly shot and, within minutes, his men had given up the fight.

The French who hadn't been killed were to be taken as prisoners—or so Washington thought. The young leader had to first prevent his fierce ally, Half King, from killing and scalping their French captives.

What happened next is still a matter of some debate. What's clear is that Half King wasn't interested in a "gentleman's war." He demanded revenge against the French for allowing their Indian allies to kill, boil, and eat his father. This was Half King's way of war: cruel, vicious, and ugly. But Washington, even at a young age, believed deeply in honor in war and life. This was no way to conduct battle, he thought, no matter how savage the enemy had been.

Washington, it is believed, eventually prevailed over the furious Indian chief, and the frightened French prisoners remained safe. The lesson? Honor does not waver in the wind; it must, to borrow a phrase from Thomas Jefferson, stand like a rock. It's something that must be practiced in good times and bad, in peace and in war.

A SAD END TO A SAD LIFE

Since Arnold's plot at West Point had failed, he received no special reward from the British. He did, however, become a brigadier general and spearheaded an attack on Virginia that led to the capture of Richmond.

That didn't surprise anyone. No one had ever doubted Arnold's prowess as a soldier, after all; they had only doubted his prowess as a man of character. And soon enough, Arnold proved them right again. After invading Fort Trumbull, which guarded the harbor of New London, Connecticut, and slaughtering the colonel who commanded it, Arnold ordered that all 105 American troops present be killed. According to a story in George Canning Hill's biography of Arnold, the "blood in the fort flowed in streams . . . the dead, dying and wounded Americans were picked up and piled together indiscriminately in a wagon, which was set going from the top of the hill, and rushed on with all speed to the bottom. It struck a tree just before it reached the foot, throwing out some of the dying ones with the shock, and extorting deep groans and piercing shrieks of anguish from lips that even then were almost mute in death. So cruel and barbarous a mode of torture to the persons of helpless captives, was never before recorded among the practices of a civilized nation."

After that, Arnold set fire to New London, a town very close to where he was born.

When the English surrender finally came, Arnold was forced to leave for England, where he advocated for restarting the war with the United States. He failed and was not at all embraced by his countrymen, many of whom saw him as a simple traitor—no matter which side he had spied for.

Soon he would sail back to North America—to Canada, where he would set up a number of businesses and speculate on land. By the time his stay in Canada was over, Arnold had been sued (a number of times) and been burned in effigy by the locals.

He seemed to be running out of places to run, so Arnold returned to England again, this time finding some honor fighting against the French. He died in 1801 at the age of sixty.

Author Clifton Johnson wrote that Arnold had always kept the Continental Army uniform he wore at the time of his treason. As his last days neared, Arnold asked for his old coat to be draped on his shoulders, saying, "Let me die in this old uniform in which I fought my battles. May God forgive me for wearing any other."

God may well have forgiven Arnold, but most of his former patriots never would. After all, as Franklin said, he had sold out his entire country for his own gain.

Perhaps no two men in our country's history better illustrate the consequences of our choices than Benedict Arnold and George Washington. Arnold valued material possessions; Washington valued eternal ones. Arnold allowed his resentment to consume him toward selfishness; Washington used it to fuel him toward greatness.

8

The War Turns at Yorktown

June 1781
Four miles southwest of Boston

The oxcart moved slowly, the large animals walking steadily but never swiftly. The road was narrow and dry, and their wide hooves kicked up little trails of dust behind each step. Traffic in and out of Boston was at a wartime pace: occasional horsemen heading toward the city at a gallop, small units of soldiers moving in formation, occasional supplies heading south, toward New Jersey.

The oxen faced the setting sun and the road grew dark, the enormous tree branches soaking up the last of the evening's light. A man walked beside the cart, followed by a single horseman with a fine leather bag resting across his saddle. Their clothes were old and salt-crusted, their worn boots made of the finest quality that could be found anywhere in the colonies.

Though the horseman couldn't see around a bend in the road, he knew there were two more horsemen up ahead. They stayed well in front of the ox-driven cart, never stopping to wait for it but closely matching its pace. All of the men were army officers, though none of them wore a uniform. And though they were heavily armed, they were careful not to show it. No reason to draw any attention to themselves. But they were ready to use their weapons if they had to. They'd lived through years of war and were not afraid to take a life if that's what was called for.

But, on this day, the soldiers were hoping that secrecy would prove to be a more useful tool than their weapons. Their cargo being as precious as it was, a fight was the last thing they wanted.

Lieutenant Colonel John Laurens drove the oxen. His close-cropped hair and youthful features belied the fact that he was the man in charge. He was also the man who had arranged for what was being transported inside the cart.

Laurens used a walnut stick to drive the oxen. The horseman rode beside him, measuring their pace. "It'll take a weary bit to get to Philadelphia," the horseman muttered, hoping that Laurens would remember that it was time for a break. But the colonel didn't answer. Dropping his walking stick along the back of the nearest ox, he prompted it along. Ten long minutes passed in silence.

With the last of the twilight dripping through the heavy trees, Laurens looked up the road and narrowed his eyes. The two vanguards had fallen back now, moving closer to the cart. Once full darkness had set in, they would ride beside them, keeping a close watch for any potential saboteurs.

"Long and dusty road to Congress," the rider said. "Don't think we'll be able to make it all the way without stopping at least once to get a drink." He hoped that this time the single-minded colonel would get the hint.

"We walk tonight," John Laurens answered quickly. "I want to get some distance between us and the bloody Tories. They infect the ports of Boston like rats crawling from a ship too long at sea."

The rider nudged his horse toward the covered cart. "Six million is a sizable sum of money to protect," he said.

"It is," was all his leader replied.

"The French were fair on to be generous."

"Very generous, I would say."

"But is it enough to make a difference? That is the question I would put you, sir."

"Enough to save our necks would be my answer. Enough to feed our army through the summer. Enough to supply more than a few forts and buy balls for our cannons. Damn the Congress for their lack of honor, but God bless our friends, the French."

The colonel paused, suppressing a smile. "Course, it probably didn't hurt to point out to them that if we fall to the British, we'd be forced to reinforce the redcoat armies. Our dear French friends realized it's easier to help us now than to fight us later—that would be my guess."

The rider thought of all the money underneath the tightly wrapped cotton tarp. The equivalent of six million French livres. An impossible sum! He was an educated man, but he couldn't fathom what even a single million meant. It was a word, not a figure. But he did know that the money completely filled the cart. He knew it was going to save his army, or at least buy them a little time. And he knew it was a miracle that they had it—one they owed to John Laurens, the officer (and son of Henry Laurens) who had been tasked by Congress to go and plead for the loan from King Louis XVI. It was a mission he had accomplished, like every other war task he'd ever been assigned.

Having recently arrived on board a ship in Boston, they were now on their way to deliver the money to the Congress, which, as one of the forward riders had noted, would surely waste it.

"You are a man of wonder," the horseman said as he stared at the load.

"No, sir, not so," Laurens was quick to answer.

"We would be lost without you."

Laurens nearly scoffed. "We can suffer the loss of any man but one, and that man is surely not me! I am not responsible for this money, George Washington is. If we had sent Washington's dog to the king then that dog would have had the money tied around his neck and sent on his way. The French generals call him one of the greatest captains of our age. The French king happens to agree with them. That is why we have this money, sir: General Washington and his honor. This had not but anything to do with me!"

The two men fell into silence once again. The horse shortened her steps to match the trudging of the cart. The moon rose over the heavy trees, casting a pale light. The road was clear before them, a trail of gray-white dirt against the darkness of the forest.

A short time later, John Laurens looked up. "We'll move all night," he said. "Much less likely to meet one of any concern while traveling at night. And Congress waits for us. So we'll walk, then make camp in the morning, taking our rest where we may."

The rider shook his head. He wanted to rest now. "Morning will come slowly."

"As does the patience of a soldier waiting to be paid. The patience of a soldier waiting for a shirt or a meal. The patience of a wife who needs a bit of penny to make up for the lost wages of her man. All good things come slowly. Victory comes slowly! Yet we have waited long enough!

"The general grows inpatient. He is ready for a final battle, a final strike to see this through. The storm winds gather for the last pitch. It is coming, I am sure. What we have in this cart may allow him to accelerate his actions. So gird yourselves and keep on walking, for tonight we do not rest."

July 1781
White Plains, New York
Twenty miles north of New York City

It was late at night. The smell of pine hung heavy in the still-humid air. A few coyotes yelped at each other from the hills along the river, but they were the only sound that could be heard—astounding when one considered that thousands of men slept nearby.

The stars were shining brightly, though occasional clouds passed by, temporarily blocking any light from the heavens. Two wax candles had been placed on the portable camp table, but both of them were burning low and would soon go out. In the dim light, General Washington stared in frustration at his map. It was roughly drawn, and not to scale, but still useful as he considered the next step in his military campaign.

The next step . . . the next step.

His chest tightened in frustration. It was becoming a familiar feeling.

He placed his arms on the table and rested his chin on them. He kept his eyes on the map, though it was getting difficult to see. In truth, he didn't really need the map anyway. He could have drawn it from memory, and, as a former surveyor, probably with greater accuracy. He had walked, ridden, marched, or sailed from the wilderness in the west to the busy ports of Boston; from his beloved Mount Vernon to points much farther south. He knew every river, town, and valley of any consequence.

And the geography wasn't all he knew. He also knew the people's strengths and weaknesses in each area. He knew what made them breathe and tick. He knew what scared and motivated them. He had fought for this land. He had watched men bleed and die here. He had commanded men to die for the soil underneath his feet. Indeed, he had surrendered his own life, every good and every pleasure, in the fight to make this land free.

But sometimes he wondered, What if it's not enough?

These were the moments that brought him the most terror; late at night, when he was alone, waves of panic crashing into him from the darkness and the quiet. Had he done everything he could? Had he paid a price sufficient to purchase the freedom of an entire people, an entire land? Did his people want it enough? Were they willing to pay the ultimate price?

He thought of his starving army at Valley Forge, his men clothed in rags, many of them shoeless in the bitter winter, eating rats and squirrels, anything for the taste of meat. Eating bark. Dirt. Worms. He thought of the humiliation he had suffered when the French general Rochambeau looked upon his army, and had then written to his superiors, begging them to "send us troops, ships and money, but do not depend upon these people nor upon their means." He thought of the fact that he had once needed to send an urgent message to Rhode Island, but had no money for the post.

Considering the frustrations of the last six years, so many dark days and disappointments, so much misery and hunger, he had to wonder if anyone outside of his army was willing to purchase liberty? Did God want this for this people? Had they paid the final price?

He didn't know. He really didn't.

And that scared him more than any bullet or bayonet on any battle-field.

The general took a deep breath, looked up at the ragged tent around him, then turned back to the map. Squinting to see, he traced his finger down the seaboard, tapping the primary locations where they'd already had major military engagements. Boston. The miracle at Long Island. Harlem Heights. Fort Lee. The majesty of the surprise victory at Trenton. A dozen more.

After a series of humiliating defeats, his new commander of the southern army, General Greene, had prosecuted the war with stunning bravery against a much more powerful foe. His throat grew tight with pride when he considered what they had done. The brilliant tactics in a pasture called Cowpens. A two-hundred-mile march through the winter in only fifteen days. A paralyzing siege at Augusta.

He was so proud of his army. He loved them, each and every man. He had spent the best years of his life in their service. He would spend his last breath, if it were necessary, to see this through—though he fervently prayed that it wouldn't be, for neither his army nor his people would last that long.

A war is an existing, living, breathing thing. It is born, it grows, it ripens then it dies. It cannot live forever, though it certainly may seem that way to the men who fight in it. And, like all living things, it changes and adapts, one side finally giving way to the grander will of the other. And this war was growing ripe now. If he knew of anything for sure, he knew that. He could feel it. Both sides were wearing down. It was time for a decisive battle. Time to break away. Time for a victory that would bring this war to an end!

But where to strike? That was the question, one that he and his war council had been arguing about for weeks with no clear decision.

Washington traced his finger down the sides of the map, moving along the coastline. The sea. Ah, the sea. It seemed to always come down to the ocean, for that was what carried the British navy and, along with it, a seemingly endless series of defeats.

No one understood the power of the sea more than he did, or how critical naval superiority was to winning the war. Earlier that year he had virtually begged anyone who would listen for a strong navy—but not even he, as persuasive and single-minded as he was, could create one out of thin air.

The Continental Congress had ordered the construction of a small navy, mostly through the purchase and conversion of existing ships—frigates, sloops, and schooners—but these were not the kind of vessels that would instill fear or hesitation in the hearts of the British admirals. Knowing they couldn't compete with the mighty British men-of-war, the colonial vessels instead limited themselves to guerrilla attacks against merchant ships, leaving him with few, if any, real naval forces under his command.

It was like a band of pirates squaring off against the most powerful navy in the world.

Washington thought back to the Battle of New York and his chest again grew tight. He couldn't think of that day in August without feeling slightly sick to his stomach. He could still picture it all as if it had just happened: the terrifying sight of the British armada sailing into New York harbor; mast upon mast and ship upon ship. The enemy warships were packed so tightly together that he thought he could have walked from one shore to the other without getting wet.

Throughout the previous six years of war, the British had controlled America's sea-lanes, harbors, and the points of entry into every important waterway or river. If that continued there was no way that the rebels could ever win. That left Washington in the unseemly position of begging the French. And while they always offered critical support, time and again they'd failed to actually deliver on it, leaving his army weakened and exposed, unable to force the hand of the British or to press any advantage they might have otherwise gained.

He hated the humiliation that came with being stood up by the French! He hated the sense of powerlessness! He hated the fate of war being in the hands of other men!

But things were turning. He could feel it.

The gods of war were smiling upon him now. For one thing, the British fleet had been caught in a violent storm, suffering significant damage (a storm that, providentially, spared the French ships). Though the fleet was eventually repaired, the setback had opened up an opportunity for the French to harass the traitor Benedict Arnold and his British troops, who had been pillaging throughout southern Virginia.

General Cornwallis, meanwhile, had been chased from most of the South (God bless General Greene again!), leaving only the areas around Savannah and Charleston under British control. Soon after, Cornwallis had virtually abandoned his southern campaign and instead decided to march his army to Virginia, where he would join forces with Benedict Arnold. But General Lafayette had cut him off, forcing him toward the coast and away from Arnold's army, making a union of their forces impossible.

Washington moved his finger two inches to the south, resting it near the mouth of the Chesapeake Bay, indicating where General Cornwallis had decided to take refuge.

It was quiet port city called Yorktown.

August 3, 1781
Yorktown, Virginia

Lord Charles Cornwallis stared at his aide-de-camp. The lesser-ranking officer lowered his eyes in fear. Cornwallis was a distinguished man in every way, imposing, handsome, impatient, and prideful to the core. It bothered him that he had spent so much of his illustrious career fighting an insurrection of these impervious colonial snips. But what had started out as frustration had grown into anger, then exploded into a nearly constant rage, making all of his subordinates toe the line when he was near.

"You've made straight the outer bastions?" the general demanded.

"Aye, Your Excellency, we have," the colonel replied smartly.

"And what have you done. What progress do you report?"

"As per your command, sir, we have now a chain of seven redoubts and batteries. They sweep from the river on the east for two thousand yards to the south. These, sir, are now linked by earthworks. Our men have been digging very proudly. Along with the earthworks, we have batteries that cover from the narrows of the York River down hither to Gloucester Point."

Lord Cornwallis smiled in satisfaction. The small city of Yorktown was almost perfectly defensible. Strong walls. Rock and earthen redoubts that could hold under the most intense attacks. Behind him, the banks dropped steeply into the Chesapeake Bay, allowing British ships to port as needed to bring him additional men or supplies. He had food. Horses. Plenty of ammunition. He could stay the entire fall here, or the winter if he had to, though he hoped it would not come to that.

Cornwallis turned to the colonel and softened his tone, if only for a moment. "Your men have done good work here. Yorktown is nigh unto impenetrable. It would take an army of ten thousand before we would even feel their presence. I commend you for your efforts. Tell your men to stay sharp, and by half a fortnight we'll have a new supply of ale."

The colonel smiled and offered the slightest bow. Like most British officers, he was a landowner back in England, a man of means and influence, and he was tired of this bloody war. What he wanted was to go home.

Lord Cornwallis ignored the bow as he moved toward the nearest wall. From where he stood, he could look south and west over most of the fortifications that would protect them.

"What do you think, colonel? Where will he strike?" he asked.

The colonel was slow to answer. He hated the uppity colonialists, there was no doubt about that, but he had also learned to respect them, even if it was the kind of respect that a master might offer to a good dog. They were not his equals—and they would never be—but they certainly had put up a devil of a fight! So, he had learned not to underestimate them. And he wouldn't underestimate them now, especially with General Washington standing at their head.

"I suppose, Your Excellency," he finally answered, "that it will be New York. Washington has shown no inclination to come against us here, sir. New York would be the logical target, it would seem."

"Which makes me wonder," Cornwallis replied, "if we are perhaps missing the mark?"

The colonel nodded slowly. It wouldn't be the first time, that was for sure.

Cornwallis leaned against the bulwark and pointed toward the river. "Do you know what I love, colonel?"

The colonel knew at least half a dozen answers to that question, none of which he was going to mention. "Sir?" was all he answered.

"I love the British navy! I *love* our royal fleet. It provides us with security that you might not appreciate. Consider what I tell you, colonel! We stand here, behind these magnificent defenses, yet we still might find ourselves in a roost. And, if that were to be the case, what would we do? Why, we'd call upon our fleet.

"In three days, they'd be here to repatriate us to the main body of our army. We'd simply sail away on the backs of the British fleet."

He stopped and wet his lips. Sweeping his arms across his defenses, he smiled for the first time since arriving in Virginia. "No, colonel, this one thing I know as sure as the sun rises over that ocean each morning: if General Washington is going to defeat us, it is not going to happen here."

August 14, 1781
White Plains, New York

Two of the most powerful men in the Western Hemisphere stood atop a small hill, looking south. The sun was just coming up, promising another hot and humid summer day. The American general stared through his looking glass, taking a quick appraisal of the scout party that was returning from another probing mission against the British fortifications in New York. He and his army had been in New Jersey for weeks before they headed north, probing and prodding at the British forces in the city, searching for a weakness, trying to determine the best use of his soldiers, the best advantage that could be gained for spilling the blood of his men.

It was a burden none could understand except those who had commanded men in battle. Every decision that he made determined the life or death of an unknown number of souls. Make a mistake—and he had made plenty of them—and some men died who otherwise might have lived. Do nothing and the war would drag on, costing yet more lives and treasure. The best outcome of the three bad options was to command with elegance, to make the right decision at the right time and prosecute the war with surgical precision and grace. Yes, men still would die, but at least they would give their lives in pursuit of victory.

It was a responsibility that General Washington took very seriously. It had caused him to be excessively cautious on more than one occasion. But he was getting better, more determined, more willing to take calculated risks. And he had proven an uncanny ability to bounce back from his mistakes: the stunning evacuation across the East River in New York; the glorious victory at Trenton; the war in the South. He had learned, and while no one would ever mistake him for the great generals in history, he knew now when to pounce and when to run.

And something was saying in his gut that he should wait a little longer. Let things develop. Let things turn. With less experience he might have made a snap decision but now he knew that timing was everything. He wasn't ready to pounce, *or* to run. Not yet.

Yet he also knew that they were approaching a critical juncture in the war. Where he and his army attacked next could decide everything—and they would have only one chance to get it right. He needed—no, *all* of them: his staff, the men in his army, the leaders who sat in Congress, the families and patriots who supported their mighty cause—desperately needed hope. He had to show them all that the war was not only going to soon end, but that when it did, they might actually find themselves on the winning side.

The French general Rochambeau stood beside Washington and watched the approaching reconnaissance party. The sounds of the military camp were just starting to build behind them. With more than forty years of combat experience, and with thousands of French soldiers under his command, General Rochambeau was the epitome of a European officer and gentleman, always deferential to his American counterpart. "I have come to serve," he often reminded the man whom he occasionally referred to as his adoptive father, "not to command."

Rochambeau was quite fond of Washington—but the two of them had been disagreeing for weeks now. The Frenchman turned toward his friend. "You know, of course, Your Excellency, that the scouts will have found nothing new in their probes of the British defenses." He struggled a bit with the words, having spoken not a word of English when he had first arrived to help the colonies a little more than a year before.

Washington stared through his spyglass, but did not respond.

Rochambeau leaned in closer. "It is time, sir, for you to decide what we should do."

Washington put the spyglass aside. "I will wait for the report from the reconnaissance party."

Rochambeau suppressed a smile. He knew that once Washington

heard what he was about to tell him, the report of the scouts about the buttress being built around New York City would suddenly seem *much* less important.

"Your Excellency," he said, "I've been trying to convince you for weeks now that New York should not be our next target. We should be marching our armies south tow—"

Washington did not let him finish. "We outnumber the British three to one here! If we strike at their headquarters while we are strong . . ."

"Yes, sir, I understand. We have heard your wise reasoning before. Yet all of your senior generals have tried to convince you that we should march south and move on toward Yorktown. General Cornwallis is huddled there, licking his wounds from his defeat in the South. We have him trapped. If we move quickly—and yes, Excellency, *time is running out*—but if we move our forces quickly we can—"

"We can what, General? What exactly will we do there? We put siege upon the town? We put the lives of our men and the reputation of our army on the line there?"

Washington paused and gathered himself before continuing. "No, I can tell you exactly what will happen there, General. We siege the city at the cost of hundreds of my men. Cornwallis waits us out. In the best case, we defeat his defenses and surround him there.

"And then what? Clinton has ordered him to maintain the deepwater port. Being there upon his order, Clinton will do whatever it takes to protect General Cornwallis and his army. The British navy will ensure that Cornwallis receives a constant string of supplies. Fresh men and reinforcements. Food. Artillery. Ammunition. Perhaps even ale to celebrate their victory!

"Even if we keep up the siege and move forward, even if things become intolerable for the British, our adversary simply calls for his navy to rescue him out of the jaws of defeat. That is precisely what will happen, General Rochambeau. We do not have him if he has a navy and a means of escape. And *if we can't defeat him*, then why do we make the march in the first place? We only end up chasing ghosts.

"It pains me to say it, but it is better to stay here, rest our army, gather our forces, and fight them while we are able to negotiate the terms of the engagement. Better to fight them here, where we might actually defeat them, rather than box them up at Yorktown only to watch them sail down the Chesapeake to fight another day!"

The two men fell into silence. Behind them, a bugle and drum roll sounded the reveille.

Washington looked away. "I know what you think," he said quietly. "All of my staff agrees with you. But I cannot do it. Against all the winds that push me, I must do what I must do. And as long as the British have their navy, I know what little at Yorktown we can do."

Rochambeau let the moment simmer. Then he smiled. "Tell me, General Washington," he said expectantly, "what if we had a navy that could stop them from fleeing?"

Washington turned to look at him. His face remained passive. He was afraid to gather any hope.

Rochambeau lifted a piece of dirty paper from his satchel. The wax seal of the French navy commander, Comte de Grasse, was clearly visible.

Washington's eyes grew wide.

The French officer smiled again. "Comte de Grasse has set sail from the West Indies. He will bring the French fleet with him. Twenty-nine warships. Three thousand men.

"He is sailing for the Chesapeake, where he will put himself at our disposal. But we only have him for a few weeks so we must strike now, General Washington! We must move our troops and strike at Cornwallis while we have him up against what is now an inescapable wall!"

Washington took the paper in his trembling hands and stared at it for what seemed like an eternity. Then he looked toward the heavens and smiled.

"Today, General Rochambeau," he said, turning to survey the vast military camp, now humming with life, "we prepare to leave for Yorktown."

August 1781
Yorktown, Virginia

The messenger rode his horse hard, driving her with his stirrups digging until she was bleeding from her flanks. He would suffer a reprimand for wasting her, but he had to deliver this stunning news as fast as possible.

The officer rode until he hit the last gate, then left his horse and ran inside an enormous house set in a clearing in the center of the town.

His lord was just sitting down to dinner. Wild turkey. Wild rabbit. Good potatoes. Better wine. He looked up at the captain.

"Your Excellency!" the breathless man cried.

The general could see from the intense look in the runner's eye that it was urgent. He beckoned him over. "What have you, lad?" he said.

The captain was embarrassingly young, maybe eighteen, with a light beard and a father who had the money to buy an officer's rank for his oldest son. "Sir . . ." He stopped and corrected himself: "Your Excellency, word has come from our sentries in Cap-Français, Haiti. Admiral de Grasse is preparing to depart with his entire fleet!"

Later that night Cornwallis and his closest advisors pondered the implications of the news. Was the French fleet heading to New York? They had no way to know for sure—but all signs pointed to yes. General Washington, after all, had been plotting against the city for weeks now.

After just a few minutes of debate, General Cornwallis had made up his mind: early the next morning he'd send another runner north. He had to warn the commander that the French fleet might very well be on its way to New York harbor.

August 14, 1781
White Plains, New York

General Washington was concerned. Yorktown was the right choice, he was sure of it—but that was only half the battle. Keeping that choice a secret was the other half.

Washington gathered his closest advisors inside his large white linen tent and explained what he'd learned. The soldiers listened in stunned silence as the significant repercussions of the news slowly became clear. "As you all know," he said, his voice notching down a level, forcing the soldiers to lean in close, "many of our plans have been severely foiled in the past. Being determined not to allow that to happen again, this is what we will do.

"First, not a word outside this council as to our intentions." He stopped and eyed each man directly. "Need I say that once again, sirs? Not a word to any of your soldiers! When we start to march, I want all of them to think we are marching on New York. Some men talk. Other men listen. They must not know where we are going, even as we are marching there."

The war council nodded their heads as one.

"We will then begin to release selected bits of information," he continued, "all designed to misdirect or confuse. We will talk to known British spies and ask them about the terrain on Long Island. We will send fake messages with intricate plans describing our intention to march through New Jersey, then fall upon New York from the rear." He stopped and a wry smile again began to take shape. "We will then prepare a siege camp on Staten Island. We will send men to start working to improve the roads throughout the island, all in preparation for an army that will never come."

Washington looked at his French commander. "Sir, if you will, assign French troops to start building oversized ovens, capable of baking bread for thousands of soldiers. All of this will, of course, be easily observed by Tory spies."

The men nodded their approval. It was a brilliant plan.

General Washington read the look of approval on their faces. "Having been betrayed by loose tongues in the past," he concluded, "perhaps we can use loose tongues to help us now."

The long dirt road was filled with troops, the brightly colored uniforms of 4,000 French soldiers standing in stark contrast to the dirty, ragged uniforms of the 3,000 Americans. The march to Virginia promised to be long and hot and, by the time they arrived, their ranks would swell to more than 17,000 soldiers ready to take on Cornwallis's 8,000 men.

As he made his way south, a growing fear gnawed at General

Washington. How many times had he relied upon the word of allies, only to be disappointed? How many times had he been forced to rely upon the grace of others, only to be left devastated when they didn't come through? What if it happened again? What if de Grasse didn't come? It wasn't an idle thought; the admiral was, in fact, already late. He should have been at the mouth of the Chesapeake Bay by now, yet there was still no word from him.

Washington surveyed the thousands of thirsty, exhausted men all around him. If de Grasse doesn't come through, he thought to himself, then God help us all.

9

Yorktown Falls

September 5, 1781
Yorktown, Virginia

The booms were muffled by the time they reached General Cornwallis's ears. Yet, muffled or not, they were unmistakably the sounds of cannons echoing over the water.

Cornwallis had been waiting for this moment—hoping it would never come, but knowing in his gut that it would. The French had not gone to New York harbor; they had instead come here, to Yorktown.

It didn't take a military officer of Cornwallis's pedigree to know what that meant: Washington and his army would be coming here as well.

September 14, 1781
Yorktown

"Tell me again!" Cornwallis snapped in fear.

"Your Excellency, the royal fleet has left the Chesapeake and has set sail for New York."

"All of them? Every ship?"

"Yes, Excellency, every single one."

"Graves has gone and left us nothing?"

The lieutenant only nodded as he processed the impetuous actions of Rear Admiral Thomas Graves, commander of the British fleet that had been sent to the Chesapeake to support them.

"It simply can't be!" Cornwallis snapped.

"Sir, beg you, but it is."

"What did the fool do, lose his entire fleet in a single battle?"

"Beg Your Excellency, he didn't lose them all. Only but one ship was scuttled, the *Terrible*, which was sent to the bottom out beyond the bay. But there was enough damage to the other ships that the admiral felt he must retire to New York for repairs."

"He's a fool not to have left us something!" Cornwallis shot back at his lieutenant. "Does he anticipate that Washington is still interested in attacking New York? Why does he think de Grasse sailed to the mouth of the Chesapeake and not to the Hudson River? Does he think General Washington such a fool that he would not have coordinated with de Grasse before they attacked!"

The British general fumed, his rhetorical questions spilling out at a rapid pace. "Even if Graves thinks Washington a fool, does he forget about the bloody French officer that paddles around Washington like a house dog, ready to jump into his lap? Does he think General Rochambeau is a fool as well? If so, then he's mistaken—Rochambeau has proven himself in battle many times before."

The lieutenant was smart enough to remain silent. He was a messenger—nothing else. Cornwallis shook his head. He was speaking to himself now. "If Graves has truly left us, then he has left us in great danger, I am sure of it."

The room was quiet but for the sounds of the night breeze blowing gently against the eaves of the old house. The humidity kept the heat locked inside for hours after the sun had gone down. Cornwallis hated the American summers. And that was not the only thing that he had learned to hate about these colonies.

He pulled a white handkerchief from the breast pocket of his magnificent uniform and patted his forehead. Moving to the window, he stared at the campfires that burned outside. The thin glass on the kitchen door distorted the image softly, adding a sense of eeriness to what he saw. Hundreds of fires flickered in the night, one for every twenty soldiers. He knew they were necessary for light and food preparation, but he still hated the idea that they added to the heat. He stood there a long time, looking out at the thousands of soldiers who would sleep well, blissfully unaware that Her Majesty's fleet had all but abandoned them.

September 28, 1781
Yorktown

The last two weeks had been pure hell.

General Cornwallis waited anxiously for what he knew was coming. He sometimes stared at the horizon for so long that his eyes would play tricks on him. On more than one occasion he had summoned his lieutenant to look through his spyglass and confirm his sighting of Washington's troops, only to be informed that nothing was there.

But on this day, his eyes did not deceive him. Thousands of troops appeared on the northern horizon. Hundreds more appeared across the York River at Gloucester Point.

The siege of Yorktown was on.

September 28, 1781
Yorktown

General Washington stood on a small embankment on the south side of the city. Seventeen thousand men lay at his disposal. Whether French or Continental, all of them were waiting to charge at his command. His men had been sleeping in the open, grateful for the summer breeze. Some hunted wild hogs while others worked to build bridges across the marshes. An ugly stench drifted from the musky beach and the general glanced in that direction.

In a desperate effort to preserve what precious food they had, the British had slaughtered most of their horses and left their bodies on the beach. There had been a time, years before the war, when such a thing would have made Washington sick. But not now. He had seen enough to have his stomach hardened to such horrors.

The air was thick with gnats and mosquitoes, and he swatted them without thinking. His uniform was clean and tidy—one did not take men into battle without looking worthy to lead—but it was as uncomfortable and impractical as any piece of clothing he had ever owned. Thinking of the coming battle, his heart leapt in his chest. Part anticipation, part anxiety, part the adrenaline of combat that couldn't be had any other way. He was ready for it now. Ready to attack. Ready to feel the thrill of an honorable victory while participating in an undertaking that could only have been designed in hell.

He and General Rochambeau had split up the battlefield. Washington's men had taken the eastern position, from the York River and marshlands that followed Wormley Creek to the south and then east. His artillery was to his left, near the center of the battlefield.

He considered the leaders he had placed in command of the various regiments: General Clinton; Lafayette; Nelson; von Steuben; Knox. All good men. Battle tested. He trusted them like brothers. He looked toward the afternoon sun, across a series of small creeks, pastures, and open fields scattered lightly with trees and brush. The French were on the west. And there, across the York River, was an army made up of both French and American soldiers ready to confront the British at Gloucester Point. Good men and generals there, too.

Washington knew they were ready to lay siege. But they didn't have to. At least not right away. For reasons that seemed unfathomable to him at the time, the British troops manning the outer fortifications around the city—fortifications that may have taken weeks and many hundreds of lives to capture—had outright abandoned their posts and pulled back into the center of the city.

The French and American soldiers took those positions and, within a week, had rolled their cannons and artillery into a position where they could provide enough cover.

Now, Washington knew, it was time for the digging to start.

That first night proved stormy, the waning moon throwing off very little light—perfect conditions to protect the massive operation that was just about to get under way. Under the cloak of darkness, the commander of the allied forces moved to within six hundred yards of the British line, where he ceremonially stuck the first pick into the ground. In less than a week, two thousand yards of trenches, stretching from directly south of Yorktown to the river, had to be finished. It was dangerous, backbreaking work. Once complete, half of them would be commanded by the Americans, half by the French.

A few nights later, Washington moved forward toward the British line once again. Standing beside a heavy cannon, he fired the first gun.

The world seemed to utterly explode around him as dozens of allied guns and artillery started blowing deadly metal toward the British de-fenses. The cannonballs were clearly visible, scorching black knots against the sky. At night they looked like flaming fireballs with white-hot tails.

Washington knew how accurate his gunners were, their skills finely honed by years of experience. They could drop a ball or shell within a few feet of its intended target, where it would whirl and spin before exploding, taking body pieces with it; arms, parts of bowels, sometimes entire heads. It was horrible to experience, dreadful and inhuman, but it was the way that war was fought.

Standing on the embankment to survey the battlefield, Washington looked down his line of heavy artillery and cannons. They had enough siege equipment. Enough ammunition. Enough men. With the French fleet in place, they could cover the river from any attempt by Cornwallis to escape.

His foe was going to fold here. There was not a doubt in his mind.

October 1781
Yorktown

General Rochambeau stared across the tent at the American general. Both of them had moved up to front lines of the battle. It was growing dark now, but the terrifying sound of cannonballs and artillery could still be heard over their heads. Most of the fireballs were going instead of coming, which brought a bit of comfort, but he never quite got used to the horrible sound of metal flying through the air. Farther to the south, in a small pasture full of high grass, the hospital tent was near overflow-ing. Behind them there was the constant sound of chains, wheels, and hooves from the supply wagons moving men and ammunition toward the trenches that were being dug ever closer to the British walls.

The Frenchman sat upon a small barrel he had turned over for a stool. He was weary to the bone. War was excruciating work. A drop of sweat dripped from his nose and he lifted an arm to wipe his sleeve across his forehead. A gust of humid air blew in from the beach and he caught a whiff of decaying flesh. Without thinking, he turned away. He never got used to it—the smell of death—and he hoped he never would.

General Washington stood with a few of his aides, giving them instructions. The men were attentive and respectful and Rochambeau couldn't help but note the look of deference in their eyes.

As he watched the American general work, his heart swelled with a love that could only be compared to the love a son might feel for his father. Why he felt such affection for the American general, he had wondered many times. Part of it was the French blood that ran through him. Far more emotional than the practical Anglo colonialists who surrounded him, he wasn't so fearful of letting his fondness show. Part of it was the way that war had of sharpening one's emotions, making the dear things more dear, men becoming brothers upon the battlefield. But most of it, Rochambeau knew, was the simple fact that Washington was so damnably easy to love. He stood above his men, but never over them, as a lord of Europe would. And he had a way of pulling you in, making you not only willing but grateful to stand in his presence. Simply put, he was a great man *and* a good man. And that was very rare, indeed.

Washington's army loved him beyond words. Because of this, their single greatest fear was that he would allow himself to be killed in battle. That was the only thing that could destroy their nation, the only thing that could destroy their cause. Rochambeau's fellow French officer, Lafayette, had once said to Washington, "If you were lost . . . there is nobody who could keep the army and the revolution for six months!"

Everyone knew that was true.

Yet Washington insisted on terrifying his men. He'd been terrifying them for years now. He took little care of himself in battle, insisting on animating his troops by the sheer force of his example. He could always be found in the very midst of battle. Time and time again, despite Rochambeau's strongest protests, he led the charge. But his life seemed to have been preserved so often that it had become accepted that God was not going to let him die. Whether Washington believed that or not, no one knew. Rochambeau had asked him once, but his friend had only frowned and waved a dismissive hand. But he certainly acted like it. Which caused even greater fear among his men.

Had God preserved his good friend? Rochambeau didn't know. But if not, Washington was the most fortunate man he'd ever known. Fortunate and reckless. A good combination for building legends—but a difficult one for maintaining friendships.

Rochambeau slid the barrel a few feet and sat across from his friend at a makeshift table that held a variety of hastily drawn maps. He thought back to what others who'd fought with Washington at the Battle of Princeton had told him. It was a story that defied belief, but by the third time he'd heard it, he'd begun to believe it was true.

Washington, the story went, had galloped to within thirty yards of the enemy's position before ordering his men to fire. Hundreds of troops discharged their muskets as one, sending a deadly rain of metal balls screeching across the battlefield. At the same time, the English also fired, most of them directly at Washington. The blast from so many simultaneous gunshots was utterly deafening—earth and sky seeming to shake from the force of the guns. The smoke was so thick that it was virtually impossible to see. The entire scene was chaos.

As the smoke began to clear and the guns grew quiet, everyone expected to see the American commander lying dead upon the ground. Instead, he sat upright upon his horse, calm and resolute. And certainly composed.

"Thank God!" Colonel Fitzgerald, Washington's trusted aide, had exclaimed. Then Fitzgerald, a man who was hardened by years of war, a man as rough and demanding as any on the battlefield, burst into tears of relief. Upon seeing this, and with the battle still raging around him, Washington had ridden over to the colonel and taken him by the hand to reassure him. "The day is our own," was all he said.

As the war had drawn on, Washington's courage only seemed to grow. Rochambeau thought back to just over a week ago when the battle at Yorktown was just getting under way. As the two armies started exchanging a relentless volley of cannon and artillery fire, no one was surprised to see Washington in the siege trenches with the engineering troops, the enemy forces barely a few hundred yards away.

Rochambeau had stood beside the general as they surveyed the battlefield. He couldn't believe his friend's calm—his steady hands holding the spyglass. Rochambeau was not quite as composed, though he did his best to maintain the appearance.

Suddenly there was a violent *CRACK!* from an exploding cannonball that had dropped out of the sky far too close to their position. Rochambeau had winced in pain as the explosion thumped against his chest and burst in his ears, leaving him to feel like he'd been hit by a hammer upside the head. The percussion thundered along the trench, sliding dirt and sand over the edges and into the hole. Instinctively he had ducked below the trench, as dirt and muck rained down like a summer storm, coating Washington and all of his men with black rain.

A nearby chaplain took his hat off to examine it, his eyes wide in fear at having survived the exploding ball. He stared at the dirty, black-singed hat as if it were something otherworldly, something that carried far more significance than a piece of gear to cover his head.

Washington, however, had never diverted his eyes from his study of the British fortifications. It was as if the cannonball had never exploded, as if the force of the blast had not almost knocked him over, as if the sky had not just rained down a hundred pounds of dirt.

Finally the general turned to see the chaplain and the astonished look of fear upon his face. "Mr. Evans," he smiled as he pointed toward the dirty hat, "you had better take that home to show your wife and children."

Thinking on it, Rochambeau smiled, too. Then he adjusted his weight on the barrel to lean back against a rough pine post that held up one corner of the tent. In a moment of indulgence, he dropped his head and closed his eyes. If he slept, he didn't know it, but eventually he felt a gentle nudge on his shoulder. Looking up, Washington was standing there. "One more survey of our progress before we lose the light," he said.

Minutes later, the two men were standing near one of the earthen barricades piled up on the American side of the trench nearest the British armaments. Below them, dozens of trees had been felled, their branches sharpened to deadly sticks and braced at the bottom of the barricade to protect against a British assault. Glancing at the branches, Rochambeau knew they would never be used. Cornwallis was in a defensive posture only, clearly in no position to attack. Sensing movement beside him, he turned and watched in horror as Washington pulled his way up to the top of the barricade, exposing himself to the deadly fire. Overhead the eerie sound of cannons flew while occasional musket balls impacted the dirt around them. Rochambeau knew they were so close the British could easily make out Washington's uniform. He imagined the commotion along the British walls. *"Look there! Is that General Washington! Quick, men, gather fire!"*

A nearby colonel rushed forward, pulling himself up the steep embankment. "Your Excellency!" he almost screamed, "Beg you sir, you must come down from this position." He reached up to pull on Washington's jacket, partly to pull the general down, partly to brace himself against falling back along the steep grade of dirt.

But Washington didn't move.

The colonel pulled again, begging him to retreat. Washington turned and looked at him. "Colonel Cobb, if you are afraid, you have the liberty to step back," he replied. Continuing his watch from his exposed position, Washington used the remaining light to survey the enemy's position.

Knowing Washington would not retreat until he had seen what he had come to see, Rochambeau climbed up the earthen embankment and stood beside his friend, praying the sun had fallen enough to make it difficult for the enemy to target them directly—but knowing in his gut that it had not.

Washington pointed toward two stone barricades on his right. "We paid a heavy price for what we gained here," he said.

Rochambeau nodded toward the redoubts that were now under their control. Two days before, Washington had sent his engineers to dig a second trench, this one a mere two hundred yards from the walls of Yorktown. The engineers had been torn to pieces by a brutal hail of fire from two British redoubts near the York River. Knowing he had to have the final trench, Washington ordered two divisions to take the fortifications. Before he had sent them out, he called his men together and gave them a rare battlefield speech in which he reminded them of their responsibility for bravery and the absolute necessity of taking the British strongholds.

Four hundred French troops had assailed the redoubt on the left. Four hundred Continentals, led by brazen Lieutenant Colonel Alexander Hamilton, had gone after the fortification on the right. Attacking on the night of October 14, the forces had charged the parapets with their bayonets at the ready. The hand-to-hand combat was brutal and frightening, but in the end, the allies captured the walls that Washington now surveyed.

"The battle is winding down now," Washington said without turning. "A few more days, and it will end."

Rochambeau didn't answer. He wasn't so sure.

"We've been showering the British with a fearsome and constant rain of cannonballs and fire. At the same time, General Cornwallis has spared no ball in his defenses. But he does not have a cache of unlimited ammunition. He must be getting desperate."

"It would seem," Rochambeau answered.

Washington waited, but Rochambeau did not say any more.

As they stood there, two men against the dying light, the British cannonballs and artillery seemed to fall silent. Rochambeau became more nervous. He knew the gunners were adjusting their aim toward them and he reached out to his friend. "Come, sir, we must climb down now," he said.

To his great surprise, Washington actually listened.

Two nights later, in sheer desperation, Cornwallis attempted to lead an evacuation across the York River in whatever small boats he could muster. Apparently, God did not intend to let them go so easily, as a violent storm appeared out of nowhere. In a rush of ferocious wind and rain, the small British boats were swept downstream.

The next morning, the allies continued raining down an unending hail of bombs and cannonballs. Relentless. Without mercy. It was noise and fear and death from every angle. The British soldiers cowered in any place of refuge they could find: along their decimated stone walls, in every trench, under any log or tree. There was nothing they could do to stop the allied forces. Most of the British troops had only one hope left: that somehow they might live.

Sometime later that morning, Cornwallis shot the last of his ammunition. An eerie quiet settled over the British lines. You could almost hear men breathing—at least the ones who were still able to do so.

About the same time as the white flag was being raised in Yorktown, the proud British fleet finally sailed out of the New York harbor, the repairs to their ships from the damage inflicted in the Chesapeake having taken almost two weeks longer than expected.

The fleet arrived at Yorktown a week too late.

October 20, 1781
Yorktown

General Cornwallis knew that this would be one of the most painful days of his esteemed life. Surrendering to the enemy was simply unimaginable. He would not lower himself, his pride, the dignity of his great nation, to lift his own sword and give it to the leader of this scrawny bunch of disreputable and illiterate men who called themselves an army!

He would die of shame if he were forced to do it.

So he sent one of his men instead.

The brigadier general selected by Cornwallis attempted to surrender to General Rochambeau, who refused, pointing to General Washington, the supreme commander of the allied forces. General Washington also refused to accept the sword of surrender from the deputy, realizing it was an attempt by Cornwallis to belittle what he and his army had accomplished. He tartly directed the British brigadier general to one of his deputies instead.

Soon after, eight thousand defeated troops marched between parallel lines of allied soldiers to surrender their arms. Many of the British soldiers were openly weeping. Instead of handing over their weapons, some smashed them against the ground and sullied off.

Many of the American soldiers were weeping, too. But they weren't crying in defeat or fury—it was with joy. They fell into each other's arms, too overcome to even talk as an uncontrollable rush of laughing, singing and dancing swept through the ranks.

Everything had just changed. While the rebels knew that the war was not over, a victory was far more important for their morale than for anything else. After all, that morale, that innate thirst for freedom that had propelled them into this war in the first place, was the patriot's greatest weapon—and it would ultimately prove to be the one thing that their enemy could not match.

The World Turned Upside Down

The power and goodness of the Almighty were strongly manifested
in the events of our late glorious revolution; and his kind interposition in our behalf has been no less visible in the establishment of our
present equal government. In war he directed the sword; and in peace
he has ruled in our councils. My agency in both has been guided by
the best intentions, and a sense of the duty which I owe my country.
—GEORGE WASHINGTON TO THE HEBREW CONGREGATIONS

As British troops marched out of their fortifications to surrender
to Washington's army at Yorktown—a moment that was un-
thinkable only a few months earlier—the English military band
began to perform the song "The World Turned Upside Down."

> *Listen to me and you shall hear,*
> *news hath not been this thousand year;*
> *Since Herod, Caesar, and many more,*
> *you never heard the like before.*

It could not have been a more fitting choice. The world had, in fact,
been turned upside down. And nothing would ever be the same again.

THE TRAP IS SET

Yorktown makes for a dramatic war story, but its real importance is that
it proves that David really can beat Goliath. It is, when read in the proper

light, the ultimate motivational story for those of us who feel like we are up against insurmountable odds and that America has been set on an inevitable course toward collapse.

But before we can appreciate the lessons of Yorktown we first have to understand how Washington pulled off the victory.

As with any complex military action, secrecy was of the utmost importance. Washington's plans had been undermined so many times before by security leaks and British spies that he was determined to stop even the tiniest trickle of information from leaking out.

Washington's plans were kept so close to the vest that his own troops didn't know when or where they'd be marching. Bets were made in camp—would they attack Clinton in New York or Cornwallis in Virginia? To confuse things even further, Washington leaked selected bits of intelligence that were either false or of no consequence. Disinformation was key. Surprise, he knew, could be his most effective weapon.

Through a controlled stream of bogus intelligence, Washington had Clinton and his British advisors convinced that the Americans were going to sneak through New Jersey, then come upon New York from the rear. Washington actually prepared a siege camp on Staten Island strictly as a diversionary ploy. Workers patched and smoothed roads while French troops across the way in New Jersey built huge ovens capable of baking bread for thousands of hungry soldiers.

Clinton took the bait. He was frightened into action and had Cornwallis send him two thousand men as reinforcements. The senior British commander was so intently concentrating his attention on Staten Island that Washington and Rochambeau were able to march their troops quietly out of New Jersey without being detected. Three days passed before Clinton even realized they were gone. As a result, Cornwallis received no warning that Washington was coming to Yorktown.

When General Greene heard that Washington's army was trekking south, he was shocked. "We have been beating the bush," he exclaimed, "and the General has come to catch the bird."

Although Yorktown is usually remembered as the pivotal land battle of the revolution, the outcome was decided as much upon the briny waters of the Chesapeake Bay as it was upon the marshlands around the heavily fortified port. Fed by more than 150 rivers and streams, the

Chesapeake is as narrow as three miles in some places and as wide as thirty miles in others. Its currents and tides are hazardous and unpredictable, with shoals, eddies, and sandbars making navigation a real challenge.

Hearing that the French fleet under Admiral de Grasse had left the French Indies, British rear admiral Sir Thomas Graves set sail from New York with nineteen warships to meet them. With the confidence of a man who had rarely been challenged, Graves fully expected to easily handle whatever French forces he might encounter. That cockiness—a disposition that Washington never displayed—might have led directly to Graves's downfall.

When Graves arrived at the mouth of the Chesapeake, he was surprised to see de Grasse's fleet already anchored in the bay. He was also surprised to see that it was much larger than he was told to expect. But if his cockiness waned at the sight of the French fleet, he certainly didn't show it.

De Grasse immediately ordered twenty-four of his warships to prepare for battle, maneuvering them into position to engage the British fleet.

The deadly dance of naval warfare had begun.

After each admiral positioned his forces as best as he could, the two sailed toward each other in a long line of warships. For two hours, cannons fired. Smoke and shot filled the air with confusion and death. At one point, two enemy ships were so close that the French considered a boarding action. The winds shifted, putting the British at a sudden disadvantage. They continued to fire, but did so from longer range, afraid to move in for a witheringly close exchange of fire. As the sun set over the Chesapeake Bay, the warring, wounded navies broke off from each other to assess the damage.

For Graves, it wasn't pretty. While the two fleets had been almost evenly matched, the British had suffered far more damage to their ships than the French.

Over the next week, the two fleets circled one another, neither willing to risk a full engagement. When the fickle wind suddenly gave the French an advantage, they threatened the British again. Graves, handicapped by several badly damaged ships, had great trouble keeping some in the line. His exhausted men worked desperately to repair them, but much of the damage was too severe to be repaired at sea.

One of his largest ships, the *Terrible*, had her foremast severely damaged, and Graves had no choice but to order it to be sunk—something that must have been an unbelievable sight to many of his officers, who were already on edge and humiliated from a battle they never expected to last this long. Meanwhile, de Grasse kept the pressure on, continuing to lure the British farther out to sea, away from Cornwallis and his troops.

Then, suddenly, de Grasse turned back toward the bay.

With a severely damaged fleet, and no meaningful way to assist General Cornwallis, Graves decided to hightail it back to New York, abandoning the British soldiers at Yorktown and forcing them to fend for themselves.

It was the only break that Washington needed.

A Man Among Men

Private Joseph Plumb Martin, who had enlisted with a Connecticut regiment as a nineteen-year-old private, and later with the Continental Army, was a prodigious diary keeper and, many years later, wrote about his many experiences in the book *A Narrative of a Revolutionary Soldier: Some of the Adventures, Dangers and Sufferings.*

Though historians have praised the book for its fascinating firsthand accounts of the war, others suggest that Martin was prone to tall tales and couldn't possibly have witnessed all those incidents as a mere private. Nonetheless, one particular story has long resonated.

Martin claims that as he was about to dig one of the first trenches around Yorktown, a stranger dressed in civilian clothes approached him and his fellow soldiers and struck up a conversation. Only after some time passed and French engineers began to refer to the man by his title, General Washington, did the Americans realize who they were talking to.

Today, politicians try everything to appear like ordinary citizens. They engage in staged populist appearances with false humility as they stop at local burger joints or state fairs to show everyone that they are authentically interested in you and your problems—not just your vote.

But Americans can spot a fake.

Knowing what we do about Washington, though, it is not very difficult to believe that he picked up a shovel and broke ground with his fellow soldiers at the siege of Yorktown. It's easy to imagine that his men appreciated it and easier still to believe that the gesture was genuine (after all, the man was not trying to win any elections at that point). Our leaders today go out and kiss babies to make them seem normal, instead of just being themselves, speaking plainly, and leading from their heart, not polling reports or carefully crafted talking points based on focus groups.

WITH AN OPEN MIND

St. James once said, "God opposes the proud but gives grace to the humble."

Yorktown is a perfect illustration of that. Graves and Cornwallis were proud (in other words, "cocky"); Washington was humble. But Yorktown is also a great illustration of the idea that God gives to those who are not only worthy to receive—but also *ready* to receive.

Washington was humble, sure, but he was also prepared. He'd always understood the necessity of sea power and had lobbied Congress for quite some time to begin building a formidable navy. When that didn't happen, he turned to the French, realizing that their navy was his only chance to match the British fleet and stop Cornwallis.

If you think about what Washington accomplished given the timeline of the battle, it's pretty mind-boggling. The very idea of coordinating the convergence of a massive French navy with French and American land forces on the coast at a specified time and a specific place is a miracle in itself. Think how difficult it is to coordinate a couple of friends for lunch—and that's with cell phones and email.

The Humility Standard

St. Bernard defined humility like this: "A quality by which a person considering his own defects has a lowly opinion of himself and willingly submits himself to God and to others for God's sake." George Washington clearly met that standard—but how many of today's politicians do? Think about that definition the next time you listen to a speech or a debate and use it as one of the standards by which you judge who should lead us. If a politician fails to pass the humility test, then chances are they'll fail every other test as well.

Washington's willingness to listen to others, including his subordinates, is what made this possible. Being humble means nothing if you don't live it every day. Plenty of bosses, for example, believe themselves to be humble but would never call in a low-level manager or secretary to take their advice about a business deal. (In my own company I've found that some of the best ideas come from the people and places that you'd least expect.) But Washington did. He listened to everyone—keeping the good ideas and discarding the bad.

According to historian David Hackett Fischer, throughout his military career Washington frequently met with subordinates and, unlike English commanders, encouraged the free exchange of ideas. He listened more than he talked (one of the rules of civility) and he not only drew from the best ideas of his men, but also credited them generously.

As a new general, Washington actually took a vote to decide how to proceed in battle. That would have been unimaginable in any European army. Later, as his confidence and skill began to eclipse those around him, he would build consensus and make strong arguments for his plan. That approach built a confidence that was at an all-time high as the war's biggest showdown approached at Yorktown.

Whereas English forces relied almost exclusively on the old-school European traditional top-down military system, Washington embodied the Spirit of '76 by allowing the experiences and ideas of others to help him find innovative and practical ways to win the war.

Timing Is Everything

Pulitzer Prize–winning Washington biographer Ron Chernow relates that the young Washington was obsessed with precision and time. "Washington," Chernow writes, "aspired to stand at the center of an orderly clockwork universe."

Washington had placed a sundial at a center spot on his estate lawn. A French businessman friend once said that "no one ever appreciated better than General Washington the value of time and the art of making use of it."

This might be one of Washington's most important lessons for us today. No one man, no matter how respected or powerful (and there certainly aren't many of those), can do it all. We all need help. We all have strengths and weaknesses and only by listening to, and working with others can we maximize the positives and minimize the negatives.

This is one of the reasons I've been so obsessed lately with physically getting people together in their communities. We all have a tendency lately—and I'm as guilty as anyone—to rely on email or the Web or cell phones to communicate with each other. But that doesn't really connect us; it doesn't let us see each other eye to eye, shake hands, and get to know each other.

I've met so many people over the last decade who so desperately want to make a difference. I tell them all the same thing: you'll never do it alone. George Washington, the author of perhaps the biggest underdog success story in history, understood that concept very well and, while others resorted to egocentric, outmoded models of war and government, he pushed past it. We must do the same.

With God on Our Side

During the revolutionary era most colonists believed that God had played a large part in all the victories of the patriots. They believed that the establishment of a free nation was destined to them by God and that fighting was a divine cause. After all, how else could they have survived against the world's greatest military power for so long?

Colonial religious leaders regularly preached that liberty was an inalienable right, handed down by a higher power. The Founders were always hardheaded realists about the chances of victory and concerned about human nature's tendency toward greed, but they never wavered in the belief that the cause of American liberty was divinely inspired. One revolutionary battle flag featured the phrase "Resistance to Tyrants is Obedience to God."

Another, the Pine Tree Flag (sometimes called "Washington's flag"), often flew during the American Revolution and featured a picture of a tree with the words "An Appeal to God" or "An Appeal to Heaven" in text underneath. It was originally used by a squadron of six ships commissioned—and paid for—by Washington.

GRACE IN VICTORY

Sometimes how you win is just as important as the fact that you won at all.

After the British ceased fire at Yorktown, General Cornwallis refused to attend the surrender ceremonies, claiming that he was not feeling well. He sent his deputy, General Charles O'Hara, in his place.

The Great Authoring ... of Two Thunderstorms

Prior to Cornwallis's surrender he'd decided to make a run for it. The plan was to cross the York River and flee through the neighboring town of Gloucester, which was far less heavily guarded than Yorktown. As soon as they were free, the white flag would be put up in Yorktown by the sick and injured troops who remained.

On a moonless night, the British gathered every vessel they could find and put their best soldiers aboard, hoping they would reach Gloucester well before dawn so that they could sleep and prepare for the fight at daybreak.

After two hours the first group of troops made it across and the sailors turned around and headed back for Yorktown to pick up the second contingent. But, as they sailed, something unexpected happened: a severe storm blew in unexpectedly. Showers turned to a full downpour and then into severe, violent winds.

The storm erupted for nearly two hours and the British boats, which were floating helplessly on the York River, were scattered—some driven back to the Yorktown shore and others blown miles downstream.

Cornwallis's escape attempt was over. He had no other choice but to face Washington's siege.

That freak storm may not have mattered if the English navy had been able to leave New York and come to the rescue of Cornwallis earlier. But they couldn't. Why? Another thunderstorm.

Perhaps because of confidence in their own might or maybe an underestimation of the colonialists, the British took their sweet time repairing their fleet in New York harbor. But finally, on October 13, the fleet was ready. If all went well they'd still have plenty of time to reach Yorktown and save Cornwallis.

And then it happened: a freak storm with huge squalls pounded New York harbor for over an hour, damaging two vital British ships, the *Shrewsbury* and *Alcide*, which then had to be towed to Staten Island for several days to be repaired. By then it was too late—Cornwallis was on his own.

These two storms may have been just as critical in winning Yorktown as anything that Washington did. And, of course, Yorktown was critical to winning the revolution. So, you decide: were these perfectly timed storms simple coincidence . . . or were they something much more?

As a traditional gesture of surrender, the English sword was offered to the French commander, General Rochambeau. The French general refused to accept the sword because it was Washington who was the overall commanding general of the troops. So O'Hara turned to Washington, who also declined and pointed toward his own deputy, Benjamin Lincoln.

Hey, if the British were going to insult the patriots by sending a deputy then Washington would return the favor. It was a manner of honor.

But Washington did not go overboard. He understood that the way he acted in victory was just as crucial as the way he carried himself in defeat. He also understood better than most the indignity and disgrace of surrender. Decades earlier at Fort Necessity, fighting one of the first battles of the French and Indian War under the British colors, Washington was forced to surrender after losing more than a third of his force in a prolonged French siege. It was only after his weapons had become useless and his troops had only three days of supplies left that he'd finally given in.

Though surrender assaulted his senses, Washington conceded and resigned himself to what he was sure would be personal disgrace. Sometimes you have to take one step back before you can take two steps forward. Sometimes the battle simply can't be won.

Yet the loss of Fort Necessity didn't tarnish his stellar reputation. Not only did his resolve in fighting the battle boost his public image, but his honorable behavior afterward enhanced it even further. When all was said and done, the House of Burgesses of Virginia adopted a resolution to thank Washington and his officers for their courageous endeavors on behalf of the British Crown.

It goes to show you that you can win, even when you lose.

Washington: Religious Zealot?

When the Continental Congress learned of the British surrender to Washington at Yorktown, representatives walked together to a Philadelphia church and prayed. Nearly a thousand other people joined America's leaders in worship around the city. In fact, Congress recommended that the entire nation might want to observe a day of "public thanksgiving and prayer" to celebrate the victory.

How times have changed. Can you imagine if Congress declared a national day of prayer after a military victory these days? The ACLU would file a lawsuit before you could say "God bless you." On the tenth anniversary of 9/11, New York's Mayor Bloomberg even banned all clergy from the Ground Zero ceremonies.

The congressional prayer resolution of 1781 is a powerful one. It says that American victory "hath pleased Almighty God, father of mercies, remarkably to assist and support the United States of America in their important struggle for liberty against the long continued efforts of a powerful nation; it is the duty of all ranks to observe and thankfully acknowledge the interpositions of his Providence in their behalf. Through the whole of this contest, from its first rise to this time, the influence of divine Providence may be clearly perceived in many signal instances. . . ."

Sure sounds like the Founders were a bunch of religious fanatics to me.

And Washington was right there with them. The best way to exhibit this kind of reverence to Providence was to remain humble in great moments just as he remained strong in difficult ones.

Two days after the definitive battle of the revolution ended, the British press reported that Washington had ordered a "Divine service" to be performed in all the different brigades and divisions in the American army in order to return "thanks to the Almighty for this great event."

Soon after the British surrender at Yorktown, Cornwallis asked for a meeting with the American general. The two ended up touring the Yorktown defenses and developing a mutual respect. Cornwallis even hosted a dinner for all the general officers—French, American, and British alike—and proposed a toast to Washington: "When the illustrious part that your Excellency has borne in this long and arduous contest," he said, "becomes a matter of history, fame will gather your brightest laurels rather from the banks of the Delaware and those of the Chesapeake."

Did Cornwallis already have an inkling of where the world was headed when he gave that toast? Maybe. Like Washington, Cornwallis was one of the most impressive men of his generation—he very well may have realized that the British loss would resonate far beyond this city on the Chesapeake.

A Complicated Rival

It's surprising, but Cornwallis, like a number of other well-known English-men (such as philosopher Edmund Burke), actually favored granting the colonies more rights before the revolution. What he opposed, and could not accept, was armed rebellion against the Crown.

By winning over the enemy, and a formidable opponent like Cornwallis, Washington showed no ill will toward a nation he had fought for and nearly died for in the past. How Washington carried himself, and how he represented the nation moving forward, went a long way toward establishing the American ideals that seem almost second nature today.

When President Chester Alan Arthur celebrated the hundredth anniversary of the revolutionary victory at Yorktown, he honored the descendants of Washington, Lafayette, Rochambeau, and many others. But, to close the ceremony, the president saluted the British flag to honor those who had fallen. This might seem a bit strange to outsiders, but Americans, starting with Washington, have fought wars to find peace. Once we do, we harbor no grudges—if you embrace freedom, we embrace you. European nations had a long way to go before they understood this concept. We have never forgotten it. Just ask the Germans, Japanese, Koreans, or Iraqis.

II

Gray in Your Service

March 14, 1783
General Washington's Headquarters
Newburgh, New York

For perhaps the very first time, George Washington felt completely alone.

He had always been able to count on the support of his men, the devotion of his staff, the dedication of his army. Through the very worst of times and from the loneliest of days, from the lowliest private to his senior generals, his men had always stood at his side.

But now they did not stand with him; they stood against him.

And that cut him to the core.

Alone, he thought. *I am alone in this.* He slowly shook his head.

A pile of gentle embers glowed below the mantel, but the fire itself had long since burned down, leaving a chill in the air. Though it was late, he was dressed in his uniform and his boots were still on. The room was quiet. He could hear himself breathe. The fire popped and he watched a dying ember grow cold upon the wooden floor. Lifting his eyes, he stared at the writing quill, then at his hands. They were strong and firm, but seemed smaller, and not as thick with muscle as they once used to be. And they were rough now. Rough from work. Rough from cold winters. His knuckles were dark and wrinkled, his palms thick with calluses from holding leather reins.

Washington turned to look at the vile piece of paper that announced the secret meeting. He had thrown it upon the rough wooden table where it now sat like a poisonous spider, dangerous and menacing. He wanted to slap it aside or throw it into the hot embers; anything to get it out of his sight. But he couldn't ignore it. He had to deal with it. And it had to be done tonight.

Of all the crises that he had lived through, this one was the worst. Out of every arrow of disappointment that had pierced him, this one cut the deepest.

This wasn't a passing fancy he was dealing with. These weren't the rantings of a few disgruntled officers or the common grumblings from the enlisted men. This was something different. Far more dangerous.

This was a conspiracy on the grandest scale.

He had been warning the Congress for years. How many letters had he written! How many leaders had he begged! Now there was no choice; they simply *had* to do something or the situation would explode.

Yes, he understood their reasons. He wasn't stupid. He understood the politics, the realities of what power they did or did not have. He knew the Congress wasn't evil; it wasn't filled with evil or lazy men. Most of them were friends. All of them loved their country. But, through the weak Articles of Confederation, they had made themselves powerless and, in the end, that is what would destroy them.

He also understood that the states felt they'd given all they had. Their cities had been occupied by the hated British soldiers for far too long. All of their citizens had suffered. But that was nothing compared with what his army had endured.

And yet they had won!

It had been more than eighteen months since Yorktown and little meaningful military action had occurred since then. The British fleet had already sailed out of the New York harbor. Some British soldiers remained, but his army had essentially won the war! He had known since watching the white flag rise at Yorktown that they were going to drive the British from their shores. But this thing, this ongoing atrocity that had befallen his army, took all the glory out of their victory.

Staring at the dying fire, he scowled. It was a bitter thing to swallow. A bitter, dangerous thing. But the simple fact was that it had proven easier to defeat the mighty British than it was to convince his people to pay the very army that had set them free!

He looked at the dreadful bulletin, then closed his eyes and took a deep breath.

His chair creaked underneath his large frame as he placed his feet atop the rock and mortar hearth. He was close enough to the dying fire that he could feel occasional puffs of heat when a downdraft channeled through the chimney.

We could still lose this! he thought.

His heart slammed inside his chest.

Everything we've done could be for nothing!

His mind drifted back across the years of war. He remembered it all: every single day of hunger, every cut of fear, every man he had watched fall upon his chest and die, every night away from Martha, every day without the smell of the pines on his beloved estate—at one time he'd been away from Mount Vernon for six years! He remembered every march in crushing heat, every night in bitter cold, his feet so numb he was certain they had frozen, every patch of thirst, every ounce of blood they'd shed.

He remembered every glorious day of victory and every awful day of defeat.

He drifted further back. Another memory; more pain. June 14, 1775. His good friend, John Adams, had introduced a motion in the Congress to adopt the army of Massachusetts and to appoint a commander in chief to lead it. Everyone knew who it would be. George Washington knew it, too. Despite the sincerity of his protests, despite the fact that he had begged a fellow Virginian to oppose his appointment, the motion to name him supreme commander was taken forward. As he had listened to his fellow delegates begin the debate, and not wanting to put them in the uncomfortable position of having to discuss him while he was in their midst, he had stood and walked out of the room.

The following day, he was given word: The vote had been unanimous. He was commander in chief of the continental army. To show their enormous gratitude for his service, the Congress had stipulated the ridiculously high salary of five hundred dollars a month.

Put in charge of an army that didn't exist, given a salary he'd never accept, with few resources behind him and a violent enemy in his path, he accepted the task with a solemn sense of duty but not much optimism. All that Congress had asked him to do was to take a ragtag group of undisciplined and inexperienced farmers and craftsmen, men who had virtually no combat experience or military training, many of whom were without supplies or even weapons, men who were hungry, without uniforms or, in some cases, boots on their feet, and turn them into a fighting force that could defeat the most frightening army in the world.

It was an impossible task. Yet he knew he had no choice.

He thought back to the letter that he had sent to Martha soon after the commission had been placed on his shoulders. He didn't remember every word, but the tone of his letter was impossible to forget. *I do not want this! Far from seeking this appointment, I have used every power to avoid it! I would rather be home with you! I have been given a trust that is too great for me. But as it has been a kind of destiny that has thrown me in this service, then I must serve.*

Unlike the letter he'd sent to Martha, he remembered with perfect clarity the words he had said to Congress upon his appointment, for he believed them with every ounce of his being: "I do not think myself equal to the command I am honored with."

He reviewed in his mind the terrible price they had already paid: 4,400 American men killed in battle; 6,200 wounded. Maybe ten thousand killed on British prison ships anchored in New York's Hudson River.

Then, the most discouraging statistic of them all: sixty thousand American soldiers dead from hunger, exposure, or disease.

Sixty thousand soldiers! Dead from causes that could have been avoided if their civilian leaders had only done their jobs.

If they only had kept their promises.

It was, in fact, those broken promises that had brought them to this point; the most dangerous moment his infant nation might ever face. Another burden thrown upon his shoulders. Another crisis to navigate.

The general opened his eyes. How much time had passed, he did not know, but the red and orange embers had turned black, leaving white and gray rims around the charcoal's edges. The room was dark, the night quiet. Knowing he had but one chance to change the outcome, he picked up a piece of paper and started writing.

ONE YEAR EARLIER

Colonel Lewis Nicola, commander of a group of wounded soldiers known as the Invalid Regiment, had had enough. The army had gone without adequate food and clothing for far too long. Starvation. Cold. Disease. Beyond the horrors of the battlefield, these were the indignities his men had been forced to suffer.

As hostilities were winding down, it became painfully obvious to Nicola that, once the army was disbanded, Congress would have little incentive to fulfill the promises they had once made: payment for their service, land, and a pension for the wounded. Every day that passed, the entire army—but especially the Invalid Regiment—found themselves less and less likely to be paid. Without help from Congress, his wounded soldiers would live a life of poverty and devastation.

The war would end, but their suffering would continue. His soldiers would be nothing but a footnote to history.

He would not let that happen. He *could* not let that happen. Not while there was a single breath inside his chest.

Nicola sat at his desk and began to write. The words came slowly at first, but soon they flowed out of him like blood from a dying soldier. He could not stop them even if he'd wanted to—this was his duty.

When he was done, he sealed the letter and called for a messenger. "For His Excellency, General Washington," he directed as he placed the letter into the messenger's hand.

LATER THAT DAY

The messenger stood quietly in the corner, his head down, his feet together, as if he were afraid to take up too much space.

George Washington glanced at him, then looked away. He was in a foul mood. But he could not blame the poor man who stood before him. It was not his fault.

Closing his eyes, he shook his head. What was Colonel Nicola thinking?

He tried to hide his anger, but the emotion burned like boiling water through his fingers and he quickly looked away.

If there's one thing he had learned by sad experience it was the unpredictability of war. The constant uncertainty tossed his emotions about like a leaf in the wind. Up and down he was thrown, the smallest dose of good news filling his day with great pleasure, bad news tossing his heart into despair. Yet, because he understood that the long run was the only thing that mattered, he kept his emotions tightly contained, letting his men see him neither celebrate nor despair.

But he was growing tired now. The war was dragging on, its ending prolonged, its final passage painful and slow. He wanted it finished! He wanted to go home! He wanted to get on with the life that he had put on hold.

Washington glanced down at the letter once again, jumping quickly from paragraph to paragraph, wanting to make certain that he had not misread or misunderstood Nicola's words.

Sir:

The injuries the troops have received in their pecuniary rights have been, & still continue to be too obvious to require a particular detail, or to have escaped your Excellencies notice.

This gives us a dismal prospect for the time to come, & much reason to fear the future provision promised to officers by Congress.

We who have born the heat & labour of the day will be forgot and neglected by such as reap the benefits without suffering any of the hardships.

We have no doubt of Congresses intention to act uprightly, but greatly fear that, by the interested voices of others, their abilities will not be equal to the task.

I own I am not that violent admirer of a republican form of government as numbers in this country are; this is not owing to caprice, but reason & experience.

Congress has promised all those that continue in the service certain tracts of land, agreeable to their grades. Some States have done the same, others have not, probably owing to their not having lands to give, but as all the military have equal merits so have they equal claims to such rewards, therefore, they ought all to be put on a footing by the united States.

This war must have shown to all, but to military men in particular the weakness of republicks, and the exertions of the army has been able to make by being under a proper head.

Some people have so connected the ideas of tyranny and monarchy as to find it very difficult to separate them, it may therefore be requisite to give the head of such a constitution as I propose, some title apparently more moderate, but if all other things were once adjusted I believe strong argument might be produced for admitting the title of king, which I conceive would be attended with some material advantages.

Republican bigots will certainly consider my opinions as heterodox, and the maintainer thereof as meriting fire and faggots, I have therefore hitherto kept them within my own breast. By freely communicating them to your Excellency I am persuaded I own no risk, & that, this disapproved of, I need not apprehend their ever being disclosed to my prejudice.

—Col. Nicola

Colonel Nicola had come to an obvious conclusion: Congress was the problem. They were too weak. They had no power. All they could do was beg from the states. A republic would *never* have adequate power to administer such a vast and unyielding group of colonies.

The solution Nicola had come to was equally as obvious, though exceedingly dangerous: a monarchy.

How could this man not see the truth? Didn't he know what they were fighting for? Didn't he understand the great experiment they were seeking to achieve? Couldn't he see the bitter irony of his proposal: fight their British masters for no reason other than to implement another king?

All through the afternoon he suffered. His restlessness continued deep into the night. Finally, knowing that sleep would not come until he had addressed the colonel's letter, he got up and penned a response to the man who had caused him such despair. His response was severe and uncompromising.

"No occurrence in the course of the war has given me more painful sensations than your information of there being such ideas existing in the army, . . . and [these] I must view with abhorrence and reprehend with severity. [Your ideas are] the greatest mischiefs that can befall my country.

"You could not have found a person to whom your schemes are more disagreeable. If you have any regard for your country, concern for yourself or your posterity, or respect for me . . . banish these thoughts from your mind."

Calling for the messenger, General Washington sent his response back to the Colonel. He expected that the matter would be dropped and not brought up again—and he was right. Nicola accepted the response reluctantly, but with genuine humility.

Unfortunately, whether expressed openly or suppressed into the deepest regions of the souls, the sentiments that Nicola had put into writing—and that were shared among many—would not go away quite so easily.

March 15, 1783
General Washington's Headquarters
Newburgh

Nearly a year after Washington had curtly denied Colonel Nicola's plea, the condition of the army had not improved.

For the previous year, the resentment of the troops and officers had simmered.

In December 1782, the British fleet sailed out of New York harbor. Though it was an uncertain situation—there were still a significant number of British soldiers in the city—General Washington was confident that the winter would be as tranquil as the summer had been before. With hostilities winding down, he hoped to spend the winter at his home in Mount Vernon.

But the army didn't disband. They realized that maintaining a united front was their best, and probably only, chance of pressuring Congress to follow through on their promises. It was a recipe for disaster: an angry and rebuffed army, their demands ignored and unmet, festering in a winter camp with no more war to fight except against the men who had betrayed them through their false promises and lies.

The building anger of the army was too much to ignore. Washington knew he could not leave them to their own devices so, despite his yearning to return to Martha and Mount Vernon, he decided to quarter with his army for the winter in Newburgh. He believed that if he stayed with them, rode among them, talked with them every day, if they saw him and felt his presence, he could keep them under his control. He could stop their anger from boiling over into rage.

"The temper of the army is much soured," he wrote in December, noting that they were "more irritable" than at any time since the war had begun.

The general was very fearful of a mass mutiny, or worse. Would the army rise up against their government? Would they resort to the sword "to procure justice?" He knew they might. And they certainly had the power; he had helped forge them into an expert fighting force.

The thought was like a dagger to his heart.

Throughout the following months, Washington expressed his concerns in a series of letters. He was direct in his appraisal of the injustices with which his army had been treated—and in his appraisal that, without intervention, these injustices would soon turn into violence. To Congressman McHenry he wrote, "The patience, the fortitude, the long and great suffering of this army is unexampled in history. But there is an end to all things, and I fear we are very near to this."

On the long winter nights, he often had to wonder: what shame is about to fall upon the colonies! Is the great experiment of building a republic based on freedom about to come to a disgraceful end, the army *not even waiting until the British army had withdrawn* before turning on their own government?

What will the British think! Indeed, the same question would sweep through all of Europe. Are the colonies about to shame themselves before the entire world?

Alexander Hamilton was even more pessimistic, feeling that an uprising was inevitable. Open revolt, he thought, was the only way the army could claim their just rewards. He also recognized that some within the army thought that Washington had failed them, unable to secure what they had been promised from the Congress. In one particularly troubling exchange, he even encouraged General Washington not to stand against the army, but to "take the direction from them."

Washington stewed over Hamilton's letter for days, before rejecting it completely. He knew that if he and his army became the arbiters of justice, it would lead to a disaster.

Then, on March 10, he had received the final blow. Very discreetly, he was handed a covert memo that he was not supposed to see. A group of senior officers had scheduled a secret meeting. It was time, they had concluded, for the army to take things into their own hands. How many of his officers were involved, he did not know. But he feared that it was many. And maybe every single one of them.

The meeting had been scheduled to take place the very next day. It took all of Washington's efforts, and all of the goodwill he'd built up over the years, to convince his men to postpone it. He needed time to prepare an answer equal to their complaints.

George Washington had always thought that Alexander Hamilton was being a bit dramatic about discord among the officers. But now, after seeing the truth spelled out on that awful circular, he knew that Hamilton was right.

After spending several hours thinking about what message to send back to Hamilton in Philadelphia, Washington retired to his office to put the words on paper.

Dear Sir,

When I wrote to you last we were in a state of tranquility, but after the arrival of a certain Gentleman, who shall be nameless at present, from Philadelphia, a storm very suddenly arose with unfavorable prognostics; which though diverted for a moment is not yet blown over, nor is it in my power to point to the issue.

There is something very mysterious in this business. It appears, reports have been propagated in Philadelphia, that dangerous combinations were forming in the Army; and this at a time when there was not a syllable of the kind in agitation in Camp.

From this, and a variety of other considerations, it is firmly believed, by some, the scheme was not only planned but also digested and matured in Philadelphia; but in my opinion shall be suspended till I have a better ground to found one on. The matter was managed with great art; for as soon as the Minds of the Officers were thought to be prepared for the transaction, the anonymous invitations and address to the Officers were put in circulation, through every state line in the army. I was obliged therefore, in order to arrest on the spot, the foot that stood wavering on a tremendous precipice; to prevent the Officers from being taken by surprise while the passions were all inflamed, and to rescue them from plunging themselves into a gulf of Civil horror from which there might be no receding, to issue the order of the 11th. This was done upon the principle that it is easier to divert from a wrong, and point to a right path, than it is to recall the hasty and fatal steps which have been already taken.

Let me beseech you therefore, my good Sir, to urge this matter earnestly, and without further delay. The situation of these Gentlemen I do verily believe, is distressing beyond description....If any disastrous consequences should follow, by reason of their delinquency, that they must be answerable to God & their Country for the ineffable horrors which may be occasioned thereby.

I am Dear Sir Your Most Obedient Servant.

Washington sealed the letter and said a silent prayer. He would soon point his men to the right path he had written about—he just hoped they would listen.

March 15, 1783
General Washington's Headquarters
Newburgh

It had been an awful few days.

After reading the letter announcing the secret meeting of his officers, Washington had tried to stay out of sight. He knew he had to talk to his men, but he didn't yet know what to say.

The previous night had been sleepless, but productive. The speech he would give to his men had come to him, slowly at first, and then rapidly, as though they were not his words at all. In the dim predawn light, he wrote them down on rough, off-colored paper with uneven edges and rounded corners. Slightly damp with sweat, the ink had smeared some of the words together. In his pocket, he had a letter from a member of the Congress who had pledged to support the army, further evidence of the argument he had to put forward on this day.

He was exhausted. His eyes were bleary and his chest was wire tight. But his mind was sharp and clear, focused as a beam of sunlight shining through a portal window. There wasn't a doubt in his mind what the right thing to do was; the only question was whether his army would listen. Would the reputation he'd built up over years of sacrifice afford him the dignity of a true debate, or would his officers consider him to be a simple figurehead for the Congress whose words counted for nothing?

It was impossible to say. After all the suffering that they had lived through, he really didn't know—but he was about to find out. The emergency meeting he had called was about to begin.

March 15, 1783
Temple of Honor
Newburgh

The air was cold and raw as George Washington stood outside a new building on the edges of the military camp. It was just before noon.

The place he was about to enter was called the Temple of Honor, and it had many uses: a dance hall, a meetinghouse, a place to gather and keep warm. Today he hoped to add another use to that list: a place to quell a fractious rebellion.

The building's wooden exterior was rough and poorly finished, with brown mortar stuck between the logs and a slightly uneven door. Standing at the large double doors that covered the main entrance, he listened to the voices booming from inside. They were waiting for him, the officers and generals of his army, men he had spent years fighting to defend, both from within the halls of Congress and upon the battlefield. Listening, he identified the voices of some of his senior generals and most trusted aides.

Were there any who were with him?

His chest tightened.

He put his hand on the door pull and an ominous spirit seemed to emanate from out of thin air, whispering feelings of darkness and despair into his mind. He had wrestled with the demons of discouragement many times before, this feeling was not unfamiliar to him, but this time was different: far more deadly, far more personal.

Taking a deep breath, he pulled the wooden door back and stepped into the hall.

The group of men instantly turned toward him, feeling his presence as he entered the dimly lit room. A deep hush fell over them. No one spoke. No one moved. The smell of smoke and newly cut pine permeated the air. The small windows, thin and poorly made, bent the sunlight across the floor into broken prisms. A potbelly stove burned at the front of the hall and the air was stuffy.

The general took two steps inside, then stopped, his eyes moving around the room. The moment of decision had finally come. For all of them.

Washington noticed that none of the officers looked away from him. And why should they? They had nothing to be ashamed about. They had done nothing wrong! They weren't plotting to destroy a nation. They weren't fighting to grab power or great riches. They weren't fighting out of maliciousness or pride or for any of the other reasons that evil men might fight. The only thing that they wanted was for the promises that had been made to them to be kept.

The general took his time, moving his eyes around the room. He needed to read the mood, to know what he was up against. Looking at the stoic faces, he realized that he faced a mountain.

He moved toward the makeshift podium that had been positioned at the front of the room. The men turned their heads to match his pace, never taking their eyes off him.

He stopped behind the podium and cleared his throat. "I apologize," he started. "It wasn't my intention to come to you in person. But upon reading this paper"—he lifted the threatening circular in his hand—"and after a long night of careful consideration, I knew I had to speak to you myself."

He began with his prepared remarks, speaking of the neglect that all of them had suffered and acknowledging the painful fact that some in the room felt that he had personally let them down.

"If my conduct heretofore has not evinced to you that I have been a faithful friend to the army," he said, "my declaration of it at this time would be equally unavailing and improper. But as I was among the first who embarked in the cause of our common country; as I have never left your side one moment, but when called from you on public duty; as I have been the constant companion and witness of your distresses . . . as I have ever considered my military reputation as inseparably connected with that of the army; as my heart has ever expanded with joy when I have heard its praises; and my indignation has arisen when the mouth of detraction has been opened against it, it can scarcely be supposed, at this late stage of the war, that I am indifferent to its interests."

He thrust the threatening circular into the air, toward the men, resentment rising in his voice.

"The anonymous addresser of this paper says, '*If peace takes place, never sheathe your swords until you have obtained full and ample justice!*'

"My God!" His voice was booming now. "What can this writer have in view, by recommending such measures? Can he be a friend to the army? Can he be a friend to this country? Rather, is he not an insidious foe?"

His words seemed to echo through the wooden hall. There was no doubt left about where he stood.

He went on, choosing his words very carefully now. Yes, the Congress has been shackled. But it was made up of good and honorable men. They *would* give the army justice! He promised to continue promoting their cause before the Congress to the utmost extent of his abilities. But they had to trust him. They had to give him another chance.

He warned them that moving forward with violence now would shade the glory that they had earned. "Let me entreat you, gentlemen, on your part, not to take any measures which, viewed in the calm light of reason, will lessen the dignity and sully the glory you have hitherto maintained; let me request you to rely on the plighted faith of your country, and place a full confidence in the purity of the intentions of Congress."

He paused and looked upon the faces. He had rewritten the end of his remarks many times over the previous days, searching for the exact right words to leave them with.

Stepping out from behind the podium and into the crowd, he began,

"[By rejecting violence] you will, by the dignity of your conduct, afford occasion for posterity to say, when speaking of the glorious example you have exhibited to mankind, 'Had this day been wanting, the world had never seen the last stage of perfection to which human nature is capable of attaining.' "

And that was it. It was all he had to say. He had put forward every argument. If they couldn't see it, if they didn't believe it, if putting his honor and reputation on the line were not enough, then there was nothing he could do now. He would fight them if he had to, but he couldn't fight them with any more words.

Silence hung in the air. No one stood to applaud. It seemed that no one even moved. A few of the men, it seemed, had softened, but most were still as hard as the nails driven into the floor. Hardened and unyielding, refusing even now to bend.

He swallowed in despair. So this is it! he thought to himself This is how it ends . . .

Washington moved his gaze from face to face. All of the men were looking at him, but none of them were smiling.

In desperation, the general thought of what more he could say. Almost as an afterthought, he remembered the letter from the congressman that he had put into his pocket. It wasn't much, but perhaps a pledge of support from a representative in Philadelphia would help tip the scales toward peace.

He reached into his pocket and unfolded the letter. He began to read but the words had been crammed onto the page and were too small for him to make out. He stumbled over them badly. A moment of awkward silence followed. He turned back to the letter. He read a few more words but there was no point in trying to continue—he was looking foolish.

With great reluctance, he reached into another pocket and pulled out a new set of spectacles. He stared at them a moment. Only a few of his closest aides had ever seen him put them on. He lifted them to his eyes, but fumbled awkwardly. He instead looked out upon his men. "Gentlemen, you will permit me to put on my spectacles," he explained in sadness, "for I have not only grown gray but almost blind in service to my country."

A reverent hush fell over every man within the room. Watching their mighty general struggle, none could pull their eyes from him.

There he was, this giant in their service, this man who towered over them in almost every sense of the word, this man who had sacrificed everything that he had ever loved, who had walked and fought beside them, suffering every indignity that they had—stood before them in utter humility, having nothing more left to give.

A few men shifted in their seats. Many of them were weeping, tears streaming down their wintry cheeks. These grizzled men—hardened first by battle and then by a feeling of betrayal—were softened to the point of tears. But they wept not out of sympathy, nor for his immense sacrifice; they wept not out of anger, nor out of shame.

They wept because they loved him.

And they were going to follow him until the very end.

General Washington read the rest of the letter from the congressman and then left the Temple of Honor. A few minutes later, the officers took a vote. The tally was unanimous: they would stand at their beloved leader's side.

March 16, 1783
General Washington's Headquarters
Newburgh

George Washington had his best night's sleep in almost a week. He dreamed not of insurrection and chaos, but of peace and prosperity.

After attending Sunday service he retired to his office to finish his report to Congress in Philadelphia, which was still very much on edge. After he'd finished writing a complete description of the meeting he penned a short cover letter.

Sir:

The result of the proceedings of the grand Convention of the Officers, which I have the honor of enclosing to your Excellency for the inspection of Congress, will, I flatter myself, be considered as the last glorious proof of Patriotism which could have been given by Men who aspired to the distinction of a Patriot Army; and will not only confirm their claim to the justice, but will increase their title to the gratitude of their Country...

With great respect, etc.
George Washington

His letter arrived in Philadelphia just in time. James Madison later wrote in his personal journal that the "dispatch dispelled the cloud which seemed to have been gathering."

While Washington likely did not know it at the time, the outcome of his meeting in the Temple of Honor had very likely stopped the Congress from voting to declare war on their very own army.

But while that storm had been deftly avoided—another one—this one involving the very Articles of Confederation that had been at the root of the Newburgh crisis—was beginning to form.

12

A Moment of Crisis,
a Lifetime of Preparation

Perhaps the strongest feature in his character was prudence, never acting until every circumstance, every consideration, was maturely weighed; refraining if he saw a doubt, but, when once decided, going through with his purpose, whatever obstacles opposed. His integrity was most pure, his justice the most inflexible I have ever known, no motives of interest or consanguinity, of friendship or hatred, being able to bias his decision. He was, indeed, in every sense of the words, a wise, a good, and a great man.

—THOMAS JEFFERSON

Sometimes everything you prepare for during your entire life can come down to one instant in time. With athletes it might be one pitch; with musicians and actors it might be one audition; and, for the rest of us, it might be one chance to influence others to make the right decision.

As we sit here today, many of us are frustrated. Some of us have gone out to rallies or town hall meetings, or written our congressmen—but rarely has that gotten the results we hope for. Some people get frustrated by that and some will, no doubt, choose the Benedict Arnold path as a result. But others get motivated by it—they use their frustrations as incentive to keep going, to keep preparing, to keep waiting for their opportunity.

George Washington was one of those people.

The unbiased march of time has proven the Newburgh Conspiracy to be one of the most important episodes of the entire American Revolution. In fact, many historians recognize it as one of the most, if not *the* most, dangerous hour the United States has ever faced. Had General Washington failed to pacify his angry army, and his men gone forward with venting their rage upon the Congress, the nation may well have drowned in the blood of a civil war.

It is clear now that Washington's speech before his army in Newburgh stopped what could have been a very dangerous turn of events. That watershed moment proved to be one of those rare turning points that shaped not only the future of our nation, but the fate of the entire world.

Think about it: What would the next two centuries have been like had the United States not been the *united* states? How different would our world be right now, how different would it have been for our ancestors, how different for our children, had the country—free from the oppression of a foreign king—turned to a monarchy of its own?

These may seem like rhetorical questions, but they're not; they're vital ones because they force us to think about the fact that one person at one moment in time can define history for generations to come.

From President to Emperor

It was not very far in the future from that day in Newburgh that Napoleon Bonaparte became "First Consul" of the French Republic. Five years later Bonaparte had literally crowned himself Napoleon I, Emperor of the French. It goes to show you just how fast a republic can become a monarchy if the wrong people are put in charge.

At Newburgh, only one man had the power to sway the embittered army and short-circuit any talk of emperors or kings or coups or rebellions. Only one man had the stature and humility to guide the nation through this dark hour. Only one man really understood not only human weaknesses but also *the stage of perfection to which human nature is capable*. Only one man had the chance to be Bonaparte—and only one man had the courage and humility to turn it down.

An officer on Henry Knox's staff witnessed how Washington met this challenge. He wrote:

On other occasions, [Washington] had been supported by the exertions of an army and the countenance of his friends; but in this he stood single and alone. There was no saying where the passions of an army, which were not a little inflamed, might lead....Under these circumstances he appeared, not at the head of his troops, but as it were, in opposition to them; and for a dreadful moment the interests of the army and its General seemed to be in competition! He spoke—every doubt was dispelled, and the tide of patriotism rolled again in its wonted course. Illustrious man! What he says of the army may with equal justice be applied to his own character. "Had this day been wanting, the world had never seen the last stage of perfection to which human nature is capable of attaining."

Well over two hundred years have passed since that fateful meeting in Newburgh, New York. For many, that dramatic showdown has been lost in the passage of time. Some historians, in their detached and educated analysis, give little importance to the event or to the power of the man who dared his army to believe in laws instead of arms, a man who had *grown gray in the service* of the men and nation that he loved. Even now, how many of our fellow citizens realize that, for an agonizing few days, the American experiment hung precariously in the balance? How many kids in school are taught that everything they've come to know and believe in literally depended on one speech and one man?

For those of us fortunate to enjoy the marvelous blessings of the original "land of the free," there is little excuse for not appreciating the extraordinary power of what happened in what many remember simply as a part-time dance hall in upstate New York.

An Appropriate Name

The assembly hall in Newburgh where the meeting took place was called the "Temple," and it was, unsurprisingly, also a part-time church. I say "unsurprisingly" because it's clear now that God was present there that day. Of course, the building's full name was "The Temple of Honor" and it could not have been a more perfect fit for the occasion. If the man who gave the speech that day had not been a man of honor, things may have very well turned out much different.

PREPARING FOR YOUR MOMENT

It was all about character, trust, and honor—three words that most current-day elites scoff at, but three of Washington's traits that likely saved America.

A year after the Newburgh crisis, Thomas Jefferson recognized Washington's accomplishment: "The moderation and virtue of a single character have probably prevented this revolution from being closed, as most others have been, by a subversion of that liberty it was intended to establish."

It wasn't Washington's military expertise that saved the day. It wasn't his oratory skills or his powers of persuasion. It wasn't the height of his stature, the enormously important political connections that he held, nor his elevated social status.

It was his soft-spoken meekness, his deep humility in a moment of utter crisis, and the trust and respect he'd garnered from his colleagues over the years that saved the country.

Angry George

Given Washington's famously humble speeches and subdued nature it's surprising to learn that he was once known for his hotheadedness and sudden temper.

"I wish I could say that he governs his temper," Lord Fairfax wrote to Mary Ball Washington about the sixteen-year-old Washington. "He is subject to attacks of anger on provocation, sometimes without just cause."

Gilbert Stuart, a man who knew Washington well, and who painted his official portrait, said of him, "Had he been born in the forests, he would have been the fiercest among savage tribes."

Yes, life as a surveyor on the unforgiving frontier was very difficult. It was demanding and hostile, with danger and deprivation at every turn. It demanded a decisive and sometimes authoritarian approach in order to survive. But Washington recognized that this didn't change the fact that his hot temper was a weakness. Whether he was on the frontier or engaged in mortal combat against the redcoats, an explosive temper detracted from his ability to accomplish his goals. It was a deficiency in his personality that would not serve him if he didn't rise above it.

Perhaps there is no better example of Washington having the self-discipline to conquer his own weakness than the fact that he grew from a hot-tempered young man into a powerful leader who had the humility to be open and honest before his men.

There is a lesson in that for all of us.

Everything that we do in life—every battle that we fight and every mountain that we climb, no matter how many times that we may fall—may be for no other purpose than to prepare us for that moment when we are called upon to make a difference in this world.

In fact, every decision that we make, even those that seem small and perhaps irrelevant—perhaps *especially* those that seem small and irrelevant—may be moving us toward that moment when we can change a life for the better.

We may only get one chance to make a difference. But there is no doubt that such a moment in each of our lives is going to come.

The only question that really matters is, Will we be ready for it?

THE BURDEN–AND THE GLORY– OF RESPONSIBILITY

Prior to taking command of the army in 1775, Washington expressed his great reluctance and deep humility regarding his ability to lead his men through the storms that lay ahead. He expressed these reservations on more than one occasion. But, unlike so many of today's leaders, once he had accepted a challenge, he rose above it. He conquered it. He did whatever it took to see that his nation and his people prevailed. He didn't bemoan the difficult circumstances he had inherited. He didn't blame his army's early failures on his subordinates (though there were many times that he could have). He didn't blame his battlefield failures on the tides of misfortune, constantly pointing out all the elements that were beyond his control. And he didn't indulge his pride after his victories; never crowing over his conquests at Boston, Trenton, Yorktown.

What Washington *did* do was accept the responsibility he had been given, beg the grace of God upon himself and his army, and then work relentlessly to accomplish his goals. What he *did* do was to keep on working, regardless of the personal sacrifices required or the setbacks that he encountered. He kept the faith, no matter who stood against him; regardless of the gossip, the naysayers and, sometimes, regardless even of the betrayal of his friends.

It wasn't easy. In every moment there was a hill to climb, in every day a sacrifice to make, in every trial a challenge that racked his soul. Had he known how very difficult it would prove to be, he might not have taken on the task. As he had confessed to a close aide, "Could I have foreseen . . . no consideration upon earth should have induced me to accept this command."

But he did accept it. And he won.

What If He Had Been King?

The monarchies that held so much control around the world hated the idea that the American people might claim a list of rights. I mean, come on, kings were divinely appointed leaders! Their absolute rule might not be the will of the people, but it certainly was the will of God.

That being the case, the royal monarchs had to be thinking, How dare the Americans mess around with thousands of years of tradition! Surely they would fail. Without the royal intellect, without the benefit of the elites and all the lessons in good governance that they had learned, without the superiority of a hereditary royalty and nobility lording over the lowly, and, most important, without the will of God behind their form of government, how could they possibly succeed?

All of that aside, it may be interesting to ask the question: what if?

What if the enormously popular and powerful Washington had decided that, why yes, as a matter of a fact, I *would* like to be the king?

Had Washington taken to the throne, who would now be our king?

Assuming the royal "House of Washington" had been able to survive all the commotion of the next 230 years (revolutions, depressions, upheavals, and world wars), the crown would likely now sit upon the head of one Paul Emery Washington, who retired after forty years as a business supply manager in Valley Forge.

According to NBC News, the royal Paul (George's third-great-grandnephew) seems to have taken the fact that he was robbed of his royal throne fairly well. Recently asked about the possibility of the monarchy that was denied him when his great-great-great-(whatever)-uncle refused the kingship, he answered simply, "I think George made the right decision."

THE SILVER LINING

All of us face moments in our lives when we're fighting for something we believe in but begin to realize that our position is far from perfect. Those who don't face those kinds of assessments will never be great leaders because they can't see any other way but theirs. If we are seeking truth then we must follow it, wherever it leads us—even if that is to a place we never thought we'd go.

For George Washington, the Newburgh Conspiracy brought to life some truths that he probably would've rather not had to deal with. Despite his efforts to assure his troops that Congress was filled with honorable men who were loyal to their nation and who would eventually see that justice to the army was done, the experience must have made him acutely aware of the potentially fatal weakness of a loosely aligned group of states. After all, they barely had the power to protect themselves from each other, let alone from foreign armies.

Though he accepted his reprimand, Colonel Nicola's harsh words regarding the frailty of the confederation (and gentle suggestion that a monarchy be considered) must have had an effect on Washington. Not only did he see the hopeless reality of the situation, but he'd experienced it firsthand in, for example, Valley Forge. A national government that didn't even have the power to procure supplies for an army was not nearly strong enough to defend a country.

And things didn't get any better from there.

Washington's Forgotten Second Message at Newburgh

Washington didn't just confront his officers at Newburgh. He also confronted Congress.

In June 1783 (just a few weeks after his showdown with his officers), he took pen in hand to warn Congress that a strong union was necessary to preserve our liberties—and he also warned how "anarchy" could lead to "Tyranny" (sounds like Cloward-Piven!). He ended by saying:

> It is only in our united Character as an Empire, that our Independence is acknowledged, that our power can be regarded, or our Credit supported among Foreign Nations. The Treaties of the European Powers with the United States of America, will have no validity on a dissolution of the Union. We shall be left nearly in a state of Nature, or we may find by our own unhappy experience, that there is a natural and necessary progression, from the extreme of anarchy to the extreme of Tyranny; and that arbitrary power is most easily established on the ruins of Liberty abused to licentiousness.

Under the Articles of Confederation, the states were never able to rise above a collection of half-starved and wilted governments that were directionless and seemingly incapable of providing even the most basic needs of their citizens. Within a few years of defeating the British, the states were in constant conflict with each other. Trade wars. Competing currencies. Bitter disputes over territories. Jealousy. Rivalries between northern and southern states and cultures. Power struggles between the large states and the small.

The states were on the edge of anarchy. And no one understood the danger more than George Washington. Having suffered through the extremely frustrating and dangerous experience that he had at New-burgh, he realized more than anyone that the Congress was too weak. They couldn't govern the states effectively. The confederation was doomed to fail.

It was this realization that led Washington to eventually agree to lead the Constitutional Convention—which, of course, ultimately decided to scrap the Articles of Confederation in favor of a much stronger federal government.

But think about how this might have played if Washington had not been someone who was open to finding the truth no matter where it led him. If he'd been a zealot for the government, a defender of the Articles at all costs, then the Newburgh Conspiracy would never have prompted him to take the actions he did.

The lessons for us today are clear—question with boldness. I know I'm like a broken record, but if you think that your version of the truth is all that exists, then not only will you fail in pursuing your agenda, but you'll also fail in motivating anyone else to join you. The search for truth is a lifelong quest without a destination. Don't fall into the trap of believing so deeply in your own ideology that you cannot even see the flaws in it.

One of George Washington's greatest traits was his understanding that man is not perfect. Imperfect men, he knew, can never create perfect government. Centuries have passed since then, but that fundamental idea has never changed, and it never will. Embrace our imperfection by constantly searching for the truth. You might just be surprised where it leads you.

13

To Please All Is Impossible

December 21, 1786
Mount Vernon, Virginia

It was four days before Christmas and Mount Vernon was ready. Large bunches of mistletoe were placed about and sprigs of holly were laid in front of each windowpane. But, despite the holiday cheer, George Washington was in a sour mood.

He sat at his desk wearing a plain blue coat, white cashmere waistcoat, black knee breeches, and black boots. His quill pen was dipped and ready, but the words were difficult to write. He was, of course, honored by the offer he'd been presented, but he simply could not agree to it. It just wasn't possible.

After a long pause Washington finally began to write, addressing his letter to Virginia's current governor, Edmund Randolph:

Sir:

I had not the honor of receiving your Excellency's favor of the 6th, with its enclosures, till last night. Sensible as I am of the honor conferred on me by the General Assembly, in appointing me one of the Deputies to a Convention proposed to be held in the City of Philadelphia in May next, for the purpose of revising the Federal Constitution; and desirous as I am on all occasions, of testifying a ready obedience to the calls of my Country; yet, Sir, there exists at this moment, circumstances, which I am persuaded

will render my acceptance of this fresh mark of confidence incompatible
with other measures which I had previously adopted; and from which,
seeing little prospect of disengaging myself, it would be disingenuous not to
express a wish that some other character, on whom greater reliance can be
had, may be substituted in my place; the probability of my non-attendance
being too great to continue my appointment.

Washington put his pen down and read aloud what he'd just written. He could not believe they were his words. Was he really going to turn down an invitation to join the convention?

He knew, of course, the perilous position the country had found itself in. Just six weeks earlier he had written to James Madison that, without a change in course, all the blood and treasure they'd expended in the war would be for nothing. The country, he wrote, was "fast verging to anarchy and confusion!"

But, still, surely there were others from Virginia who could take his place. He had put Martha through so much over the years, it simply wasn't fair to leave her again. And that wasn't the only thing giving him pause; it was also his own health: he was experiencing painful rheumatism that was nearly debilitating.

And then there were the other personal and professional commitments he had made for the time during which the convention was scheduled. It was all just too much.

George Washington signed his name to the letter and put his pen away. It was time for others to lead.

April 5, 1787
Mount Vernon

The last three months had been torturous. Washington's decision to not attend the upcoming convention had weighed on him daily. When he was able to forget about it for a moment, others were all too happy to remind him.

But it wasn't just the gentle prodding of friends that had forced him to rethink his position; he also saw what was happening to his country. Shays's Rebellion—in which the Massachusetts legislature had almost been overthrown—was a startling reminder of just how fast a spark of anarchy could ignite the entire country. The Articles of Confederation were far too weak and, Washington knew, it was only a matter of time before a crisis would eventually tear them apart.

"I won't do it! I just won't do it, Martha!"

"Yes, George," Martha Washington answered very quietly and calmly, not even looking up from her knitting. The world rarely saw her husband's great passions bursting forth, but he was comfortable enough with her that he allowed her to see the person he really was.

"Look at me! Just look at me! My arm in a sling from this blasted rheumatism! I'm in no shape to travel. And who would run this place? Lund? Why it would all finally go to rack-and-ruin!"

He was speaking of his cousin, Lund Washington, his estate's overseer. Martha might have reminded her husband that she and Lund had operated Mount Vernon together for eight years during his wartime absence—and the building they now conversed in had not fallen down even once in that whole time. Nonetheless, she maintained a discreet silence on the subject and instead played to her husband's strength. "You are certainly right about not having to go if you don't want to—you *have* done enough."

"Yes, exactly, Martha. That's what I've been saying!"

And so their conversation, if one might call it that, ended, with Martha excusing herself, leaving George alone to continue his fuming.

Martha ducked into the servants' quarters and found her husband's manservant Billy Lee in the kitchen, carving slices of ham. In a low voice, the tiny woman ordered him: "William, start thinking about packing Master Washington's trunks—for a long trip—and yours as well, of course."

"Yes, Miz Washington. Where are we going to?"

"Philadelphia, William."

Lee looked quizzically at Martha.

"Does General Washington know he's going to Philadelphia, Miz Washington?"

"Not yet, William—but he will."

Lee bowed and was about to leave when he turned back to face her. "Miz Washington, I believe everyone in the country—*except the general*—knows he's going to Philadelphia. I started packing his trunks two weeks ago."

May 13, 1787
Mrs. Whitby's Inn
Chester, Pennsylvania

George Washington was enjoying a pleasant lunch with old acquaintances from his army days, including Henry Knox, when the clatter of horses interrupted their discussion about their past triumphs and the challenges posed by the Constitutional Convention, which Washington would soon join.

It was the Philadelphia Light Horse, resplendent in their brilliant white breeches and dark, plumed hats. In 1775, this unit had escorted Washington from Philadelphia to Boston to assume command of the new Continental Army. On this afternoon, however, these cavalrymen would escort his coach twenty miles north to Philadelphia. He had hoped to be just another delegate (he was, after all, not even chair of the Virginia delegation) and to share modest quarters at a Market Street boardinghouse with James Madison, but this splendid greeting was a clue that his wish was not going to be granted.

Despite threatening skies, the whole city turned out to cheer Washington's arrival in Philadelphia, a thirteen-gun salute ensuring that even those in the surrounding areas would be aware of the celebration. Every steeple bell (and the city had so many that visitors thought it downright "papist") clanged its praises. The banker, Robert Morris, "the Financier of the American Revolution," eagerly descended upon Washington and demanded that he forgo the boardinghouse and instead reside with him at his magnificent newly built mansion.

It was a welcome worthy of a king on coronation day. And, if many citizens had their way, that's exactly what George Washington would soon be.

June 27, 1787
State House
Philadelphia

Benjamin Franklin wanted the floor.

He was never one to say much, and he said even less than usual during this convention. He was eighty-one years old and had to be transported about the city in an ornate, French-made, glass-enclosed sedan chair, carried upon the shoulders of four convicts from the Walnut Street Jail.

But today, because things were not going well at all at this Constitutional Convention, he spoke. And what the old freethinker said surprised everyone:

> *In this situation of this Assembly, groping as it were in the dark to find political truth, and scarce able to distinguish it when presented to us, how has it happened, Sir, that we have not hitherto once thought of humbly applying to the Father of lights to illuminate our understandings?*
>
> *In the beginning of the Contest with Great Britain, when we were sensible of danger we had daily prayer in this room for the divine protection. Our prayers, Sir, were heard, and they were graciously answered. All of us who were engaged in the struggle must have observed frequent instances of a Superintending providence in our favor. To that kind providence we owe this happy opportunity of consulting in peace on the means of establishing our future national felicity.*
>
> *And have we now forgotten that powerful friend?*
>
> *I have lived, Sir, a long time, and the longer I live, the more convincing proofs I see of this truth—that God governs in the affairs of men. And if a sparrow cannot fall to the ground without his notice, is it probable that an empire can rise without his aid?*
>
> *We have been assured, Sir, in the sacred writings, that "except the Lord build the House they labour in vain that build it." I firmly believe this; and I also believe that without his concurring aid we shall succeed in this political building no better than the Builders of Babel: We shall be divided by our little partial local interests; our projects will be confounded, and we ourselves shall become a reproach and bye word down to future*

ages. And what is worse, mankind may hereafter from this unfortunate instance, despair of establishing Governments by Human Wisdom and leave it to chance, war and conquest.

I therefore beg leave to move, that henceforth prayers imploring the assistance of Heaven, and its blessings on our deliberations, be held in this Assembly every morning before we proceed to business, and that one or more of the Clergy of the City be requested to officiate in that service.

George Washington, now the presiding officer of this convention, beamed—but Alexander Hamilton did not. He told the delegates that he believed asking for this kind of "foreign aid," as he so condescendingly put it, could reveal to the world just how poorly things were going.

Washington was not pleased at all by his protégé's words. In some ways, he thought, young Hamilton still had much to learn. But in the end, it was not Hamilton's objections that ruled the day; it was same dreadful finances that had plagued the old Confederation Congress: there was not a silver dime available for such purposes. Franklin's motion failed.

Virginia governor Edmund Randolph quickly rose to propose that a "sermon be preached at the request of the convention on the 4th of July, the anniversary of Independence, and thence forward prayers be used in ye Convention every morning." And that was done, with George Washington leading delegates to church on Race Street that Independence Day.

Prayer was now a part of this great constitutional enterprise. However, Washington also knew that prayer without action was a losing proposition.

So, he decided to give the convention a boost of his own.

Saturday, June 30, 1787
North of Philadelphia

It was not yet July, but Philadelphia was already hot as blazes. George Washington had asked Alexander Hamilton to set off with him on an early morning ride into the countryside to escape the heat and Hamilton had readily agreed.

But, perhaps to young Hamilton's surprise, the weather was simply an excuse; what Washington was really looking for that day was a private place to speak with him.

"What a muddle this has become!" Hamilton exclaimed. "We are getting nowhere. We are a debating society that settles nothing. Big states at small states' necks—and no one willing to give an inch! We made a good start, agreeing to junk those damned Articles—but now this! I might as well go home!"

"Why don't you?" Washington responded, in a manner that seemed a little too matter-of-fact.

Hamilton knew his commander too well not to suspect something. He also knew better than to ask anything more than the basic questions. He simply nodded.

"When should I leave, General?"

"Immediately!" Washington replied. He pulled a packet from his satchel and handed it to Hamilton. "Don't return to Philadelphia. Instead, ride to New York and present this to the secretary of the Continental Congress. Wait for his response—and return with it to me immediately."

Hamilton just stared at him.

"Does that sound crazy, Colonel?"

"About as crazy as Trenton on Christmas Night, General." With one hand on the reins and one on the whip, Hamilton galloped north toward New York City.

Sunday, July 1, 1787
City Tavern
Philadelphia

"General Washington, what are you doing here on the Sabbath?"

"Just running an errand, Colonel Few," Washington answered, handing him a packet. "This arrived for you and Major Pierce. Odd that it was delivered to me, and not to you gentlemen directly."

William Few, one of Georgia's two delegates, tore the packet open. As he did, his fellow Georgia delegate, Major William Pierce, could not help but notice that Alexander Hamilton had accompanied Washington on this visit. This was not unusual by itself, but Hamilton's dust-covered appearance certainly was. The unshaven Hamilton, who usually looked like he had spent his Saturday nights with the ladies, instead appeared to have not bathed or slept for days.

"Well," Few said after reading the letter he'd pulled from the packet, "it seems they demand that myself and Major Pierce be in New York. They need a quorum in the Confederation Congress—to do what, I don't know, but they claim it will be some business affecting Georgia that we will be quite interested in." Georgia, it seemed, took duties of both the Constitutional Convention and the Confederation Congress lightly, and to save on expenses, had appointed Few and Pierce to serve on both.

"Don't worry, gentlemen, nothing will happen here in your absence," Washington assured the Georgians. "Nothing ever does . . . By the way, I think there's a coach bound for New York still waiting at the Indian Queen Tavern. Perhaps, if you hurry, you can still make it!

"In fact, Mr. Hamilton, why don't you ride there right now and ensure the coach is held for them."

Sunday, July 1, 1787, Afternoon
Home of Robert Morris
Philadelphia

George Washington sat at his friend's desk and stared blankly into space. The previous day, Gunning Bedford from Delaware had offended nearly everyone in the room with an inexcusable tirade over the Virginia Plan, which would allow for national representation based on state population.

"The small states," Bedford had exclaimed, "can never agree to the Virginia Plan because the small states will end in ruin. And if we are to be ruined, I'd rather let a foreign power take us by the hand. The little states have been told, with a dictatorial air, that this is our last chance to build a good government. The large states dare not dissolve this confederation. If they do, the small ones will find a foreign ally, one with honor and good faith!

"Let me be clear. It's treason to annihilate our duly established government. Treason! Gentlemen, I do not trust you! The sword may decide this controversy."

Bedford's words were still weighing on Washington's mind. He knew that things were becoming perilous. The delegates would not last much longer without a breakthrough.

Washington dipped Morris's quill pen and composed a letter to a friend.

Incompatibility in the laws of different States, and disrespect to those of the general government, must render the situation of this great country weak, inefficient, and disgraceful. It has already done so, almost to the final dissolution of it. Weak at home and disregarded abroad is our present condition, and contemptible enough it is.

To please all is impossible, and to attempt it would be vain.

A great compromise was the only possible solution.

He waited at the Morris home the rest of the afternoon, half expecting news to come that the convention had been dissolved. He could barely eat, and sleep was out of the question—but he did continue to think.

Monday, July 2, 1787, Mid-morning
Pennsylvania State House
Philadelphia

It continued just as Hamilton had described—debate after debate, nothing settled, acrimony growing, not diminishing. The large states kept winning votes, but their victories only prevented any real progress from being made. The small states felt pushed aside. They would never agree to trade Britain's power for that of Virginia or Pennsylvania. Something had to be done to grab the large states by their collars and haul them to the bargaining table—to hammer out a new government that every state, no matter its size, could agree to.

George Washington slid into his Windsor chair and, with no further direction, the delegates quit their gossiping and hastily took their own seats at their baize-covered tables. The mid-morning air was already hot, stale, and infested with blackflies. The blistering Philadelphia summer had been made worse by the secrecy of these meetings. Windows were nailed shut. Guards patrolled outside. Inside, tempers flared.

Washington knew the convention was about to blow apart, but he kept his face stoic. He could not show weakness. So much was at stake.

A vote on Connecticut's proposal to provide each state with equal representation in the Senate would be the first order of business. Washington stood and addressed the convention.

"It is," he began, his voice unwavering, "probable that no plan we propose will be adopted. Perhaps another dreadful conflict is to be sustained. If, to please the people, we offer what we ourselves disapprove, how can we afterwards defend our work? Let us raise a standard to which the wise and the honest can repair."

The room was silent. Dozens of eyes stared at him and he seemed to make contact with each of them.

"Gentlemen," he continued, "the event is in the hand of God."

Connecticut's proposal had been around for weeks, but the large states had always easily defeated it, demanding representation only on the basis of population. Washington remained unsure regarding which was the better plan but he knew this: if the convention was to succeed, compromise was essential.

Today's vote, which would be taken among the eleven states represented, should have broken down this way: Rhode Island, unwilling to bow to any national government that would limit its right to print worthless fiat currency, simply hadn't shown up—and never would. New Hampshire's delegates were taking their sweet time to arrive and still hadn't gotten there. That left the "large state" bloc (Virginia, Massachusetts, Georgia, Pennsylvania, Maryland, North Carolina, and South Carolina) in a position to easily defeat the small states alliance (Connecticut, Delaware, New Jersey, and New York—which had joined the small state voting bloc because their governor had grander plans than to cede power to a national government).

With such a sizable majority, the large states would never agree to even talk of compromise—and that was a major problem. The small states, realizing their lack of leverage, had threatened to walk out of the convention if the Virginia Plan were to pass. That would spell disaster for both the convention and the country.

A compromise was needed, but without something dramatic to shake the entrenched confidence of the delegates, it looked unlikely. Without it, the small states would never agree to union and an ungovernable country was just as bad as having no country at all.

Washington rapped his gavel and requested a roll call. States voted from north to south, and everything proceeded as anticipated, until . . .

"Maryland?"

Despite his self-discipline, Washington felt his back stiffen. He gazed out over the assembly, but the mood was still the same. Very few people were paying attention. That, he knew, was about to change.

"Maryland aye."

Washington saw a few heads lift, and a couple of delegates nudging elbows, but most remained buried in their notes or conversations. Maryland usually voted with the large states or stalemated when Washington's longtime friend, Daniel of St. Thomas Jenifer, canceled out his fellow delegate Luther Martin's vote. Today, however, Jenifer was inexplicably absent. This should have raised more eyebrows, Washington thought. Being absent on such an important day was, to put it mildly, uncommon.

One delegate did realize that something was off kilter: James Madison. Washington caught his inquiring look out of the corner of his eye, but avoided looking at him directly.

Again, all moved forward normally and Washington still saw only disinterest throughout the chamber. Most of the delegates were probably more concerned about how much vitriol they would have to endure after the small states lost yet again.

The secretary barked. "Georgia?"

After a theatrical pause, Harvard-educated Abraham Baldwin responded in a steady voice, "Georgia is divided."

The chamber went still. Every head turned toward Georgia's table. Colonel Few and Major Pierce were missing. It was no secret that they had suddenly departed for New York City to take their seats in the Confederation Congress, but no one had expected their absence to matter. The vote should've remained the same "yes" it always had. Yet somehow, inexplicably, Georgia's two remaining delegates had split their ballots.

Washington gave a single rap with his gavel. "Mr. Secretary?"

"The vote is a tie, five to five with one state divided. The motion fails."

The Connecticut motion had failed once again. That was not a surprise—but *how* it failed certainly was. The large state coalition had not won; they had merely *not lost*. The distinction was not minor.

The room erupted. Chairs scraped against the floor. Heads bent conspiratorially close. Voices rose in anger or wonderment. Washington saw the same question on every face: *How could this have happened?*

They would soon find out.

Into this uproar sauntered George Washington's longtime friend, Maryland's Daniel of St. Thomas Jenifer. The delegates stared at him as he casually took his seat beside Luther Martin, then their gaze shifted toward Washington.

The youthful but balding Massachusetts delegate Rufus King stood.

"Mr. President, Mr. Jenifer appears to have been unavoidably detained. I make a motion for a new vote."

Washington rapped with more force than usual. "Denied. The rules do not allow a second vote on the same motion in a single day." Washington laid the gavel on the table and moved his hand away from it. The finality of the gesture was not lost on the delegates.

Washington recognized South Carolina's General Charles Cotesworth Pinckney.

"Mr. President, some compromise seems to be necessary. The states are exactly divided on the question for equality of votes in the second branch. I propose a committee consisting of a member from each state be appointed to devise a compromise."

James Madison jumped up to object to Pinckney's scheme. He wanted no part of compromise.

But his objection did not stand—Madison lost, and a committee was to be formed. For the first time since the convention started, compromise had a real chance.

Monday, July 2, 1787, Late Afternoon
Indian Queen Tavern
Philadelphia

"You manipulated the vote," Madison fumed. "I don't know how you did it—but you did it!"

Madison was as angry as Washington had ever seen him. Washington uncharacteristically put his hand on his shoulder and led him to a corner. Over Madeira, Washington tried to calm him. "Jemmy, you ardently believe that both houses should be proportional to population, and I agree that the national government has to be strengthened beyond the Articles—but I don't wish to subjugate my beloved Virginia to oppression from an unchecked national government."

Washington held up two fingers to halt Madison's objection. "Two houses. A Senate with equal state representation. A House based on population."

"With all due respect, sir, you are mistaken. The balancing and checks must reside within the national system itself. The states can add little but corruption to the mix."

Washington admired Madison's intellect and knowledge of classical thought, but he was uncomfortable with his inflexibility. The Virginia Plan was undoubtedly superior to the Articles, but it could not possibly be the *only* good design. Many feared the increased authority of the national government. Who would check a runaway national government if not the states? One would have to rely on a perfectly balanced system, and Washington knew enough of men to never believe in perfection. And besides, Washington thought, how could Madison argue so vehemently for states' rights on the one hand and call the states so corrupt on the other?

"Jemmy, you need to be open to the ideas of others. Giving the states a voice at the national level will help control the new government, appeal to our citizens, and facilitate ratification."

Washington would've expected Madison to soften his stance as their conversation continued, but, on this day, his manner was as black as the wardrobe he normally sported. "Sir, I cannot step away from my principles."

"Jemmy," Washington responded, "don't worry—you will come around to defending this way of government."

He wasn't sure, however, if that was really true or not.

Dusk, Monday, July 2, 1787
State House Yard
Philadelphia

Washington was alone. And in more ways than one.

He paced the State House Yard's circular footpath. No delegates had joined him when he left the Indian Queen. No member of the public could get past the yard's guardhouse. Tonight, this space was the quietest spot in the city.

As Washington contemplated the work ahead, he grew more confident. His pace quickened. He had finally come to peace with this compromise—now he must bring it to fruition.

A light breeze had cooled the night air. He lifted his gaze to the buildings across the street. He loved Mount Vernon, but there was one brief moment of the day when he preferred Philadelphia. At dusk, when there was still enough natural light to see, and lamps began to illuminate windows, he imagined contented families inside feeling safe and free to go about their business. This is what he wanted to bequeath to his nation.

Last year, he had written to a friend, "No morn ever dawned more favorable than ours did; and no day was more clouded than the present! Wisdom, and good examples are necessary at this time to rescue the political machine from the impending storm."

Washington turned his face to the sky. It appeared the storm was finally subsiding.

Monday, September 17, 1787, Mid-morning
Pennsylvania State House
Philadelphia

It was finally done. Today the new Constitution of the United States of America would be signed.

Washington touched the edge of the document before him as he listened to Benjamin Franklin's final appeal for all to sign. Franklin ended his speech by moving that the document be signed "Done in Convention by the unanimous consent of the States present the 17th of September."

Washington felt enormously gratified. After four grueling months, they were presenting the nation with a proposal for an entirely new government. Not just something that would be new to America, but new to the entire world.

Once they settled that each state would have two senators, they were able to rebalance all the remaining elements until they had an excellent design. Not a perfect design, of course, but certainly the most thoughtful and debated republic in world history. A nation formed not with the sword, but with reason. Now it would be up to the people to ratify their work.

At the conclusion of Franklin's speech, Nathaniel Gorham, a Massachusetts Congregationalist, asked for the floor. "Gentlemen," he said, "I wish that the clause declaring, 'the number of Representatives shall not exceed one for every forty thousand,' be changed to 'thirty thousand.' "

Washington slowly rose to call for a vote, hesitated, and then expressed his opinion publicly for the first time during official proceedings. "Although I have hitherto restrained myself, my wish is that the proposal be approved. Many consider the small proportion of representatives insufficient to secure the rights and interests of the people. Late as the present moment is, it will give me great satisfaction to see this amendment adopted."

It passed unanimously. No one dared deny the hero of the revolution his sole request over these many months.

Washington kept his visage properly masklike as the vote concluded, but James Madison, sitting nearby, could see Washington's head turn ever so slightly toward him. Madison knew that his fellow Virginian's little speech was a gift to him, in appreciation for Madison finally agreeing to—as Washington had predicted—the great compromise that had made this new constitution possible.

Washington summoned the delegates geographically, north to south, to advance. He signed first, inscribing his name with a flourish. Hamilton signed, too, though he represented no one but himself.

Pennsylvania's Gouverneur Morris hobbled forward on his wooden peg leg to sign. When Georgia's delegates—including Colonel Few and Major Pierce—had finished, Washington commended the delegates for their accomplishment, but with a warning. "Should the states reject this excellent constitution," he said, "the probability is that an opportunity will never again offer to cancel another in peace.

"The next will be drawn in blood."

Benjamin Franklin quizzically looked toward the back of Washington's chair—and pointed to a painted half sun.

"Painters find it difficult to distinguish a rising from a setting sun," Franklin said aloud to the delegates standing around him. "I have often in the course of these sessions looked at that painting behind my dear friend without being able to tell if it was rising or setting.

"Now, at length, I have the happiness to know that it is a rising sun."

14

Little Short of a Miracle

A few short weeks will determine the political fate of America for the present generation and probably produce no small influence on the happiness of society through a long succession of ages to come. Should every thing proceed with harmony and consent according to our actual wishes and expectations; I will confess to you sincerely, my dear Marquis; it will be so much beyond any thing we had a right to imagine or expect eighteen months ago, that it will demonstrate as visibly the finger of Providence, as any possible event in the course of human affairs can ever designate it.

—GEORGE WASHINGTON TO
THE MARQUIS DE LAFAYETTE, 1788

Sometimes success can be fleeting. It vanishes into the mist so fast that, if you blink, you've missed it.

Life's funny that way. You struggle for years to attain the prize, and, suddenly, you discover that what you sweated and bled for wasn't everything that you thought it was. Was it all really worth it?

Yorktown didn't bring a magic end to America's troubles—and George Washington was the first to know it. There was no constitution yet; the Articles of Confederation still governed the thirteen independent states—except that it didn't actually govern very much at all. The country lacked a sound currency (even by today's standards). There was no real standing army or navy to speak of. Each state fielded its own militia, and eleven states had their own navies. Patrol the frontier? Good luck.

Fight the terrorists of the day—the Barbary pirates? Try doing that without a national navy. It's nearly impossible for a government to accomplish anything without the power to raise revenue. The feds—or rather the confeds—had to live off handouts from the states.

It was a bizarro world. The national government couldn't tax you—or anybody else. (That's good, at least up to a point, as even conservatives would admit that there are *some* things, like national defense, for example, that the government needs revenue for.) But worse, the national government was the biggest welfare *recipient* on the continent.

George Washington hated this setup. He knew how much damage a weak government had caused during the war. The country couldn't equip an army. It didn't pay its soldiers. It issued worthless paper money. It didn't do much of anything at all, in fact, except beg from the states and interfere with Washington's command.

At the end of the war Washington was the most popular man in America. He might have been the most popular and admired man in the world (fortunately for us, public opinion polls weren't around yet), yet all he wanted to do was go home. He'd done his job. He'd established his reputation. He'd sacrificed everything he had. If there had been a lifetime Oscar for service to the country, he would have already won it.

But there was a major fly in the ointment: What if all his work came undone? What if, after all they had been through, the American experiment still failed? And if it did fail, what would happen to his reputation, to the popular regard he had worked so hard for? Being the father of a miserably *failed* country really wasn't much of an honor, was it? Could Valley Forge, Trenton, and Yorktown, and all of the Divine Providence that went along with them, really have been for nothing?

Washington desperately wanted for that to not be the case. Life on the Potomac at Mount Vernon was pretty sweet. "[H]aving happily assisted in bringing the ship into port," he wrote to New York's John Jay in September 1786, "and having been fairly discharged, it is *not my business to embark again on a sea of troubles.*"

But he kept hearing the thunder of disunity rumbling in the distance—and, as time moved on, it only grew louder. His old friends like Henry Knox began sounding the alarm. Troubles percolated with both Britain and Spain along our western frontiers. London refused to evacuate its forts in our northwest territories. Madrid was choking off our access to the Mississippi River. Some westerners even talked of seceding and joining the Spanish Empire.

Washington was worried, and not only for his country. He was worried that he would be called out of retirement. A five-state convention meeting in Annapolis in 1785 had demanded that the Confederation Congress call an all-state convention to amend the Articles. Virginia appointed Washington to attend as one of its delegates. But he still didn't want to go—at least, not until a very unpleasant situation got his attention.

A DIFFERENT KIND OF LEADERSHIP

Massachusetts, like the rest of the country, lacked a sound currency. Creditors demanded to be paid in gold or silver, and when they weren't, they went to court to seize the debtors' lands. Farmers who lost their land were not happy and they stormed courthouses, seized the armory at Springfield, and started a full-fledged insurrection called "Shays's Rebellion," named after one of its leaders.

But the rebellion soon moved from debt repudiation to something far more dangerous. There was something in the air—and it was not good. "[The rebels'] creed," Henry Knox warned Washington in October 1786, "is that the property of the United States has been protected from the confiscations of Britain by the joint assertions of *all*, and therefore ought to be the common property of all, and he that attempts opposition to this creed is an enemy to equity and justice, and ought to be swept from off the face of the earth."

Sounds a little bit like communism, doesn't it? This new government couldn't even maintain order or protect private property right. His beloved nation was descending into anarchy.

He wrote to Henry Lee Jr.:

The picture which you have drawn, & the accounts which are published, of the commotions ... in the Eastern States [New England], are equally to be lamented and deprecated. They exhibit a melancholy proof of what our

*trans Atlantic foes have predicted; and of another thing, perhaps, which
is to be still more regretted, and is yet more unaccountable, that mankind
left to themselves are unfit for their own government. I am mortified
beyond expression whenever I view the clouds which have spread over
the brightest morn that ever dawned upon my Country. . . . For it is hardly
to be imagined that the great body of the people . . . can be so enveloped in
darkness, or short sighted as not to see the rays of distant sun through all
this mist of intoxication & folly.*

Because of the threat it posed to the nation as a whole, Shays's Rebellion got Washington's attention, and it got the Confederation Congress's as well. In February 1787 the Congress finally authorized the all-state convention that had been demanded at Annapolis. But only then, when Washington knew that he was participating in a legal, authorized revision of the Articles, rather than a coup d'état, did he agree to attend the new convention.

He had served before, and he would serve again.

If you're a soldier who's served America you may be able to relate to the way Washington felt. Maybe you did a tour in Vietnam or Iraq and then 9/11 happened and you heard the call again. Those who love America understand that service to our country never really ends—whether that means taking part in elections or being active in charity or being part of the community in different ways.

Washington knew he would serve again. Why else would he have immersed himself, with James Madison and John Jay, in a long-distance "correspondence course" on the theory and practice of republican governments? One of Washington's great skills was that he led by listening. First he got the information. Then he synthesized it. Then he acted.

There were roughly three dozen lawyers at the Constitutional Convention, and Washington may have had as little formal schooling as any man in the room, but when he arrived, he was ready to discuss constitutional law with any one of them.

A Lifetime of Learning

I know that getting a formal education in political science or economics is wonderful, but I can also confidently tell you that a formal education can also mean politically motivated teachers and a lot of closed-minded thinking. After all, how many professors do you know that will teach kids Friedrich Hayek, Milton Friedman, or Thomas Sowell? Not many. Sometimes educating yourself is not only a necessity but a blessing. It allows you to explore ideas in a way professors like to inhibit with their preconceived ideological notions. As the columnist Heather Mac Donald recently pointed out, in the past academic year at Bowdoin College, "a student interested in American history courses could have taken 'Black Women in Atlantic New Orleans,' 'Women in American History, 1600–1900,' or 'Lawn Boy Meets Valley Girl: Gender and the Suburbs,' but if he wanted a course in American political history, the colonial and revolutionary periods, or the Civil War, he would have been out of luck."

America allowed the Founders to test ideas that were considered radical elsewhere. They were allowed to think freely without worry of repercussion. Though highly educated in classical texts, most of the Founders were not weighed down by conventional thinking or pseudoscience and gender studies. That was a blessing.

Washington remained self-conscious about his lack of a formal education his entire life. Ironically, it was this fact that drove his intellectual curiosity and ensured that he would always be overly prepared for any debate.

And that wasn't the only homework he'd done to prepare. During the war he had employed an extensive network of spies. We've already met some of them: Yale's Nathan Hale in 1776; the farmer James Honeyman at Trenton. James Armistead at Yorktown is another. Good intelligence, Washington knew, was a key to victory.

If he were to agree to attend the Constitutional Convention, he needed to know in advance if it had a reasonable chance of success. Would there be enough boots on the ground to really create a stronger national government—or would it crash and burn? Washington needed to know where to pick his fights.

He turned to James Madison to gather the intelligence he needed. One by one, as each state had chosen its delegates, Madison sounded them out and found a solid core of federalists among the attendees. He reported the news back to Washington.

Washington got on board because he had done his homework—he knew there would be a ton of work to do, but he also knew there was at least a chance that it would all pay off. As baseball's Branch Rickey (the man who brought Jackie Robinson into the big leagues) once said, "Luck is the residue of design."

LET'S WALK BEFORE WE RUN

Washington arrived at the convention on time. That may not seem like much, but it was. It showed responsibility and organization—and respect. Remember, back then you weren't jumping on a flight or driving your car to Philadelphia. The planning required to be on time was immense, and it meant that you would be taking the proceedings seriously.

On Monday morning, May 14, 1787, the day the Constitutional Convention opened, there was no quorum. In fact, it wasn't even close. There wouldn't be one until Friday, May 25, and, even then, only twenty-nine delegates showed up—barely a majority. But Washington was there on day one, ready to go when hardly anyone else was.

Washington was a great listener, but he was also a very active man, and sitting around paying attention as the delegates repeated the same points for four to seven hours each day couldn't have been much fun. But he knew he wasn't there for fun; he was there for work, and just by being present he would add weight to the proceedings.

Washington didn't just show up in Philadelphia on "opening day"; he showed up *every* day. And he rarely excused himself for a break. When he did, they were short, unlike other delegates, who might be gone for weeks. Some delegates hardly attended at all.

But Washington was there. He was persistent. As Calvin Coolidge said:

Nothing in the world can take the place of Persistence. Talent will not; nothing is more common than unsuccessful men with talent. Genius will not; unrewarded genius is almost a proverb. Education will not; the world is full of educated derelicts. Persistence and determination alone are omnipotent. The slogan 'Press On' has solved and always will solve the problems of the human race.

When Woody Allen once said, "Eighty percent of success is just showing up," he offered some good advice. Life isn't all glamour. It's putting one foot in front of the other—and to do that you'd better be there in the first place.

This is such an important lesson for us today: to make a real impact you've got to get involved. That doesn't mean firing off emails or letters: It means really *getting involved*. Showing your face, proving your commitment, earning your respect.

It doesn't have to be anything on the scale of a national convention. You can visit the sick or the elderly or pay your respects at a wake or a funeral. Showing up counts—sometimes in ways that we don't even realize on the surface. If there's a rally for something you believe in—go to it! You might be the person standing at the back of the crowd, but your presence matters. Others will take notice. So be there. George Washington was.

CHECK YOUR POCKETS

Washington insisted on great secrecy during the deliberations. Given his own reliance on intelligence gathering in the past, he knew better than anyone that information in the wrong hands could prove disastrous. He didn't want the media reporting—or distorting—the delegates' words. He didn't want "leakers" or spinmeisters. He wanted delegates to speak their minds freely—and to be free to change their minds if the facts demanded it—without regard to public outrage.

The Rumor Mill

Sometimes it feels like we can't even have an honest conversation anymore. I'm sure this is nothing new. The great thing about technology is that today, unlike in Washington's time, I am able to quickly respond and give the full context of the quotes and arguments that have been distorted. But in those days, rumors and false accusation were very hard to correct. If enough of them got out there they would soon be accepted as truth and could sink the entire convention.

When the Constitutional Convention started, each delegate received a copy of Edmund Randolph's Virginia Plan. There were many changes made to it, but basically this was the road map to a new constitution. Obviously, copies of the Virginia Plan were to be kept top secret at all costs.

One day, Pennsylvania's Thomas Mifflin found a copy of the plan lying around at the State House. He brought it to Washington, who waited until day's end to announce he had it. "Gentlemen," Washington grimly announced, "I am sorry to find that some one member of this body has been so neglectful of the secrets of the convention as to drop in the State House a copy of their proceedings which by accident was picked up and delivered to me this morning. I must entreat Gentlemen to be more careful, lest our transactions get into the newspapers, and disturb the public repose by premature speculations. I know not whoso paper it is, but there it is [throwing it down on the table]; let him who owns it take it."

The delegates shook in their boots. Imagine being reprimanded by George Washington! They fished into their pockets and desk drawers to find their own copy—and prayed that the copy on Washington's desk wasn't theirs. The panic-stricken South Carolina delegate Pierce Butler rushed home to find his in the pocket of his other coat.

Unsurprisingly, no member of the delegation ever dared to claim the lost document and risk Washington's ire. But the message had been delivered.

There is a second moral to this story: the Thomas Mifflin who brought the lost papers to Washington was none other than General Thomas Mifflin, the grotesquely incompetent quartermaster general of the army who had caused so much of the suffering at Valley Forge. Yet

Washington had clearly not ostracized Mifflin. In fact, Mifflin, along with Henry Knox, was among the old army buddies who had lunched with Washington just before he first arrived in Philadelphia for the convention.

Washington believed that men of good faith and character could be forgiven.

... on the other hand, there *was* that Arnold fellow.

AMERICA'S SPHINX

For 4,500 years the ancient, immense figure of the Sphinx at Giza has fascinated mankind.

And so has its eternal silence.

What profound secrets does this great stone beast of the desert hold? What wonders—and horrors—have its limestone eyes beheld through the millennia?

Its silence captivates us. We use it as a metaphor and we compare it to that of famous figures of our own history. But the greatest sphinx of all is George Washington. While the University of Virginia is publishing his papers, and they are expected to reach ninety volumes—his diaries alone are six volumes—he reveals very little about himself in all those pages. He is remarkably self-effacing, and, if he is introspective at all, he does not commit his self-questioning to paper.

That is one reason why recent generations have found him so remote. It's not right to say that he wasn't a man of words; he certainly was—they just weren't the type of words that we're used to hearing. He didn't pen an autobiography or a memoir, nor did he grant interviews about his decisions and life. He merely achieved.

Almost nowhere in his career is Washington more sphinxlike than during the Constitutional Convention. He is not merely guarded concerning his role in that crucial drama; he is unalterably silent and self-censoring. He seals off the convention's deliberations from the general public. He posts armed guards outside its door. He takes almost no part in its official deliberations, merely ruling on its coming and goings and limiting himself to an occasional arched eyebrow or the rare hint of a smile. Those gestures, as influential as they may have been at the time, are, of course, completely lost to history. He kept no diary of those days. He took no chance of written notes falling into the wrong hands.

Silence. Absolute silence.

And yet we know his influence must have been immense. He was not one to leave things to chance. He would not have left Mount Vernon once more to merely be a spectator at the birth of a new nation. Life—and patriotism—were not spectator sports for George Washington.

That's why our story of the convention contained a very special twist. It's a historical detective story, and the mystery we wanted to solve was this: How did that fateful voting deadlock regarding senatorial representation come to be broken? The large states had always swept every vote. Yet, on that day, they stumbled badly and were forced back to the bargaining table. As a result, a constitution was ultimately born.

Was it again the hand of Providence intervening?

Perhaps. Or, maybe, it was a different hand: Washington's.

No direct evidence exists that Washington was behind the mysterious series of events that unfolded that day, but a wealth of circumstantial evidence that we merely hint at in our chapter certainly does. We have connected the dots, and the dots may finally paint a picture of how Washington worked so ably behind the scenes throughout his entire life to influence public affairs. At dinners and dances and at taverns and even at the theater, Washington subtly, but tirelessly, lobbied his associates to reach certain conclusions.

This may have been Washington's greatest such coup, but, if it was not, if it was merely once again the remarkable hand of Providence, then well . . . that is not such a bad thing, either.

Watch Your Step

Washington almost never lived to become president—or even to return to Mount Vernon.

He wanted to rush home after the convention. He'd been away for over four months, and that was a lot longer than he had ever expected the proceedings to last.

Unfortunately, he hurried too much. In Maryland he ran into a raging storm. Rain poured down in sheets. The deluge was so heavy that his party could not make it across the swollen Elk River. But he wanted to get home so badly and was in no mood to wait—particularly not when waiting meant sitting around and getting soaked.

He ordered his driver to take his carriage across a rickety bridge—a bridge so old that it had been abandoned.

It was one of George Washington's few wrong decisions.

As the carriage started across, something seemed to warn him of the danger. He climbed out, and, then suddenly—*CRASH!!*—one of the horses pulling it fell straight through the rotted planks, plunging fifteen feet into the raging river below. Some workers from a nearby mill rushed in to save the situation, but it was a close call.

Once again, the Invisible Hand seemed to have spared George Washington.

KING FOR (NOT EVEN) A DAY

One of the major issues facing the Continental Congress was the presidency.

Some people wanted the country's new chief executive to be a king—or something very similar to a king. Some wanted him to serve for life. Some wanted him to possess unlimited veto power. People felt safe proposing such things because they assumed Washington would be their president. They knew that whatever powers they gave him would be respected.

At the convention one day, wise old Ben Franklin commented that "the first man put at the helm will be a good one."

Wink. Wink.

But the real question that Washington and others wrestled with wasn't who would be first, but who would be *next*. Who would be fifth, seventeenth, or sixtieth? Would that person be as honorable and trustworthy with their power as Washington, or merely another George III?

South Carolina's Pierce Butler remembered that "many members cast their eyes toward General Washington and shaped their ideas of the powers to be given to a president by their opinions of his virtue. So that the man, who by his patriotism and virtue contributed largely to the emancipation of the country, may be the innocent means of being, when he is laid low, oppressed."

Washington was accustomed to command. He gave the orders at Mount Vernon. He issued orders as commander in chief. He might have demanded that he possess virtually unlimited powers as president. But he knew that wouldn't be right. And, just as important, he was asking himself the same questions that troubled Pierce Butler. The presidency was not about him. If, however, he became the first to fill the office, then he had to ensure that the presidency served the nation—and not the other way around.

No section on the Constitution is complete without revisiting the topic of slavery. It's become accepted fact that the Founders believed that blacks were worth only "three-fifths" of a human. That, however, is simply wrong.

The "three-fifths" clause was really about the census and, consequently, state representation in Congress. Slave populations in the southern states were huge at that time. If slaves were counted on a one-for-one basis then southern states would have far larger populations, and therefore, far more federal representation than the northern ones. As a result, slavery would have been nearly impossible to abolish.

Some revisionists would have you believe that those slaves were not going to be counted at all and that the three-fifths clause actually gave the southern states *more* power than they otherwise would have. (This allegation is, I think, supposed to "prove" just how racist and hateful our Founders really were.) But think about that logically: would the South really have been that willing to give up so much federal representation right off the bat? Of course not—they would have fought to have slaves counted as full people along with everyone else. The three-fifths compromise was just that, a *compromise*. It appeased the South, got the Constitution ratified, and paved the way for slavery to eventually end.

COMPROMISE...BUT NOT YOUR PRINCIPLES

George Washington wasn't crazy about everything in the new constitution.

At one point, he complained to Alexander Hamilton: "I almost despair of seeing a favorable issue to the proceedings of the Convention, and do therefore repent having had any agency in the business."

Translation: I regret ever attaching my name to this.

A while later, he wrote to the Marquis de Lafayette: "I am fully persuaded it is the best that can be obtained at the present moment under such diversity of ideas that prevail." And, in a separate letter to Lafayette, he was even more plainspoken:

> *It appears to me, then, little short of a miracle, that the Delegates from so many different States (which States you know are also different from each other in their manners, circumstances and prejudices) should unite in forming a system of national Government, so little liable to well founded objections. Nor am I yet such an enthusiastic, partial or undiscriminating admirer of it, as not to perceive it is tinctured with some real (though not radical) defects.*

A little better, but still not exactly a rousing endorsement.

Look carefully at Washington's words and you'll see something else besides his lackluster vote of confidence: the art of compromise, or as he said, "the best that can be obtained at the present moment."

He didn't get his way on everything; *nobody* got everything they wanted. And, sometimes, at the end of such a process, nobody can explain quite what happened—that's why they call it the art of compromise and not the science of compromise. If it were science we'd have a formula and we'd know right from the start what the end result was going to be.

But Washington and the rest of the convention got enough of what they wanted—without sacrificing their core principles. They forged a large enough coalition, not only in their little meeting room, but nationwide. They got enough people behind them to launch words and ideas and values into action.

Today the Republican Party doesn't agree with the Tea Party on everything. Libertarians differ with Republicans. Social conservatives may disagree with fiscal conservatives. And, of course, Democrats and Republicans can't even seem to have lunch together anymore. On and on and on it goes. But like-minded people *can* work together on what they *do* believe in. It's not impossible to do that. In fact, it's more necessary now than ever. "The person who agrees with you 80 percent of the time is a friend and an ally," Ronald Reagan taught us, "*not* a 20 percent traitor."

But some people will never see it that way. Some people are just cranky. Robert Kennedy once said, "Twenty percent of the people are against everything all the time." And some people always want it "my way or the highway." But the problem with that approach is that everybody, except the people you *really* disagree with, end up on the highway, including *you*. The liberals, the progressives, the big union bosses, and the red-tape-creating bureaucrats all whiz past you in their Chevy Volts (okay, maybe they don't "whiz"), while you stand there with your thumb pointed to Utopia.

My point is that you should never surrender your core principles. Never—ever—never. But don't try to get 100 percent of what you want from an ally, while giving up zero percent

And don't expect to get everything you want this instant; this is going to be a long fight. It won't be decided in the next election. It may not be decided ever. The key is to continually push the needle in your direction and lay the foundation for the next group of people to push it a bit further.

Washington had his qualms about the new constitution, but he signed it anyway. Three members of the convention—Edmund Randolph (presenter of the Virginia Plan), George Mason (Washington's very close friend), and Massachusetts's Elbridge Gerry (inventor of the gerrymander)—all refused to sign the U.S. Constitution, period. New York's Robert Yates hated the idea of a constitution so much that he just up and left early on in the proceedings.

George Washington, on the other hand, toughed it out and worked with others. He didn't like everything in the end, but he liked enough. He didn't let the perfect be the enemy of the good and the results have been nothing short of extraordinary.

Washington got the nation's capital, the state I was born in, and several monuments named in his honor. Robert Yates got a housing project in Schenectady.

15

A Final Farewell

April 29, 1796
Executive Mansion
Philadelphia

It was well past suppertime and on cobblestoned Market Street, not five hundred feet to the north of Independence Hall, the public lamplighter had already made his rounds, setting torch to wick on the oil lamps just outside the Executive Mansion.

In George Washington's second-floor office, the president rummaged through his desk to locate his metal eyeglass case. His young manservant carefully lit the room's tallow candles. Billy Lee, the trusted servant who had served with him throughout the war, had grown lame years earlier and no longer traveled from Mount Vernon.

The president's day had been filled with meetings, reports and letters read, and decisions made. But though daylight had long since departed, Washington's day was not yet complete. There would be no genteel card games this evening, no dances or lingering dinners. Work—and, as always, duty—still summoned him to his desk.

He stared almost blankly at the lengthy manuscript before him. George Washington was sixty-four years old and bone-weary but neither fact would stop him from thoroughly examining every comma of this text. His fingers moved stiffly as he retrieved his spectacles and placed them over his tired eyes.

He had commissioned this document four years ago, requesting

Virginia congressman James Madison, the "Father of the Constitution" and a coauthor of the *Federalist* papers, to prepare it for him. Then he had put it aside. The time had not been right for it to be issued.

But now, the hour had arrived. In anticipation of its revealing, Washington had asked Alexander Hamilton to review this Farewell Address one more time. He was leaving the presidency, and this would be his valedictory.

George Washington now squinted and peered through his tortoise-shell eyeglasses to fine-tune the last draft. As he did, he couldn't help but think back to the other times that he'd unsuccessfully tried to bid good-bye to public service. That a military leader would not grasp civil power as well was unprecedented. When George III learned of Washington's departure from the military to Mount Vernon, the monarch exclaimed in profound admiration, "If he does that, he will be the *greatest man in the world!*"

For once, George III had it right.

Washington similarly abandoned power following the Constitutional Convention. Each time, he had prayed that his service to his nation was complete and that he might finally return permanently to a "most delectable" life at home. But each time, duty's solemn trumpet sounded yet again.

Duty. It was among the virtues he held most dear. Duty and service and honor and courage—he stood for all those things. But the virtue that George Washington may have held most dear of all is one that seems to have lost its way over the years: civility.

May 16, 1747
Ferry Farm, Virginia

George Washington sat at his desk. A far different kind of document lay before him.

He needed no glasses. His fingers did not ache. His muscles were not stiff.

George Washington, sixteen years old, dipped his quill pen into ink and began to write, though he did not intend to compose a single original word.

Washington copied the words written in the slim book open in front of him, inscribing them in a wonderfully round, legible script that might have been appropriate for a facsimile of the Declaration of Independence or the Magna Carta. But this was nothing of the sort. The book he now copied from was simply titled *Rules of Civility & Decent Behavior in Company and Conversation.*

The truest ideas are never new; they are eternal. And the 110 rules that young Washington so laboriously duplicated on that day were just that—eternal ideas. While they had originally been composed overseas nearly a century and a half earlier by French Jesuits looking to instruct the young gentlemen entrusted to their care, the truth was that these words were based on sentiments far older than that.

Some sneered that the maxims the young Washington reproduced so faithfully spoke merely of small matters. Some derided them as a mere grab bag of table manners ("*101. Rinse not your mouth in the presence of others*"). But, when taken together, these often ordinary watchwords fashioned an extraordinary mosaic that spoke of consideration toward others and of modesty regarding self. That a sixteen-year-old copied them with such precision was, in itself, quiet remarkable, but that the adult George Washington actually *lived* them with such faithfulness and precision was even more uncommon.

"Every action done in company," the young Washington wrote, as he copied the very first rule, "ought to be with some sign of respect to those that are present." That, in fact, was the basis of each guideline that followed—just as all of the Father's Ten Commandments were founded upon the Son's Two Great Commandments: " *'Thou shalt love the Lord thy God with thy whole heart, and with thy whole soul, and with thy whole mind.' This is the greatest and the first commandment. And the second is like it, 'Thou shalt love thy neighbor as thyself.' On these two commandments depend the whole Law and the Prophets."*

Loving thy neighbor as thyself means placing neighbor *above* self, and in the decades to follow, Washington would place his nation above himself so many times: in taking command of the Continental Army and subordinating military leadership to civilian control; in chairing the fractious Constitutional Convention and patiently allowing competing passions and interests to fuse themselves into a new nation; and in creating this new position of the presidency, fashioning it through his every nuance and action, molding it into an office of republican service rather than of royalist autocracy.

Many times, especially while watching the often gut-churning process of democracy play out, he must have been sorely tempted to merely decree that his will would be followed. He might easily have gotten away with it. But, on each occasion, the words of the Declaration of Independence's complaint against the Crown rang in his ears: "He has affected to render the Military independent of and superior to the Civil Power."

Each time, Washington's sense of duty surmounted his ego. Each time, patience overcame his pride.

March 8, 1796
Executive Mansion
Philadelphia

Gilbert Stuart dabbed not ink but paint.

He was accustomed to gazing into men's faces and into their very souls. He had to. It was his stock-in-trade. Tradesmen artists paint faces. Great artists paint souls, and Gilbert Stuart was indeed a very great artist.

He paused as George Washington sat awkwardly before him, rigidly, perfectly still—once again doing his duty. But the truth revealed by Washington's features suddenly galvanized Stuart's conception of the man. His subject's eye sockets were immense. The nose and the space between his eyes were as broad as any that Stuart had ever witnessed.

Stuart had made a veritable science out of interpreting human faces and he viewed them as a scientist might peer intently through a microscope. And through the powerful lens of his considerable experience, Stuart concluded that George Washington's features constituted irrefutable evidence of a man who embodied immense passion.

Yet, as Washington learned from an early age, it was those same passions that could be a man's downfall.

And so he worked to control them. As a boy, he painfully copied over seven dozen Jesuit maxims on civility because he knew that he was in need of self-control. Those *Rules* were signposts to what he wanted to become; a road map to ensuring that his passions were always a blessing and never a curse.

But following that map would not be easy. Grand enthusiasms and antipathies remained at his core. So Washington made a choice—or rather he made a choice every single day of his life: he would tread the hard but straight path of duty and service, no matter the cost.

June 12, 1747
Dockside, Potomac River
Below Mount Vernon, Virginia

George Washington's trunk was packed tight and already lay belowdecks.

His blue eyes shone with anticipation. The sea would now be his life. For years, his revered older half brother Lawrence had regaled him with tales of his own service in His Majesty's Navy. From the romantic West Indies to the bloody storming of the Spaniards' South American fortress at Cartagena—young George had heard all about his brother's amazing exploits.

Lawrence had served under the bewigged Admiral Edward "Old Grog" Vernon—and had eventually named his Virginia estate, Mount Vernon, after him. But even beyond Lawrence's stories, the open sea meant adventure and glamour to fifteen-year-old George Washington. Virginia, after all, was a humdrum world of isolated plantations. Even Williamsburg and Alexandria were little more than villages. But the ships—they held the promise of excitement and adventure! They were not mere assemblages of heavy wooden beams and thick canvas sails. Far from it! A life aboard a ship was a passport to the great ports of the world—to London and Amsterdam, to the exotic Caribbean, even to the Indian subcontinent and perhaps to the greater Orient itself. Life in colonial Virginia was a predictable treadmill of tobacco and white-tailed deer and slaves. But, as the adolescent Washington saw it, life at sea was life itself.

Washington received a royal midshipman's warrant and prepared to board the ship for his first voyage. He stiffly embraced his strong-willed mother, the widowed Mary Ball Washington. The tall, jut-jawed woman feared her oldest son going off upon the ocean, perhaps facing enemy cannon fire. She knew for certain that he would face prejudice as a colonial in a navy ruled by British-born and bred officers. She thought of her three other sons and of her daughter Betty—all younger than George. She thought of how much she needed George's help at home—he had grown up fast since his father's death three years earlier.

But George needed to get away. The authoritative Mary Washington was, in fact, one of the primary reasons why Lawrence had advised George to exchange the comforts of hearth and home for a hard midshipman's berth. She was a tough woman to live with.

Yet, as tough as Mary Washington was, she still found it difficult to tell her oldest son that he could not realize his most cherished dream. And time was quickly running out.

Now they stood together on the dock below Mount Vernon's rolling hillsides, his naval ship stocked and ready to leave.

"Good-bye, mother," George said, embracing her.

She pulled away. "George, you must not go—I need to have you at home."

He stood there, stunned, his mouth agape, his eyes open wide in shocked disbelief.

He was stunned and humiliated—his mother had done this at the very last possible minute, and in public!

But humiliation and anger soon turned to rage. His fists clenched, he turned and walked slowly up the shaky wooden gangplank. He grasped no guide ropes. At that moment he did not care whether he tumbled into the shoreline muck or not.

Mary Washington's thick black eyebrows arched. "George! Where are you going?" she said sharply.

He paused and turned to face her, his face reddened in anger. Before he spoke, he lowered his voice. "To retrieve my trunk, mother," he answered coolly. "It is already on board."

Rule number 108 from *Rules of Civility* was weighing on his mind: "Honor and obey your natural parents although they be poor."

Honor and obedience ruled that day, but perhaps some measure of Divine Providence did as well. After all, had George Washington gotten on that ship he may very well have gone to grand destinations like

London and Calcutta—but there's a very good chance he would've never made it to far more humble locations, like Valley Forge and Yorktown.

April **29, 1796**
Reviewing the Farewell Address
Executive Mansion
Philadelphia

George Washington took off his spectacles and rubbed his eyes. He could not believe that he was sitting behind this desk in Philadelphia, let alone working on an address to his fellow Americans explaining why he would not run for a third term as their president. A third term, he thought to himself. I did not even want the first two!

Seven years earlier, Washington, having completed his duties of presiding over the Constitutional Convention, had returned to Mount Vernon to peacefully live the rest of his days outside the public eye. It was all he'd ever wanted.

Mount Vernon—he had grown to love the place, to take quiet joy in cantering across its rolling fields and hillsides upon horseback, in surveying the white-masted schooners plying the Potomac's waters below, of ensuring that harvests would be plentiful and guests would be graciously welcomed at his table. He'd mounted his horse and rode away from Mount Vernon so many times for his nation. To the west against the French. To Philadelphia and to the Continental Congress. To war for eight long years—and all with no salary. He had put his family, and himself, through more than should ever be asked of even the greatest patriot.

Then, when he thought he'd finally left it all behind, he'd been beckoned back to Philadelphia in 1787 to chair a new Constitutional Convention. He tried his best not to go. He made excuses that business was bad at Mount Vernon. He complained of his painful rheumatism. And he plaintively asked if he had not yet done enough for his nation. The answer, of course, was *yes*, he had done enough. But he knew the truth: doing enough was not sufficient—his country demanded more. And so he left Mount Vernon and rode north once again.

After a long, hot summer in Philadelphia he returned to Mount

Vernon to spend the rest of his days at home. But, less than two years later, his country had again called and asked him to serve—this time as its president. It was a painful choice.

As Washington once again bade adieu to Mount Vernon, private life, and domestic tranquility, he became tense and anxious. He had, of course, the best of intentions to render the service that his country required—but he had far less hope of answering its expectations.

And back at home, Martha was equally as troubled. "I am truly sorry to tell that the General is gone to New York . . . ," Martha would mournfully write to her nephew. "Whether he will ever come home again God only knows. I think it was much too late for him to go in to public life again, but it was not to be avoided. . . ."

Given the precarious state of the country, some people had wanted George Washington to be ruler over this new United States—to be its monarch. But he consented only to serve, to be a president, a chief magistrate. Kings never freely abdicate their power, but Washington tried to step away in 1792—and was called back to serve again. His glorious burden was not yet ready to be lifted. But now, in 1796, he sensed, it finally was.

The American nation was advancing from infancy to headstrong youth. Its father might finally take his leave. Its people would have to choose another to lead them.

George Washington reached the end of his farewell message's first paragraph and read these words softly to himself: "I should now apprise you of the resolution I have formed, to decline being considered among the number of those out of whom a choice is to be made."

That was it: farewell, retirement, peace, and rest. It was time for the country to select a new president.

His message might have ended there, but difficult questions confronted the nation, threatening to sunder its newfound unity: issues of sectionalism and of partisanship and of a dangerous world beyond our shores. Issues that dealt with the very underpinnings of the freedoms they had all fought so hard for.

He might have now walked away from it all and allowed a fractious nation to stew in its own juices, or handed over all the issues to a new leader to figure out—but that would be abandoning duty. So, though he was leaving, Washington could not remain silent. He had so much to say and as he thought how to relay them all in the proper spirit, the memories of what had brought him to this place in life began to flood his mind.

February 3, 1776
Continental Army Encampment
Cambridge, Massachusetts

There was a chill in the air, but it had nothing to do with the weather.

The new Continental Army was assembling at Cambridge, across the Charles River from British-occupied Boston. In truth, it was hardly an army, and it was hardly continental—being composed largely of flinty New England yeoman farmers and tradesmen and merchants and fishermen.

At the same time, some Virginian riflemen had tramped their way north, and their fringed white linen uniforms had quickly caught the attention of their Yankee allies—particularly the stout seamen of the Marblehead, Massachusetts, militia. Yes, it was a bit chilly here in Massachusetts—and it was a feeling that seemed to be shared by both sides.

As the two sides met, one stinging word led to another. Snowballs soon began to sail across Harvard Yard, and that soon escalated into methods that the southerners were far more experienced with: exchanging kicks and punches, gouging eyes, and biting. A thousand Americans bloodied one another in as wild a brawl as the continent had ever seen.

As the fight worsened, a white man and a black man appeared on horseback. The white man bounded off his mount, tossed its reins to his companion, and rushed into the very heart of the melee. He roughly grabbed the two largest combatants he could find, one in each hand, pulling them apart from each other, and solemnly talking sense to them. A thousand other amazed soldiers quickly grasped the identity of the blue-cloaked giant who had waded into their midst and quickly dispersed.

In the wake of George Washington's abrupt arrival, the two warring factions settled down; the fighting was over. Washington, who watched the aftermath from atop his horse on a nearby hill, did not take any great satisfaction in what had happened. All he could think about was what still lay ahead. It will be difficult, he thought, to forge one army—let alone a single nation—out of these men.

But he had no other choice.

April 29, 1796
Reviewing the Farewell Address
Executive Mansion
Philadelphia

Washington plodded on, continuing to scan his address. There were so many issues to confront; so many things he had to say. The night would be a long one.

Even though the war was over, the Constitutional Convention in 1787 illustrated just how much animosity remained between the different regions. Large states and small states battled over the system of representation. Northerners and southerners suspected each other. Rough-hewn pioneers on the frontier grew leery of the merchants and traders of the seaboard. Northern states were already working to abolish slavery. Farming states resented the new federal tariff.

Tonight, Washington took note of those divisions. He cautioned against "local discriminations" and reminded Americans that "with slight shades of difference, you have the same religion, manners, habits, and political principles . . . common dangers, sufferings, and successes."

George Washington had relied on his gut his whole life. He judged people well and he saw events coming over the horizon when few others could. And now, once again, he saw ahead—perhaps beyond Yorktown to Fort Sumter, beyond Valley Forge to Gettysburg—and it sent an ominous chill down his spine.

January 12, 1777
Valley Forge, Pennsylvania

George Washington was angry.

"Why is your cart empty, soldier?" he demanded as he saw an empty wooden oxcart rumbling back into his army's encampment. He had ordered his men out into the Pennsylvania countryside to secure food and blankets for his starving troops. Now he saw that this cart and the ones behind it were all returning as forlorn as when they'd departed.

A sergeant, a veteran of the Delaware militia, stammered nervously at his commander. He had never addressed George Washington, nor any general, before—and he was not enjoying the experience.

"No one would sell to us, General! They won't accept our Continental dollars!"

Washington waved his hand to dismiss the man. No, it wasn't his fault, Washington had to admit. It was the fault of a currency that had no real value—and of a debt-ridden government that asked its people to place its trust in worthless IOUs instead of hard currency.

April 29, 1796
Reviewing the Farewell Address
Executive Mansion
Philadelphia

Washington fiddled with the small, shiny silver piece that lay upon his desk. It was a half dime, minted not far from the Executive Mansion. Some said that it was Martha's likeness that graced this, the first of all American coins. Washington laughed as he thought of this. No, it was no more Martha on the front than that plucked chicken on its reverse was an American eagle.

The modest half dime—it was only worth five cents—was a small beginning for American finance, but it was a start. A nation had to exist on a firm financial footing. As a farmer, Washington knew the difference between profit and loss, the benefits of prudence and frugality and the cost of borrowed capital. As a commander of an army, he sorely knew that a civil government must stand on sound financial footing to equip its forces. As a citizen, he knew the damage a worthless, inflated currency— money not "worth a continental"—could inflict.

Tyranny, he thought to himself, is a hard master. Arithmetic is a harder one, and the tyranny of debt is the heaviest of them all.

Now, how to convey that sentiment to the people?

After a few minutes of thought, Washington took up his quill pen and began to write. "Cherish public credit . . . ," he warned, "use it as sparingly as possible . . . by cultivating peace . . . not ungenerously throwing upon posterity the burden which we ourselves ought to bear. The execution of these maxims belongs to your representatives, but it is necessary that public opinion should cooperate."

Yes, Washington was warning any future presidents or congressman or senator, but he also was warning the people themselves.

In the end, he knew that the survival of freedom would depend primarily on them.

January 8, 1791
Executive Mansion
Philadelphia

Thomas Jefferson shot up out of his seat and slammed his fist on the table. His flushed complexion nearly matched his red hair.

"You have no right to do this! None whatsoever!" Washington's secretary of state screamed, his anger directed toward the nation's first secretary of the Treasury, Alexander Hamilton.

"How many times are we going to go through this, Mr. Jefferson?" Hamilton responded rather matter-of-factly. While the issue they were debating, Hamilton's plan for a national bank, was a serious one, it's always easier to maintain one's calm when one holds the winning hand.

And Hamilton's winning hand was having the support of George Washington.

Jefferson knew this, of course, but it didn't quell his rage. "You are trampling on states' rights! You are ripping up the Constitution itself! You don't even know what the Constitution is! Ask Madison! He'll tell you why you have no right to do this! None! You're creating an autocracy! A monarchy!"

Washington looked anxious. It was his habit to allow his subordinates to argue their positions freely, but this debate—actually, *all* the debates—between Jefferson and Hamilton were becoming far too personal. Jefferson's last remark was too much for Hamilton. He bolted from his seat, rushing at Jefferson. They would have been nose-to-nose, save for the fact that Jefferson's nose was a good six inches higher than Hamilton's.

"I don't know the Constitution?" Hamilton sputtered. "How many of these vexations must I endure from you? Need I remind you, Mr. Jefferson, that I cowrote *The Federalist*, while you were gallivanting around France?" Hamilton was only warming up. "And where were you at Valley Forge? Oh, I almost forgot—you were governor of Virginia—and you were so popular in Williamsburg you couldn't even get reelected!"

"Gentlemen, enough!" Washington finally exclaimed, placing his powerful frame between his most marvelously talented, and yet most antagonistic, cabinet members. "Is this what we spared so much blood and treasure for? Personal attacks on other patriots? Are we not all Americans?"

April **29, 1796**
Reviewing the Farewell Address
Executive Mansion
Philadelphia

Washington gently ran his fingers up the parchment until he found the first words in the document. "Friends and Fellow-Citizens," they read, though it seemed to him that he had far fewer friends now than he did when those words were first drafted for him.

His mind returned, as it so often did, to the rules of civility he had copied so neatly a half century earlier. *Rule 69: If two contend together take not the part of either unconstrained, and be not obstinate in your own opinion. . . .*

Obstinate opinion now threatened to wreck the new nation. Thomas Jefferson and James Madison, both great patriots, could unfortunately no longer be counted among his friends. Their enthusiasm over a revolution in France blinded them to its excesses. Jefferson clashed at seemingly every turn with Hamilton. Disagreements turned into animosities and animosities hardened into political parties. Jefferson and Madison's Democratic-Republicans declared war on Hamilton's Federalists—and vice versa.

It was just a short step for criticism of policy to degenerate into personal slander. Washington knew that firsthand as his Democratic-Republican critics falsely accused him of padding his pockets from the national treasury. Some even dredged up old British forgeries that painted him as a royalist traitor.

These ridiculous charges, Washington had painfully noted, could be "applied to a Nero; a notorious defaulter, or even a common pick-pocket." For a man so painfully conscious of his reputation, these were wounds more painful to bear than a Valley Forge or Monmouth winter.

He examined a passage in the draft of the address that lay before him. Ambitious men, it noted, "serve to organize faction; to give it an artificial and extraordinary force; . . . to make the public administration the mirror of the ill concerted and incongruous projects of faction, rather than . . . of consistent and wholesome plans. . . ."

Washington dipped his quill pen and prepared to make an addition for the next draft. "Cunning, ambitious, and unprincipled men," he wrote, "will be enabled to subvert the power of the people and to usurp for themselves the reins of government, destroying afterwards the very engines which have lifted them to unjust dominion."

Party and partisanship, Washington recognized, must never come before principles and patriotism if America were to ever have a chance to fulfill its potential.

May 17, 1793
Executive Mansion
Philadelphia

It was a madhouse outside.

Men, women, and children thronged the city streets on all sides. Whistling, cheering, and even singing, they could not contain themselves. Men enthusiastically flung their three-cornered hats in the air. Women shrieked in joy. Children ran back and forth across the street maniacally. A cannon boomed in the distance. It was as if this were Christmas, the Fourth of July, and Inauguration Day all rolled into one.

But the excitement was not for Washington, who waited inside the mansion—nor for Jefferson or Hamilton.

It was for Edmond Genêt.

Citizen Edmond-Charles Genêt was the newly arrived ambassador of the new French Republic—and Americans were going absolutely wild for both France and Genêt.

Unfortunately, the men and women on the street that day had little idea what they were really celebrating.

The French Revolution had promised a glorious spring of human freedom, but it had degenerated into a series of long, hot summers of sheer blood-spattered terror. France guillotined its king, declared war on Britain—and demanded that America take its side.

Washington had issued a Proclamation of Neutrality to keep the peace, but Genêt was already working amazing mischief by organizing clubs of Americans to work against George Washington and for a foreign power. The Frenchman had even authorized privateers, operating out of American ports, to seize British ships.

Washington grimly surveyed the crowd—or was it a mob?—outside his window. In the distance he watched Genêt's carriage approaching. Just outside he saw Americans wearing red, white, and blue, but not out of any sense of American pride. No, it was in support of the French Revolution's new national flag.

"I cannot believe it," Washington mourned. "Do these good people really want to abandon allegiance to our Stars and Stripes so soon?"

April 29, 1796
Reviewing the Farewell Address
Executive Mansion
Philadelphia

Washington laced his hands together, cupping them behind his head. He looked to the heavens and sighed. There seemed to be no end to the issues he had to address before leaving office—or in completing his Farewell Address—and foreign policy was among the most vexing of them all.

His right index finger traced the words of his warnings against foreign entanglements and the dangers of basing American foreign policy on emotion rather than national interests. "Nothing is more essential than that permanent, inveterate antipathies against particular nations and passionate attachments for others should be excluded and that in place of them just and amicable feelings towards all should be cultivated."

He smiled that the words first drafted four years ago still applied today. But now there was more to add, he thought; the Genêt affair had proved that. He began writing in his large, round script. "The nation, prompted by ill will and resentment, sometimes impels to war the government, contrary to the best calculations of policy.

"'The peace often, sometimes perhaps the liberty, of nations, has been the victim."

He put his pen down and closed his eyes. America was too vital an experiment in human liberty to risk by emulating and aligning itself with fashionable—but miserably flawed—foreign social experiments.

November 10, 1793
Notre-Dame Cathedral
Paris, France

A mob, wild-eyed, disheveled, and self-satisfied, burst through the doors of Paris's greatest house of worship. Above the doors the words "To Philosophy" had been hastily carved in centuries-old stone.

Musicians from the National Guard and the Paris Opéra blared forth newly composed hymns. These songs were not in honor of God but to the revolution. Their tunes mixed raucously with the obscene lyrics sung by the "worshippers" who rushed into the centuries-old cathedral not in piety but in crude, drunken revelry.

The sanctuary itself had already been stripped bare. Statues of the Old Testament kings of Judah were beheaded. There were no clergy present in the ordinary sense, no tabernacles. Readings of the revolutionary acts replaced those from the gospels. "Reason" itself would be exulted this day in song and blasphemy. On other days, it received the sacrifice of guillotined heads. Eventually, of course, those who officiated that sacrifice would find their own necks resting on the same blood-soaked executioner's block.

Completing the day's blasphemy, the mob escorted a blowsy "Goddess of Reason"—some said she was an actress, some said she was a prostitute—down Notre-Dame's crowded main aisle. Those Created were no longer worshipping their Creator. They were worshipping themselves.

Satan, after all, had said it first, a very long time ago:

"Ye shall be as gods . . ."

April 29, 1796
Reviewing the Farewell Address
Executive Mansion
Philadelphia

Yes, it was time to think of God.

"When you speak of God or His attributes," Washington's *Rules of Civility* noted, "let it be seriously and with reverence."

Washington had once served as a vestryman and warden of his parish. Now he smiled as he recalled delaying his first inauguration to have a Bible rushed to him from over on Water Street so that he might place his powerful hand upon the more powerful words of Genesis 49–50 and gain strength from them. Concluding his inaugural oath, he had bent his massive frame down low to kiss the holy book before him.

Later that same year he maneuvered Congress into requesting that he declare a national day of public thanksgiving to "that great and glorious Being who is the beneficent author of all the good that was, that is, or that will be. . . ." George Washington, like Thomas Jefferson, recognized that humanity enjoys whatever rights it possesses because it has, in fact, been endowed with them by its Creator.

But in France, "Reason" supplanted—no, it crushed—that concept. It preached tolerance, but it strangled opposition. Proudly trumpeting its new morality, it conveniently forgot the morality of "Thou shalt not kill."

Washington thought about the French Revolution and how different it was from the revolution he'd helped lead.

Americans fought and died to preserve their long-standing rights as freemen from a grasping Parliament, he thought. We fought to limit government, not to create a vengeful, all-powerful state. A revolution to support the existing order of freedom was one thing, but it is quite another to revolt in pursuit of a Godless tyranny.

Washington mourned the fact that Paris's mobs had lost their faith in God. The guillotine's blade commenced its work with Louis XVI. It continued with the heads of revolutionary radicals like Hébert and Danton and Robespierre severed on the same executioner's block. Thomas Paine, whose words had been read to Washington's troops prior to the pivotal crossing of the Delaware River, barely escaped their fate.

The Altar of Reason was, in fact, an Altar of Blood.

He whispered aloud the words written in the draft in front of him. "Of all the dispositions and habits which lead to political prosperity, religion and morality are indispensable supports. . . . And let us with caution indulge the supposition that morality can be maintained without religion. Whatever may be conceded to the influence of refined education on minds of peculiar structure, reason and experience both forbid us to expect that national morality can prevail in exclusion of religious principle."

A people without God, Washington knew, would soon turn to darkness.

October 16, 1794
Encampment of the Army of the United States of America
Bedford, Pennsylvania

"It still fits."

"Pardon me, Mr. President, but did you say something?"

"Oh, nothing," George Washington responded to General Light Horse Harry Lee. Washington, in full military uniform, was mounted atop his horse, inspecting an American army ready to march. "I was just marveling that this old blue uniform still fits this even older gray body."

"Ah, just like old times, Mr. President," chuckled Lee.

"No, General," Washington mournfully responded, "not like old times at all. Then we only fought the British and Hessians. Today we march against fellow Americans."

The Americans Washington spoke of were those western Pennsylvanians who had resorted to arms and violence to oppose the new federal whiskey excise tax. But the whiskey tax was no Tea Act or Stamp Act—it had been legally passed by a Congress that fully and fairly represented its citizens. Yet these insurrectionists still refused to pay it.

Washington could not tolerate that.

Either the Constitution will prove stronger than the Articles of Confederation, thought Washington, or America will not long survive. And if he needed to squeeze into his old blue uniform once again to preserve this new constitution, then by God he would.

Preserving his nation required taking action against all enemies, foreign *and domestic*.

April 29, 1796
Reviewing the Farewell Address
Executive Mansion
Philadelphia

The night was growing long and George Washington still had much work to do. His review of the address, and the memories it had triggered, had taken its toll. He was growing frustrated with how much he still had to convey; and with how much of it seemed like it should be self-evident.

Was it really necessary, he thought, to explain to his countrymen that foremost among their new nation's essential "political principles" was allegiance to the Constitution and to the rule of law?

The colonies had not rebelled because of taxes on tea or official documents. They had taken up arms because of taxes illegally imposed on them by a government that had arrogantly failed to grant them a voice in their own affairs. The United States now enjoyed lawful, representative governments whose laws had to be obeyed if freedom, if civilized society itself, were to survive.

This, Washington knew, was such a simple but important concept. It was something he'd written about nearly a decade earlier, when the Articles of Confederation were the supreme law of the land. He'd written: "[L]et the reins of government then be braced and held with a steady hand, and every violation of the constitution be reprehended: if defective let it be amended, but not suffered to be trampled upon whilst it still has an existence."

Tonight, as he sat in his Philadelphia office and recalled his words from 1787, he realized that the citizenry needed to be reminded of the very same message. He took out his quill pen for the last time and prepared to add a notation to the draft.

"The Constitution which at any time exists, until changed by an explicit and authentic act of the whole people, is sacredly obligatory upon all. The very idea of the power and the right of the people to establish government presupposes the duty of every individual to obey the established government."

The tallow candles flickered and burned low.

George Washington slumped back in his chair. Even when he was alone, it was not his habit to slump. But now he did. He was tired. And there was still so much to do.

He removed his spectacles and dropped them on his desk. The sound roused his manservant, who was sitting just outside. He reentered the room.

"Are you through, Mr. President?"

"Yes," George Washington said, carefully rolling up the document before him. "I think I finally am. Put out the lights.

"My work is done."

Three Years Later, December 1799
Mount Vernon, Virginia

George Washington was sick.

Three inches of snow had blanketed Mount Vernon, but that had not prevented Washington from inspecting the exterior of his sprawling estate. For five hours he had ridden its grounds, and his neck and hair were now wet with snow. Tobias Lear, his secretary, advised him to change out of his damp clothes, but Washington ignored him.

That turned out to be a bad decision. The next day Washington felt even worse. Lear suggested that he take some medicine for the cold that seemed to be coming on, but Washington hated taking anything except in the most serious of circumstances. "Let it go as it came," he answered Lear, repeating his longtime mantra for dealing with illness.

As the afternoon wore on, the chills only got worse. By evening they were accompanied by nausea and a sore throat. By midnight he was having trouble swallowing.

He knew it was time to try to get some sleep.

Washington entered the bedroom as quietly as possible, but the creaky wooden floors betrayed him. Martha spoke gently. "George, you are not well, why have you stayed up so much later than usual?"

He found it difficult to speak with his usual firm tone, so he lowered his voice to a whisper. "I came as soon as my business was accomplished," he said. "You well know that through a long life, it has been my unvaried rule, never to put off till the morrow the duties which should be performed today."

"Yes, George," she replied, "I know."

Night brought no comfort. His throat burned. His chills became relentless. Sometime between two and three that morning he awoke to confess to Martha that he felt extremely ill. Perhaps, he suggested to her, he might have the ague. She wanted to summon help, but he would have none of it. He did not want anyone disturbed. He would be fine.

When dawn finally broke, Martha took stock of her husband's deteriorating condition and immediately sent a courier to nearby Alexandria for Dr. James Craik. The 69-year-old Craik had served with Washington since the days of the French and Indian War and they'd been friends ever since. He came without hesitation.

"I believe you have inflammatory quinsy, General," the Scottish-born Craik said. "Treatment is straightforward: gargle some sage tea with vinegar and then we'll bleed you a little."

By that afternoon, a lot of tea had been gargled and Washington's veins had been cut in three different places to allow for bleeding. Still, he was only getting worse. His throat was so swollen that it was becoming difficult to breathe.

Two more local physicians were summoned: Dr. Elisha Cullen Dick of Alexandria and Dr. Gustavus Richard Brown of Port Tobacco. "Perhaps," Dr. Dick, who, at 37, was by far the youngest of the doctors present, suggested, "we should consider a tracheotomy. It would allow him to breathe much better."

It was a shocking proposal—cutting a hole in a patient's throat to allow for airflow was a new technique practiced by only a minority of doctors. Dr. Craik would not hear of it. "No, Dr. Dick," Craik replied, "we would never try such a dangerous, unproven procedure out on a man like this. We must continue with the tried-and-true remedies. Now, let's find another vein and bleed him some more."

"But he needs all his strength—," Dr. Dick protested, "bleeding him more will only diminish it."

They cut into Washington's veins a fourth time. This time his blood ran thick and slowly. He could barely speak, but he continued to issue instructions about what needed to be done regarding his estate. He asked that his will—a magnificent document, written on a specially watermarked paper, adorned with the image of the goddess of agriculture wearing a liberty cap—be brought to him. He had personally inscribed it so that the right end of each line perfectly matched that of every other line. But it was more than just a beautifully composed document—it was also one with a beautiful purpose: it would free all of his slaves upon the death of his wife.

Hope was fading as fast as winter's sunlight.

The doctors, friends, and family who gathered around the seemingly invincible man could not avoid the reality that whatever now ailed him was far more deadly than the enemy bullets he had faced down for so many years. Martha, the three doctors, and Tobias Lear all waited faithfully. Three female slaves—Caroline, Molly, and Charlotte—acted as nurses and stood near the door awaiting instructions.

Washington noticed that his personal black servant Christopher Sheels had been standing for a very long time at his bedside. He motioned for the young man to sit down, seemingly far more concerned for his comfort than for his own.

Those who stood around Washington in the dimly lit room could not help but admire his courage. He was in excruciating pain, but never complained. He did not sob or cry out in anguish. He lay silently, seemingly at peace with his suffering—and the life he'd led.

Dr. Craik asked him to sit up in the bed. "I feel myself going," Washington replied. "You had better not take any more trouble about me. Let me go off quietly; I cannot last long."

Everyone filed out of the room to leave the general alone for a bit, but Dr. Craik remained and took his friend's hand. Washington looked him in the eyes and mustered a hint of a smile. "Doctor," he said, "I die hard, but I am not afraid to go."

Craik squeezed Washington's hand but could not find the right words to say, so he said nothing. He left the bedroom and joined the others by the fire, his grief overwhelming him.

An hour later, Tobias Lear stood next to Washington, holding his hand. With great effort, the general relayed precise instructions on how he wanted his body to be handled. "Do you understand me?" he asked after he had finished. "Yes, sir," Lear replied.

Washington squeezed his secretary's hand for the last time. " 'Tis well."

Washington let go of Lear's hand and checked his own weakening pulse. Then he closed his eyes, folded his arms across his chest, and exhaled one final time.

The father of his country had finally returned to his Father in heaven.

16

A Humble Agent of Heaven

I was but the humble agent of favoring Heaven, whose benign in-
terference was so often manifested in our behalf, and to whom the
praise of victory alone is due.

—GEORGE WASHINGTON, 1789

After the Revolutionary War ended a newspaper published an
account of a British soldier leaving his ship to retrieve some
personal items that he had left in New York City:

"This is a strange scene indeed! Here, in this city, we have had an
army for more than seven years, and yet could not keep the peace of
it. . . . Now [that] we are gone, everything is in quietness and safety. The
Americans are a curious, original people. They know how to govern
themselves, but nobody else can govern them."

It's difficult to comprehend just how radical the idea of self-
governance was to the average person in the eighteenth century. (Actually, if you look around the world, at places like North Africa or the
Middle East—or Berkeley, California—it's still a radical idea.) To most
people back then, the notion that man didn't need titles or authority to
be successful was alien. The idea that God, not man, bequeathed a person liberty and the right to pursue happiness in any way he saw fit—so
long as the rights of others were not infringed—was utterly absurd.

The Founders' generation glorified self-rule, not government service. They trusted that people could take care of themselves outside of
government. And, of course, they were right.

You only have to read basic history (or watch politics in Washington,

D.C.) to understand how rare acts of selflessness are among political leaders. How many consequential people in history have exhibited the character—or the willpower—to relinquish the perks of power and fame when they were there for the taking?

Giving Up (Power) Is Hard to Do

When I left my cable news show to embark on a new risky venture, a lot of people thought I was crazy. Or, I should say, a lot of people thought I was even crazier than they did before. Walking away from a prestigious position with that kind of platform was not easy, so I can only imagine how hard it is for people with real power to surrender it.

But that's also the problem with a lifetime of government work. People are too comfortable. Think of how many famous entrepreneurs have left the coziness of big companies or top schools to start something new and "crazy." Taking risks is part of life. It's the only way to spark real innovation. But government is risk-averse. It doesn't allow for innovation or critical thinking. And we have too many smart people turning into complacent bureaucrats.

CRAFTING THE FAREWELL

Some people think that Alexander Hamilton was the brains behind Washington's Farewell Address and Washington merely rubber-stamped it.

Not true.

Washington put an amazing amount of thought into his farewell.

He asked Madison to compose its first draft back in 1792. Then, in 1796, Hamilton and John Jay took a look at Madison's version. At one point Washington provided Hamilton with these instructions: "My wish is that the whole may appear in a plain style, and be handed to the public in an honest, unaffected, simple part."

Later, Hamilton provided Washington with two drafts. One was a very simple edit of the Madison version. The second draft was much more involved but basically retold the same content in different form. Washington preferred Hamilton's second version "greatly to the other draughts, being more copious on material points, more dignified on the whole, and with less egotism; of course, less exposed to criticism, and better calculated to meet the eye of discerning readers (foreigners particularly, whose curiosity I have little doubt will lead them to inspect it attentively, and to pronounce their opinions on the performance)."

Then Washington polished it some more. He had three cabinet members—Secretary of State Timothy Pickering, Secretary of the Treasury Oliver Wolcott Jr., and Secretary of War James McHenry—all review it as well. When they returned their comments, Washington personally went over them line by line before turning a final draft in to the printer.

The process then was very much like Washington's position as wartime commander in chief. He called in his officers. Got all sides of the issue. Then he alone made the final call.

The Blessing of Self-Sufficiency

George Washington had a very healthy aversion to professional government service. But the flip side to that was his lifelong fondness for self-reliance.

Not only would Washington have scoffed at the idea of using government as a permanent politician job program, but he would have been dismayed at the dependency it has created in the average citizen. More Americans rely on government today than ever before. From obvious programs, like welfare, to less obvious ones, like federal flood insurance and disaster relief, the federal government touches most citizens every year in one way or another.

Not long ago, I got a lot of flak for saying that a hurricane was a blessing in disguise because it was a reminder that bad things can happen, that we need to be prepared and rely on ourselves and our communities rather than wait for FEMA trucks to roll in. We can be charitable, help our neighbors, and rally around community. One day that FEMA truck may not be there—then what?

George Washington set a great example for self-sufficiency (after all, he had no choice). There was no government to rush in. But if he were alive today, I'm pretty sure he wouldn't sit around after a natural disaster and wait for some bureaucrat to send in food and water.

ORIGINAL INTENT WAS THE ONLY INTENT

Washington's Farewell Address, despite being called an "address," was never given as an actual speech. It was dated September 17, 1796 (the ninth anniversary of the signing of the Constitution), and initially printed in Philadelphia's *American Daily Advertiser*. Soon after that it appeared in numerous other newspapers across the country.

Washington, modest as ever, began by offering his words to his countrymen as the parting counsel of "an old and affectionate friend." He then unequivocally announced that he would not be considered for a third term in the presidency.

I am influenced by no diminution of zeal for your future interest, no deficiency of grateful respect for your past kindness; but am supported by a full conviction that the step is compatible with both.

Always treating his fellow citizens as equals, Washington then mentioned his desire to leave people with some farewell counsel, hoping they would receive it as "the disinterested warnings of a parting friend."

The union of the states was vitally important, he reminded them, cautioning that there were those who would seek "to weaken in your minds the conviction of this truth." Americans must therefore watch "for its preservation with jealous anxiety, discountenancing whatever may suggest even a suspicion that it can in any event be abandoned, and indignantly frowning upon the first dawning of every attempt to alienate any portion of our country from the rest."

Washington had basically just summed up the future of partisanship: lobbyists, biased media, fearmongering "think tanks," and the divisive political environment that plagues our nation today.

He then went on to strike a note of unity. Though different regions of the country often had different needs and interests, he explained, our diversity was our strength. "Your Union ought to be considered as a main prop of your liberty, and . . . the love of the one ought to endear to you the preservation of the other."

The primary support of the Union, other than the people's commitment to liberty, he explained, was the Constitution. "Toward the preservation of your government and the permanency of your present happy state," he wrote, "it is requisite, not only that you steadily discountenance irregular oppositions to its acknowledged authority, but also that you resist with care the spirit of innovation upon its principles, however specious the pretexts. One method of assault may be to effect in the forms of the Constitution alterations which will impair the energy of the system, and thus to undermine what cannot be directly overthrown."

Wow. I know the language doesn't necessarily flow off the tongue, but read that two or three times. He is clearly talking about the idea that people would eventually make the case that the Constitution is outdated and can be improved. Their goal is to simply water down the document through constant "innovations." Is there any better way to summarize what is happening right now? We constantly hear that original intent is irrelevant and that we need a "living document." Of course, if any of the people proposing such a thing took the time to read Washington's farewell then they'd realize that he called them out hundreds of years before they were even born.

No Good-bye to the Farewell

The U.S. Senate retains at least one tradition that has nothing to do with putting its hands into our pockets. Once a year, on Washington's Birthday (as opposed to "Presidents' Day"), a member of the Senate reads Washington's Farewell Address aloud.

This tradition has been going on since 1862, and its history involves a future president. In that Civil War year, Tennessee's U.S. senator Andrew Johnson proposed that "in view of the perilous condition of the country, I think the time has arrived when we should recur back to the days, the times, and the doings of Washington and the patriots of the Revolution, who founded the government under which we live."

Since 1893 members of the Republican and Democratic parties have alternated each year in reading the Farewell Address in the Senate chamber. On finishing, that person then inscribes his or her name into a black, leather-bound book maintained for that purpose and adds brief comments.

In 1956, it was Minnesota's Hubert Humphrey's turn. "It gives one a renewed sense of pride in our republic," wrote the future vice president. "It arouses the wholesome and creative emotions of patriotism and love of country."

MAKING THE CASE

Given how clear Washington was about the need to protect the underlying principles of the Constitution, it makes sense that he then took a good amount of time going through almost each tenet of the document.

1. The Constitution recognizes the existence of natural law. In the Declaration of Independence Thomas Jefferson referred to "the laws of Nature and of Nature's God." Natural law recognizes the existence of God and acknowledges that God established a natural order of things for this earth and the people of this earth.

2. Over and over, Washington made sure to credit God for the success of the revolution. Liberty for man *was* the natural order of things. Washington lived this credo, as we've seen—as a general, as a president, and as a person. It didn't matter who the officeholders were as long as they followed the Constitution. As he reaffirmed in his Farewell Address, we are governed by God and by the Constitution, not by men.

    For the Constitution to work, the citizens of a republic must be virtuous and moral. Benjamin Franklin once wrote, "Only a virtuous people are capable of freedom. As nations become corrupt and vicious, they have more need of masters." Who tried to live their lives more virtuously than Washington? Who acted more bravely and more nobly than the nation's first general and statesman? Who more vigorously applied a code of decent behavior and morality in his personal life than our first president?

Washington strongly believed in the need for morality and virtue among all Americans. He wrote to Lafayette that America's constitutional government would only protect us "so long as there shall remain any virtue in the body of the people." And, in his Farewell Address, he emphasized it again. "Of all the dispositions and habits which lead to political prosperity," he wrote, "religion and morality are indispensable supports."

Washington himself set the finest possible example of that.

Do Sweat the Small Stuff

Modern voters—and especially the media—always ask if presidential candidates have the required "gravitas" (the Roman virtue of seriousness or dignity) for the position. Washington certainly didn't need any help in that department. He understood that paying attention to the details, the discipline of everyday life, was necessary if one was going to do the right thing when the big decisions came along. It seems simple, but it's something that contemporary politicians can't seem to figure out.

Washington, of course, wasn't born with these attributes. God might have put him in the right place at the right time, but he taught himself these virtues at a young age. Sometimes I wonder how my childhood might have been different if I had had the discipline to live the Rules of Civility growing up. It seems impossible to imagine Washington falling into a life of drinking or blowing his money on material possessions when his biggest concern was sitting up straight or crossing his legs in public.

The Rules of Civility let Washington display poise in the small moments and thus gravitas in the big ones. He applied these prescriptions to everyday life and they became second nature. The lesson for us is that leadership and vision don't exist in a vacuum—or spring to life all at once. They must be practiced, and they can grow within you until they become a part of you.

3. The Constitution acknowledges that the people are the true sovereigns in a republican government. The Founders rejected the notion that a king has a "divine right" to rule. Under natural law, no man has a right to rule over another, unless the subject gives his or her consent. Alexander Hamilton emphasized this in the *Federalist:* "The fabric of American empire ought to rest on the solid basis of the consent of the people. The streams of national power ought to flow immediately from that pure, original fountain of all legitimate authority." James Madison added, "The ultimate authority, wherever the derivative may be found, resides in the people alone."

   Washington obviously agreed. "The power under the Constitution will always be in the people," he wrote. And what better way to show the people that he was serious than through his own actions. Washington would not be king. He would not abuse the people's trust. And certainly he would not overstay his welcome. The presidency demanded virtuous men. God and law would take care of the rest.

4. The Constitution was created on the assumption that America would function under a free-market economy, recognizing and protecting property rights. John Adams wrote: "All men are born free and independent, and have certain natural, essential, and unalienable rights, among which may be reckoned the right of enjoying and defending their lives and liberties; that of acquiring, possessing, and protecting property; in fine, that of seeking and obtaining their safety and happiness."

   The federal government the Constitution created was only a protection from tyranny, not a way of life and certainly not a career. It allowed men to worship freely and to trade freely and peacefully among themselves. It granted the protection of property rights—the hallmark of capitalism—and gave men the right to pursue their own happiness.

   It is no wonder that Washington was enthusiastic as he penned his name in large letters at the top of the list of signatures on the Constitution. It is no wonder that even as he left public life he was still teaching us a lesson. And it is no wonder he never took the moniker "His Excellency" to heart.

More Civility

Some of the other Rules of Civility that Washington copied as a young boy:

- "Let your countenance be pleasant, but in serious matters somewhat grave."
- "Show not yourself glad at the misfortune of another, though he were your enemy."
- "In writing or speaking, give to every person his due title according to his degree and the custom of the place."
- "When a man does all he can, though it succeeds not well, blame not him that did it."
- "Strive not with your superiors in argument, but always submit your judgment to others with modesty."
- "Associate yourself with men of good quality if you esteem your own reputation; for 'tis better to be alone than in bad company."
- "Let your conversation be without malice or envy. And in all causes of passion admit reason to govern."
- "Undertake not what you cannot perform, but be careful to keep your promise."
- "When you speak of God and his attributes, let it be seriously and with reverence."
- "Labor to keep alive in your breast that little spark of celestial fire called conscience."

A NEARLY PERMANENT RULING CLASS

For Washington, holding power was the sacrifice; giving it up was easy. Government was something a citizen took part in as a patriotic duty, not a career. It is sadly ironic, then, that this lesson has been forgotten by nearly everyone who now lives in the city named after him.

Time to Move On
Senator Daniel Inouye of Hawaii must be the modern-day opposite of Cincinnatus. He has been a senator for nearly forty-nine years.

Washington probably never could have imagined a professional politician. Yet, these days, there is no shortage of them. Put it this way: twenty-one present senators have served more than twenty years in Congress. *Forty* senators are sixty-five or older and twenty-two are age seventy or older. These are political lifers. This is the ruling class that the Founders feared.

George Washington, on the other hand, is often compared to the great Roman statesman Lucius Quinctius Cincinnatus. Cincinnatus had given up his idyllic life on the farm to serve as Magister Populi— a title giving him all dictatorial powers and the ability to deal decisively with any emergency threatening the republic. Once Rome had defeated its rival tribes and the threat had passed, Cincinnatus voluntarily surrendered those powers and returned to the Roman Senate, and back to plowing his fields and living the life of the average citizen.

The Society of the Cincinnati was an association founded after the Revolutionary War by military officers to honor their own "Cincinnatus" and to "preserve the rights so dearly won; to promote the continuing union of the states; and to assist members in need, their widows, and their orphans."

The society's motto, *Omnia relinquit servare rempublicam*, means "He relinquished everything to serve the Republic."

Not surprisingly, in December 1783, George Washington was elected as the society's first president.

That was all Washington wanted. Throughout his entire career he had fought, both literally and figuratively, against the idea of an American royalty or nobility. Nothing did more to cement that legacy than his voluntary decision to leave the presidency after two terms.

In retrospect, it's not surprising that Washington made another difficult decision—he'd been making them his entire life. The harder the choice, the higher he seemed to rise above it. In the end, he made the hardest decision of all—one that has confounded even the most well intentioned people over the years—he turned his back on power.

Through that act he not only set a precedent for those who would follow him (FDR being the one notable exception), he also set an example for all Americans. After all, it's one thing to talk about raising a standard for the wise and honest—it's another thing to actually do it. We can talk about things like honor and character and humility until we're blue in the face, but if we're not ready to live our lives according to those principles, then we're really no better than those we claim to resent.

Being George Washington was not easy—and neither is attempting to live by the standard he set. But if Washington taught us one thing, it's that doing the easy thing is rarely the right thing, and doing the right thing is rarely easy.

Conclusion

True Greatness Dwells in the Soul

The name of Washington will live when the sculptured marble and statue of bronze shall be crumbled into dust—for it is the decree of the eternal God that "the righteous shall be had in everlasting remembrance, but the memorial of the wicked shall rot."

—RICHARD ALLEN, A FORMER SLAVE,
FROM HIS EULOGY OF GEORGE WASHINGTON, 1799

George Washington's overriding fear in life was that he might be dishonored in death.

His reputation with his family, his fellow countrymen, and his God meant everything to him and it constantly motivated him to become a better person. It's why he taught himself the rules of civility. It's why he was always loyal, honest, and humble. It's why he educated himself on policy, history, science, and human nature. It's why he pushed himself out of his comfort zone time and time again. It's why he did the tough things and made the difficult choices—even when every ounce of his being was pulling him in the opposite direction.

George Washington, like you and I, was a flawed, imperfect man. He was born that way, and he died that way. He had no exceptional powers or unique abilities, except for one: he did not care for public accolades, only private honor. As William Bentley said during one of the many eulogies that were delivered in Washington's honor, "True greatness dwells in the soul." Washington lived his life as though that were his motto. If we live as though it is ours, we will be well on our way to following in his footsteps.

Being George Washington in today's world means a daily struggle between your heart and your brain; between instant gratification and enduring greatness.

Being George Washington means passing up awards, honors, and public admiration in exchange for real honor and the admiration of only those who know you best.

Being George Washington means looking out for our families, our neighbors, and our countrymen—standing for them when they can't stand for themselves. Washington wrote: "How pitiful, in the eye of reason and religion, is that false ambition which desolates the world with fire and sword for the purpose of conquest and fame when compared to the milder virtues of making our neighbors and our fellow men as happy as their frail conditions and perishable natures will permit them." In other words, choose small but real victories over false idols such as fame.

Being George Washington means putting country above party. Washington loathed the idea of partisanship because it "serves always to distract the public councils and enfeeble the public administration. It agitates the community with ill-founded jealousies and false alarm; kindles the animosity of one part against another; foments occasionally riot and insurrection." Have his words ever rung more true? That doesn't mean that we can't disagree on policy—of course we can—but it does mean that we need return to the core ideas of our founding because they are the concepts—life, liberty, and the pursuit of happiness—that all Americans, regardless of party, can agree on.

Being George Washington means becoming a leader. Not of a country or an army, but of yourself, your community, and your own family. It means taking personal responsibility for your actions and holding those around you to the same standard.

Being George Washington means accepting that this country was chosen for Divine protection because the struggle for freedom is worthy of God's protection. It means believing that miracles can happen to all of us because a great Author is writing the script. But it also means not sitting around waiting for them. George Washington certainly didn't wait—and look at what he experienced. As a young man he was a mere subject of the British Crown; as an old man he was one of the few people in the history of the world to ever experience true freedom.

That is a miracle.

What other mortal can lay claim to a legacy that has allowed so many to experience freedom around the world?

We need to continue that legacy, but we've been searching for the "next" George Washington in all the wrong places. The truth is that he doesn't exist—yet. It's up to us to build him—and it starts inside every single one of us.

So the real question is this: Are you willing to lose everything to do what's right?

Washington did. He risked it all—his life, his fortune and his sacred honor—to complete a journey that, quite often, he didn't even want to be on. Nothing less than that level of dedication is required of us today.

Being George Washington will be the hardest thing you ever do. There will be days you'll want to give in, moments where you'll wonder if all of the hard work and personal sacrifices are really worth it. Trust me, they are. You may die without awards, there may not be any monuments built in your honor, and your face may not be printed on our currency, but you'll leave this earth with something else, something far more enduring and valuable: the reverence of your family, friends, and God, all of whom will know that true greatness dwelled in your soul.

Glossary

Aide-de-camp—A personal assistant, secretary, or adjutant to a person of high rank; Washington's aides-de-camp included Hamilton, Lafayette, Joseph Reed (a great critic of Benedict Arnold), and Edmund Randolph (America's first attorney general).

Cock hat—A three-cornered hat worn in colonial times.

Comte—The French equivalent of a count.

Cornet—A now-abolished British and early American military rank, most equivalent to a second lieutenant.

Diphtheria—An illness of the upper respiratory tract.

Dragoon—A light cavalryman.

Drumhead—The portion of a drum formerly made of animal skins (usually lamb, but often goat) upon which the tune was beat.

Durham boat—A flat-bottomed boat used to transport iron, wood, grain, and whiskey. They measured three feet deep and were generally thirty to forty feet in length. On occasion they might reach sixty feet in length. Built originally for the Durham Iron Works in Bucks County, Pennsylvania.

Feu de Joie ("fire of joy")—A celebratory running of musket fire.

Gibbet—The gallows structure upon which a dead criminal was left on public display after his execution.

Grenadier—An elite infantryman. Originally so called because they were specialized in throwing grenades. The high, peaked caps worn by Hessian troops, akin in shape and design to a bishop's mitre, are called "grenadier's caps," even though they might be made of brass.

Guinea—A former unit of British currency. Made of gold and equivalent to twenty shillings. Issued from 1663 to 1813.

Hesse-Kassel—A central German state of the Holy Roman Empire ruled by a "landgrave" or count. The landgrave of Hesse-Kassel at the time of the American Revolution was Friedrich II, uncle of Great Britain's King George III.

Hessian—Specifically refers to a soldier from Hesse-Kassel, which supplied so many mercenaries to Great Britain, but applied broadly to any German mercenary soldier who fought for the British in the Revolutionary War.

Loyalist—An American colonist loyal to the British Crown.

Musket—A muzzle-loaded, flintlock-fired firearm, a predecessor of the modern rifle.

Pleurisy—An inflammation of the cavity surrounding the lungs.

Prussia—Former north German kingdom, which formed the core of the new German Empire in 1871. Famous for its military prowess.

Quinsy—A complication of tonsillitis.

Sloop—In the eighteenth century, a warship with a single gun deck, armed with less than twenty guns.

Spanish dollar—The Spanish dollar was originally a silver coin worth eight reals, and thus the dollars were often called "pieces of eight."

Sugar House—A notorious British prison built in 1763 at lower Manhattan's Duane and Rose streets. Hundreds of American prisoners of war died there from 1776 to 1783.

Tory—A sympathizer of the British; royalist; Loyalist.

Cast of Characters

John Adams (1735–1826)—Massachusetts attorney and patriot. At the Second Continental Congress, Adams will nominate Washington to be commander of the Continental Army. Ambassador to the Netherlands and to Great Britain. Washington's vice president and his successor as president. Appoints Washington commander of the American army in 1798.

Ethan Allen (1738–1789)—Vermont patriot. Alongside Benedict Arnold, Allen's "Green Mountain Boys" will seize Fort Ticonderoga in May 1775. With Washington at Valley Forge.

Major John André (1750–1780)—Cultivated and highly popular chief of British intelligence. A close friend of Benedict Arnold's wife Margaret "Peggy" Shippen. Offered Arnold twenty thousand dollars to betray the American cause. Captured by patriots. Ordered hanged as a spy by Washington.

Major General Benedict "the Hannibal of the Revolution" Arnold (1741–1801)—Connecticut merchant and patriot. The real hero of Ticonderoga, Valcour Bay, and Saratoga. Court-martialed for corruption as military governor of Philadelphia. Arnold's treasonous plot to betray West Point—and Washington—to the British fails and he is appointed as a British brigadier general. Has an illegitimate child in exile in Canada. Dies of dropsy in London.

Margaret "Peggy" Shippen Arnold (1760–1804)—Benedict Arnold's second wife. Member of a prominent Philadelphia family, the daughter of suspected Loyalist judge Edward Shippen IV. Friend of John André.

General John "Gentleman Johnny" Burgoyne (1722–1792)—His march down from Canada is key to the British plan to dividing the colonies and crushing the rebellion. Burgoyne's defeat in the Second Battle of Saratoga in October 1777 is crucial to bringing France into the Revolutionary War on the American side.

General Edward Braddock (1695–1755)—Washington's British commander in the French and Indian War (1754–63). Mortally wounded in the Battle of the Monongahela.

John Cadwalader (1742–1786)—Wealthy Philadelphia merchant and American military officer. Unable to cross the Delaware to join Washington at Trenton. General Howe will occupy Cadwalader's home during the British occupation of Philadelphia. Challenges Horatio to duel following the Conway Cabal affair.

General Sir Henry "the Knight" Clinton (1730–1795)—The final and perhaps the ablest of Britain's three North Americans commanders during the Revolutionary War. Clinton will, nonetheless, tarry in New York City with his mistress, Mary Baddeley, the Irish-born wife of a sergeant in his army, and fail to relieve Cornwallis at Yorktown. Major John André is his adjutant and spymaster.

General Thomas Conway (1735–ca. 1800)—Irish-born French general whom Congress will appoint inspector general of the Continental Army. Ambitious and conceited. At the heart of the Conway Cabal against Washington.

General Charles Cornwallis (1738–1805)—British veteran of the battles of Long Island, Brandywine, Monmouth, and Charleston. Defeated at Princeton. In charge of Britain's Southern Campaign after Henry Clinton's departure for New York. Victorious at Camden and Guilford Courthouse. His surrender at Yorktown effectively ends the Revolutionary War.

Admiral François-Joseph-Paul, Comte de Grasse (1722–1788)—Commander of French naval forces in the West Indies. At General

Rochambeau's urging, the massively built Comte de Grasse will sail northward to trap Cornwallis at Yorktown. Victory in hand, de Grasse will ignore Washington's entreaties to remain in American waters, and return to the Caribbean.

Brigadier General James Ewing (1736–1806)—The western Pennsylvanian who despite valiant efforts failed to ferry his men across the hopelessly ice-choked Delaware River to assist Washington at Trenton.

Benjamin Franklin (1706–1790)—Printer and newspaper editor. Inventor. Author of *Poor Richard's Almanack*. Member of the Committee of Five, which drafts the Declaration of Independence. American envoy to France.

General Thomas Gage (1719 or 1720–1787)—Survivor of the Battle of the Monongahela. British commander at Boston during the Boston Massacre, the march to Lexington and Concord, and the Battle of Bunker Hill. Replaced by William Howe.

General Horatio Gates (1727–1806)—British-born Revolutionary War general. Served alongside Washington during the French and Indian War. Refuses to join Washington before the Battle of Trenton—and connives against him with Congress. American commander at Saratoga. Part of the Conway Cabal. Disgraced at the Battle of Camden.

Edmond-Charles Genêt (1763–1834)—Revolutionary France's incendiary envoy to America. He will try to incite opinion in his nation and against the policy of neutrality practiced by Washington.

Rear Admiral Sir Thomas Graves (1725–1802)—British naval commander at Yorktown, defeated by the Comte de Grasse.

General Nathanael Greene (1742–1786)—The Rhode Island Quaker merchant who became Washington's most-trusted general. Appointed quartermaster general at Valley Forge. His campaign against Cornwallis in the South (including Cornwallis's pyrrhic victory at Guilford Courthouse) helped lead to Yorktown.

Half King (ca. 1700–1754)—Seneca leader (real name: "Tanacharison") allied with the Virginians against the French. With George Washington, he defeats the French under Ensign Jumonville in May 1754.

Alexander Hamilton (1755 or 1757–1804)—West Indian-born aide-de-camp to Washington. Coauthor, with James Madison and John Jay, of the *Federalist* papers. America's first secretary of the Treasury. Rival of Jefferson. Founder of the Federalist Party. Assists with the Farewell Address. Killed in a duel with Aaron Burr.

John Honeyman (1729–1822)—Scottish weaver turned New Jersey farmer. An American spy, key to victory at Trenton.

Admiral Richard Howe (1726–1799)—Brother of General William Howe. He accompanies his brother William on Britain's successful 1776 and 1777 campaigns to capture New York and Philadelphia. Sympathetic to the colonists, he left his command in September 1778. Replaced by Henry Clinton.

Major General Robert Howe (1732–1786)—North Carolina–born Continental Army general. Lost Savannah to the British. Replaced by Benedict Arnold as commandant of West Point. Helped crush January 1781's troop mutiny in New Jersey.

General William Howe (1729–1814)—Second commander of British forces during the Revolutionary War. Howe evacuates Boston after Washington fortifies Dorchester Heights but defeats him at Long Island and Brandywine. Howe's occupation of New Jersey proves disastrous and helps lead to Rall's defeat at Trenton and Cornwallis's defeat at Princeton. In 1777, Howe captures Philadelphia but refuses to move against Washington at Valley Forge. Disgusted with the war, he resigns his command and returns to England in 1778.

John Jay (1745–1829)—New York attorney. President of the Continental Congress (1778–79). Coauthor of the *Federalist* papers. First chief justice of the United States. Negotiator of the controversial Jay Treaty with Britain.

Thomas Jefferson (1743–1826)—Virginia planter. Author of the Declaration of Independence. Governor of Virginia. Minister to France. Washington's first secretary of state. Rival of Alexander Hamilton. Third president of the United States.

Daniel of St. Thomas Jenifer (1723–1790)—Maryland planter. Attended the Mount Vernon conference of 1785. Among the oldest of delegates to the Constitutional Convention.

General Henry "the Ox" Knox (1750–1806)—The 280-pound Boston bookseller who became the Continental Army's chief of artillery. He served at Bunker Hill, during the New York campaign, Trenton, Princeton, Brandywine, Germantown, and Monmouth. Knox's transporting of fifty-nine cannons and mortars from Fort Ticonderoga and Crown Point to Cambridge triggered the British evacuation of Boston. In overall command of December 1776's Delaware crossing.

Marquis de Lafayette (Marie-Joseph Paul Yves Roch Gilbert du Motier) (1757–1834)—Scion of one of the wealthiest families of aristocratic France. Passionate believer in liberty. Volunteer in the Continental Army. Almost a son to the childless Washington. Key to trapping Cornwallis at Yorktown.

Henry Laurens (1724–1792)—South Carolina rice planter and slave merchant. President of the Continental Congress (1777–78). A firm Washington ally. Captured by the British, he will be the only American prisoner in the Tower of London. Exchanged for General Cornwallis. Ultimately opposes slavery.

John Laurens (1754–1782)—Son of Henry Laurens. Aide to Washington. Assisted von Steuben in authoring the army instruction manual. Attempted to raise a black regiment in South Carolina. Helped negotiate Cornwallis's surrender.

General Charles Lee (1732–1782)—British-born Revolutionary War general. Slovenly and strangely ill-mannered for his highborn background. Served alongside Washington during the French and Indian War and later in armies on the European continent. Resentful of Washington. Collaborates with the British after his December 1776 capture by Lieutenant Colonel Banastre Tarleton at Basking Ridge, New Jersey. Disgraced at the Battle of Monmouth.

General Henry "Light Horse Harry" Lee III (1756–1812)—Revolutionary War general. Governor of Virginia. Commander of American forces during the Whiskey Rebellion. Eulogizes Washington as "First in War, first in Peace, and first in the hearts of his Countrymen." Killed by a Democratic-Republic mob in Baltimore.

Richard Henry Lee (1732–1794)—Virginia patriot. Author of the Continental Congress resolution first calling for independence from Britain. Signer of the Declaration of Independence.

William "Billy" or "Will" Lee (ca. 1750–1728)—Washington's slave and personal assistant. He serves with Washington throughout the Revolutionary War. An invalid by the late 1780s. Freed by Washington in his will.

Elizabeth "Betsy" Lloyd Loring (ca. 1752–1831)—Wife of Joshua Loring Jr. Mistress of General William Howe. Howe's tarrying with Betsy Loring may have saved Washington at Valley Forge.

Joshua Loring Jr. (1744–1789)—Loyalist deputy commissary of prisoners. Under his command thousands of American prisoners of war will perish from starvation and disease.

James "Jemmy" Madison (1751–1836)—Virginia-born planter. "Father of the Constitution." Contributor to the *Federalist* papers. Author of the Bill of Rights. Virginia congressman. Drafts the 1792 version of Washington's Farewell Address. Fourth president of the United States.

General Francis "the Swamp Fox" Marion (1732–1795)—South Carolina–born Continental Army officer. Master of guerrilla warfare in the southern campaigns. Given his nickname by Banastre Tarleton.

Luther Martin (**1748–1826**)—Maryland attorney. Delegate to the Constitutional Convention. He will, however, refuse to sign the Constitution. Aaron Burr's defense lawyer in the shooting of Alexander Hamilton.

George Mason (**1725–1792**)—Virginia planter. Author of that state's Declaration of Rights. Delegate to the Constitutional Convention. Refuses to sign the new constitution and argues for a Bill of Rights.

James Monroe (**1758–1831**)—Virginia planter. A member of the advance party at Trenton, where he is seriously wounded in the left shoulder. Secretary of state and of war under James Madison. Fifth president of the United States.

General Daniel Morgan (**1736–1802**)—Commander of Virginia's "Morgan's Riflemen." Poorly educated. Virulently anti-British. Among Washington's able generals and firmest supporters. Defeated Lieutenant Colonel Banastre Tarleton at Cowpens in January 1781.

Gouverneur Morris (**1752–1816**)—Peg-legged New York lawyer and merchant. Influential Pennsylvania delegate to the Constitutional Convention. His hand may have literally "written" most of the Constitution. Ambassador to France.

Robert Morris (**1734–1806**)—Philadelphia banker. "Financier of the American Revolution." Signer of the Declaration of Independence. Hosts Washington during the Constitutional Convention. Sent to debtors prison in 1798.

Colonel Lewis Nicola (**1717–ca. 1807**)—Dublin-born Continental officer. Writes to Washington in May 1782 suggesting Washington assume "the title of king."

Thomas Paine (**1737–1809**)—English-born American pamphleteer. Volunteer in the Philadelphia Associators militia unit. Aide-de-camp to Nathanael Greene. Author of *Common Sense* and *The Crisis* ("These are the times that try men's souls. . . ."). A supporter of the French Revolution, Paine would write *The Rights of Man* before being imprisoned by French revolutionaries.

Colonel Johann Gottlieb "the Hessian Lion" Rall (c. 1726–1776)—Hessian commander at Trenton. Buffeted by attacks from New Jersey patriots, he nonetheless refuses to fortify the town. Killed there by a musket ball as he turns to aid a wounded fellow officer.

Dr. Benjamin Rush (1746–1813)—Philadelphia physician. Signer of the Declaration of Independence. Member of the Continental Congress. Surgeon general of the Middle Department of the Continental Army (1776–77). Persistent harsh critic of Washington. Supporter of the Conway Cabal.

Judge Edward Shippen IV (1729–1806)—Suspected Loyalist. His third daughter is Margaret "Peggy" Shippen, Benedict Arnold's second wife.

Joseph Stansbury (ca. 1742–1809)—London-born Loyalist and Philadelphia china merchant. Commissioner of the city watch during General Howe's occupation. Go-between in the Arnold-André conspiracy.

Gilbert Stuart (1755–1828)—Rhode Island-born portrait painter. His 1796 portrait of Washington is found on the one-dollar bill.

Benjamin Tallmadge (1754–1835)—Washington's New York–born chief intelligence officer. Yale classmate of Nathan Hale. A key to unmasking the Arnold-André conspiracy.

Lieutenant Colonel Banastre "Bloody Ban" Tarleton (1754–1833)—British cavalryman. Infamous for his massacre of surrendered American troops at the Battle of Waxhaw Creek. Captured General Charles Lee at Basking Ridge, New Jersey. Defeated by General Daniel Morgan at Cowpens. Surrendered with Cornwallis at Yorktown.

Count Carl Emilius von Donop (**1732–1777**)—The Hessian colonel who tarried with a beautiful young widow at Mount Holly, New Jersey, and failed to reinforce Colonel Johann Rall at Trenton. Was that widow Betsy Ross? Killed at the Battle of Red Bank.

Baron Friedrich Wilhelm von Steuben (**1730–1794**)—Prussian-born volunteer with the Continental Army—sent to Congress and Washington by Benjamin Franklin in Paris. Despite speaking little if any English at the time, he successfully trains the rebel forces at Valley Forge. Later inspector general of the Continental Army and Washington's chief of staff. A division commander at Yorktown.

George Washington (**1732–1799**)—Father of his country. Virginia planter. Youthful hero of the French and Indian War. Delegate to the first and second Continental Congresses. First commander of the Continental Army (1775–83). President of 1787's Constitutional Convention. First president of the United States (1789–97).

Martha Dandridge Custis Washington (**1731–1802**)—Widow of Virginia planter Daniel Parke Custis. Among the wealthiest women in the colonies. She marries George Washington in January 1759.

Timeline

1732

February 22 [new calendar; February 11 old calendar]—George Washington born at Westmoreland County, Virginia Colony.

1746

September 8—Lawrence Washington writes to Mary Ball Washington requesting permission for George to enter the Royal Navy as a midshipman.

1747

May 19—Joseph Ball writes to his sister Mary Ball Washington advising against George entering the Royal Navy.
Plans to go to sea abandoned upon his mother's plea.
Copies *Rules of Civility & Decent Behavior in Company and Conversation.*
Moves to Mount Vernon to live with Lawrence.

1751

September 28—Travels to Barbados with his half brother Lawrence Washington.
November 17—Shows first signs of smallpox.
December 12—Released from doctor's care for smallpox.
December 22—Departs for return to Virginia.

1752

January 28—Lands at Yorktown.

Spring—Suffers from "a violent pleurisy."

May 20—Writes to William Fauntleroy, requesting to marry his daughter Betsy.

July 26—Death of Lawrence Washington of consumption.

September 1—Joins the Fredericksburg Masonic Lodge.

November 6—Commissioned as a major in the Virginia militia.

1754

May 27—With the Seneca leader Half King defeats the French under Joseph Jumonville; incident starts the French and Indian War.

July 3—Surrenders Fort Necessity to the French under Jumonville's brother Louis.

1755

July 9—French defeat British at the Battle of the Monongahela; Braddock is killed.

August 14—Appointed a colonel and head of Virginia's colonial militia.

1759

January 6—Marries Martha Dandridge Custis.

1773

May 10—Parliament passes the Tea Act.

December 16—Patriots conduct the "Boston Tea Party" at Boston Harbor.

1775

April 19—The battles of Lexington and Concord.

May 10—Fort Ticonderoga captured by Ethan Allen and Benedict Arnold.

May 10—Crown Point captured by Ethan Allen and Benedict Arnold.

June 15—Washington appointed head of the Continental Army.

June 17—The Battle of Bunker Hill.

November 12—Signs order banning recruitment of blacks from the Continental Army.

December 5—Henry Knox commences mission to retrieve artillery from Fort Ticonderoga and Crown Point.

1776

January—Washington lifts ban on black recruitment.

January 10—Thomas Paine publishes *Common Sense*.

January 24—Knox reaches Cambridge with artillery.

June—Allegedly works with Betsy Ross on creation of the American flag.

July 4—American independence proclaimed in Philadelphia.

July 9—Washington celebrates independence in New York City.

September 15—Defeated at the Battle of Kips Bay in Manhattan.

September 15—American spy Nathan Hale is captured and executed.

September 16—Washington defeats Major General Alexander Leslie at the Battle of Harlem Heights.

October 28—Washington defeated at the Battle of White Plains.

November 16—U.S. ship *Andrew Doria* (carrying a copy of the Declaration of Independence) arrives at Sint Eustatius in the Dutch West Indies and is tendered an eleven-gun salute, thus receiving America's first recognition by a foreign power.

November 30—Enlistments of more than two thousand Maryland and New Jersey militiamen expire; they go home.

December 8—British occupy Newport, Rhode Island.

December 13—General Charles Lee captured at Basking Ridge, New Jersey.

December 19—Thomas Paine publishes the first installment of *The Crisis* in the *Pennsylvania Journal* and has additional copies shipped back to him for Washington's army.

December 25—Washington has Paine's *The Crisis* read to his troops.

December 25–26—Crosses Delaware River, defeats Colonel Rall's Hessians at Trenton.

December 30—At Maidenhead (now Lawrenceville), New Jersey, pleads with troops to extend their enlistments.

December 30—Writes to Congress that "free Negroes who have served in the Army, are very much dissatisfied at being discarded."

1777

January 2—Defeats General Charles Cornwallis at the Second Battle of Trenton (also known as the Battle of Assunpink Creek).

January 3—Dr. Rush writes to Patrick Henry criticizing Washington.

January 13—Dr. Rush writes to John Adams criticizing Washington.

January 25—Washington issues proclamation ordering those who had sworn loyalty to the Crown to swear allegiance to the Congress within thirty days.

January 30—Dr. Rush resigns as surgeon general.

February 19—Congress appoints five new major generals—Stirling, Mifflin, St. Clair, Stephen, and Lincoln—bypassing Benedict Arnold.

May 3—Congress promotes Benedict Arnold to major general.

July 11—Arnold submits his resignation to Congress.

July 31—In Philadelphia, Washington first meets the Marquis de Lafayette.

September 3—Washington defeated at the Battle of Brandywine; Lafayette is wounded in the leg.

September 19—The Battle of Freeman's Farm (First Battle of Saratoga); Horatio Gates strips Arnold of his command.

September 21—The Battle of Paoli ("Paoli Massacre").

October 4—Washington defeated at the Battle of Germantown in Pennsylvania.

October 6—British capture Fort Montgomery in New York State.

October 7—Battle of Bemis Heights (Second Battle of Saratoga); Benedict Arnold wounded in the leg.

October 17—General John Burgoyne surrenders at Saratoga.

November 3—General Lord Stirling informs Washington of the Conway Cabal.

November 3—Thomas Mifflin resigns as quartermaster general.

December 19—Washington arrives at Valley Forge.

December 29—General Thomas Conway arrives at Valley Forge; rebuffed by Washington.

1778

January 19—Conway Cabal collapses; Congress supports Washington.

February 4—General Henry Clinton appointed British commander in chief for North America.

February 6—French-American alliance signed in Paris.

February 23—Baron von Steuben arrives at Valley Forge.

February 24—Great Britain declares war on France.

March 2—Nathanael Greene appointed quartermaster general.

May 5—Washington receives word of the American-French alliance.

May 6—At Valley Forge, celebration (*feu de joie* or "fire of joy") of French alliance.

June 8—Martha Washington departs Valley Forge.

June 18—British evacuate Philadelphia; Washington appoints Arnold its military governor.

June 19—Washington leaves Valley Forge.

June 28—Battle of Monmouth.

June—Fortifications at West Point, New York, are named "Fort Arnold."

July 4—Generals Cadwalader and Conway fight a duel in the aftermath of the Conway Cabal.

1779

March 5—Congressional committee clears Arnold of corruption charges.

March 19—Arnold resigns his commission.

April 3—Congress forwards charges against Arnold to Washington.

April 8—Arnold marries Loyalist Margaret "Peggy" Shippen.

May 5—Arnold writes Washington; demands a quick trial.

May 10—Messenger reaches Major John André in New York City with offer from Arnold to defect.

May 21—Arnold sends first encrypted message to the British.

May 31—British land troops on both sides of the Hudson to seize West Point.

June 1—Arnold court-martial commences; interrupted by attack on West Point.

July 2—Congress returns to Philadelphia.

August 6—Major André writes to Peggy Arnold.

August 19—"Light Horse Harry" Lee's victory at Paulus Hook, New Jersey.

September 12—Birth of a son to the Marquis de Lafayette—named "George Washington Lafayette."

1780

January 1—Pennsylvania troops mutiny.

January 26—Court-martial convicts Arnold of two minor counts of corruption.

April 6—Washington officially rebukes Arnold.

May 12—General Cornwallis assumes command of the British southern command.

May 25—Two Connecticut regiments are narrowly dissuaded from deserting.

July 7—Arnold writes to Clinton that he is certain he will receive command of West Point.

July 14—Arnold offers to Clinton to betray West Point for a price.

July 31—Near Stony Point, Washington informs Arnold that he is being restored to active command (left wing of Washington's main army); Arnold declines.

August 3—Washington appoints Arnold as commandant of West Point, replacing General Robert Howe.

September 11—Planned meeting of Benedict Arnold and Major André fails to occur.

September 17—Washington meets with Arnold at Joshua Smith's house.

September 18—Crosses the Hudson on Arnold's barge on way to Hartford.

September 21—Arnold dispatches Joshua Smith to *Vulture* to fetch André to him.

September 25—Arnold learns of Andre's capture and flees to the *Vulture;* Washington inspects West Point, later learns of Andre's capture; orders Arnold's arrest; Arnold writes to Washington.

September 27—Peggy Arnold leaves for Philadelphia.

September 29—Board of Inquiry convicts André of espionage.

October 2—André executed at Tappan, New York.

1781

January 5—British forces under Arnold burn Richmond.

January 20—New Jersey troops mutiny at Pompton, New Jersey.

January 21—Washington orders General Robert Howe to crush the New Jersey mutineers.

January 27—Two New Jersey mutineers executed.

March 1—Articles of Confederation ratified.

August 1—Cornwallis occupies Yorktown.

September 5—French naval forces defeat the British in the Battle of the Virginia Capes; trap Cornwallis.

September 6—Arnold leads attack on New London, Connecticut.

September 9—Washington arrives at Mount Vernon; first visit home in the course of the war.

September 11—Admiral Graves orders HMS *Terrible* scuttled.

September 28—Siege of Yorktown commences.

October 19—Cornwallis surrenders.

1782

February 27—The British House of Commons votes against continuing the war.

March 22—The Washingtons depart Philadelphia for army headquarters at Newburgh, New York.

March 31—The Washingtons arrive at Newburgh.

May 22—Washington responds to Colonel Lewis Nicola.

August 7—Establishes the Order of the Purple Heart.

1783

March 15—Washington speech to officers at Newburgh.

September 3—Treaty of Paris grants American independence.

December 23—Resigns his commission.

1786–87

Shays's Rebellion disrupts Massachusetts.

1787

February 21—Continental Congress authorizes Constitutional Convention.

May 13—Arrives in Philadelphia for Constitutional Convention.

May 14—Delegates arrive for the scheduled start of Constitutional Convention but lack a quorum.

May 25—A quorum is reached; Washington is unanimously selected as Constitutional Convention's president.

May 29—Edmund Randolph submits Virginia Plan to Constitutional Convention.

June 15—New Jersey plan presented to Constitutional Convention.

July 2—States deadlock on Connecticut motion for senatorial representation; committee appointed to draft a compromise.

July 16—Constitutional Convention passes Benjamin's Franklin's compromise proposal on legislative representation 5–4.

July 24—Five-man committee appointed to draft a constitution.

July 26–August 6—Constitutional Convention adjourns.

September 12—"Committee of Style" begins work on final draft of U.S. Constitution.

September 12—Constitutional Convention receives final draft of Constitution.

October 27—Publication of the first of the *Federalist* papers.

December 7—Delaware becomes first state to ratify Constitution.

1788

June 21—New Hampshire becomes the ninth state to ratify Constitution; it takes effect.

June 25—Virginia ratifies Constitution.

July 26—New York ratifies Constitution, but with a recommendation that a bill of rights be enacted.

August—Publication of the last of the *Federalist* papers.

September 13—Continental Congress declares Constitution to be in effect; declares New York City to be the nation's capital.

1789

January 7—First presidential electors selected.

February 4—Electors unanimously elect Washington president.

April 16—Washington leaves Mount Vernon to assume the presidency.

April 30—Inaugurated president at New York City's Federal Hall.

July 14—Fall of the Bastille in France.

August 26—Death of Washington's mother, Mary Ball Washington.

1790

May 29—Rhode Island is the last of the original thirteen states to ratify the Constitution.

May—Washington writes to the Jewish congregation of Savannah.

August—Letter to Hebrew Congregation at Newport.

December—Writes to the Hebrew Congregations of Philadelphia, New York, Charleston, and Richmond.

Capital is relocated from New York to Philadelphia.

1791

March—Passage of the Whiskey Excise Tax.

September—Convention to oppose Whiskey Excise Tax held in Pittsburgh.

September 11—Tax collectors tarred and feathered in Washington County, Pennsylvania. Washington tours the South.

December 15—Bill of Rights is ratified on Virginia's action.

1792

July—The first United States coinage is minted—the "half-disme."

September 15—Washington issues proclamation denouncing illegal resistance to Whiskey Excise Tax.

October 13—Lays cornerstone of the White House.

December 5—Reelected president.

1793

January 21—King Louis XVI of France guillotined.

April 8—Citizen Edmond Genêt arrives in the United States, at Charleston.

November 10—French Constituent Assembly authorizes a "Goddess of Reason."

November 22—Protestors against Whiskey Excise Tax break into the home of tax collector Benjamin Wells in Fayette County, Pennsylvania.

December 29—Thomas Paine arrested by the French revolutionaries.

1793-1794

British seize hundreds of American ships on the high seas.

1794

August 1—Seven thousand anti-Whiskey Excise Tax protestors gather at Braddock's Field, talk of burning Pittsburgh and seceding from the Union.

August 4—U.S. Supreme Court justice James Wilson certifies that western Pennsylvania is in a state of rebellion.

August 7—Washington summons the militia to quash the Whiskey Rebellion.

1796

March 15—Washington submits Madison's four-year-old draft of Washington's Farewell Address to Hamilton for review.

December 7—Washington gives last message to Congress; proposes establishment of a navy and a military academy.

December 7—Electors cast votes for the presidency—Adams defeats Jefferson.

1797

March 4—Leaves the presidency; John Adams inaugurated.

1798

July 7—Washington appointed by John Adams to command the American army in anticipation of war with France (effective July 4).

July 9—Prepares will, frees Billy Lee on his death and grants Lee a life pension; frees remainder of his slaves upon Martha's death.

1799

December 13—Composes his last letter (to his farm manager).

December 14—Dies at Mount Vernon.

December 18—Body interred at Mount Vernon.

December 26—Huge memorial services held for Washington in Philadelphia; "Light Horse Harry" Lee eulogizes Washington as "First in War, first in Peace, and first in the hearts of his Countrymen."

1801

January 1—Will takes effect.

1802

May 22—Death of Martha Washington.

George Washington, in His Own Words

Perhaps no person in history has had more written about him than George Washington. But despite all of the analysis and commentary published over the centuries, the best way to really get to know the man is to read his own words. Below is a selection of quotes, sorted alphabetically by topic, from Washington's own speeches, letters, and orders. Many of these quotes are not famous, but I think they give great insight into the person George Washington really was—and what it will take to become him today.

ADVANCEMENT, Should Stem from Own Efforts.—Let your promotion result from your own application and from intrinsic merit, not from the labors of others. The last would prove fallacious and expose you to the reproach of the daw in borrowed feathers.—To George Washington Parke Custis. (1796)

AMERICA, To Be Preserved by God.—It is indeed a pleasure, from the walks of private life, to view in retrospect all the meanderings of our past labors, the difficulties through which we have waded, and the fortunate haven to which the ship has been brought! Is it possible after this that it should founder? Will not the all-wise and all-powerful Director of human events preserve it? I think he will. He may, however (for wise purposes not discoverable by finite minds), suffer our indiscretions and folly to place our national character low in the political scale; and this, unless more wisdom and less prejudice take the lead in our governments, will most assuredly be the case.—To Jonathan Trumbull. (1784)

AMERICA, To Be an Example to All the World.—It should be the highest ambition of every American to extend his views beyond himself, and to bear in mind that his conduct will not only affect himself, his country, and his immediate posterity, but that its influence may be co-extensive with the world and stamp political happiness or misery on ages yet unborn. To establish this desirable end, and to establish [a] government of laws, the union of these states is absolutely necessary; therefore in every proceeding, this great, this important object should ever be kept in view; and so long as our measures tend to this, and are marked with the wisdom of a well-informed and enlightened people, we may reasonably hope, under the smiles of Heaven, to convince the world that the happiness of nations can be accomplished by pacific revolutions in their political systems, without the destructive intervention of the sword.—To the legislature of Pennsylvania. (1789)

ARMY, An Appeal for Christian Soldiers.—The General hopes and trusts that every officer and man will endeavor so to live and act as becomes a Christian soldier defending the dearest rights and liberties of his country.—General Orders. (1776)

ARTICLES OF CONFEDERATION, Too Weak to Build Unity.— I see one head gradually changing into thirteen. I see one army branching into thirteen; and instead of looking up to Congress as the supreme controlling power of the United States, [these armies] are considering themselves as dependent on their respective states. In a word, I see the powers of Congress declining too fast for the consequence and respect which is due to them as the grand representative body of America, and am fearful of the consequences of it.—To Joseph Jones. (1780)

ARTICLES OF CONFEDERATION, Must Be Revised.—That it is necessary to revise and amend the Articles of Confederation, I entertain no doubt; but what may be the consequences of such an attempt is doubtful. Yet something must be done, or the fabric must fall, for it certainly is tottering.—To John Jay. (1786)

BORROWING, A Dangerous Practice.—There is no practice more dangerous than that of borrowing money; . . . for when money can be had in this way, repayment is seldom thought of in time, the interest becomes a moth, exertions to raise it by dint of industry cease, it comes easy and is spent freely, and many things indulged in that would never be thought of if [they were] to be purchased by the sweat of the brow. In the meantime, the debt is accumulating like a snowball in rolling.—To Samuel Washington. (1797)

CHARITY, Advice on Giving.—Let your *heart* feel for the affliction and distresses of everyone; let your *hand* give in proportion to your purse, remembering always the estimation of the widow's mite. But . . . it is not everyone who asketh that deserveth charity; all, however, are worthy of the inquiry, or the deserving may suffer.—To Bushrod Washington. (1783)

CONGRESS, The People's Representatives.—Congress are in fact but the people; they return to them at certain short periods [and] are amenable at all times for their conduct. . . . What interest, therefore, can a man have, under these circumstances, distinct from his constituents?—To Governor Benjamin Harrison. (1783)

CONSCIENCE, Often Comes Too Late.—Conscience . . . seldom comes to a man's aid while he is in the zenith of health and revelling in pomp and luxury upon ill-gotten spoils; it is generally the *last* act of his life, and comes too late to be of much service to others here, or to himself hereafter.—To John Price Posey. (1782)

CONSTITUTION (U.S.), Future Generations Qualified to Amend— Is there not a constitutional door open for alterations or amendments? And is it not likely that real defects will be as readily discovered after as before trial? And will not our successors be as ready to apply the remedy as ourselves, if occasion should require it? To think otherwise will, in my judgment, be ascribing more of the *amor patria*, more wisdom, and more virtue to ourselves than I think we deserve.—To Henry Knox. (1787)

CONSTITUTION (U.S.), God's Hand in Framing and Adoption of.— A few short weeks will determine the political fate of America for the present generation and [will] probably produce no small influence on the happiness of society through a long succession of ages to come. Should everything proceed with harmony and consent according to our actual wishes and expectations, I will confess to you sincerely, my dear Marquis, it will be so much beyond anything we had a right to imagine or expect eighteen months ago that it will demonstrate as visibly the finger of Providence as any possible event in the course of human affairs can ever designate it. It is impracticable for you or anyone who has not been on the spot to realize the change in men's minds and the progress towards rectitude in thinking and acting which will then have been made.—To the Marquis de Lafayette. (1788)

CONSTITUTION (U.S.), Changes in, to Be Made with Care.—In all the changes to which you may be invited, remember that time and habit are at least as necessary to fix the true character of governments as of other human institutions; that experience is the surest standard by which to test the real tendency of the existing constitution of a country; that facility in changes upon the credit of mere hypotheses and opinion exposes to perpetual change, from the endless variety of hypotheses and opinion. And remember, especially, that for the efficient management of your common interests in a country so extensive as ours, a government of as much vigor as is consistent with the perfect security of liberty is indispensable. Liberty itself will find in such a government, with powers properly distributed and adjusted, its surest guardian.—Farewell Address. (1796)

CURRENCY, A Strong, Basic to National Well-being.—Every other effort is in vain unless something can be done to restore [the currency's] credit. Congress, the states individually, and individuals of each state should exert themselves to effect this great end . . . But it is virtue alone that can effect it.—To Edmund Pendleton. (1779)

DEMOCRACY, Limitation of.—It is among the evils, and perhaps is not the smallest [evil], of democratical governments that the people must *feel* before they will *see*; when this happens they are roused to action. Hence it is that this form of government is so slow.—To Henry Knox. (1787)

EDUCATION, Evils of Foreign.—It has always been a source of serious regret with me to see the youth of these United States sent to foreign countries for the purpose of education, often before their minds were formed or they had imbibed any adequate ideas of the happiness of their own, contracting, too frequently, not only habits of dissipation and extravagance, but principles unfriendly to republican government and to the true and genuine liberties of mankind, which thereafter are rarely overcome.—Last Will and Testament. (1799)

FINANCES, Policies for National.—As a very important source of strength and security, cherish public credit. One method of preserving it is to use it as sparingly as possible, avoiding occasions of expense by cultivating peace, but remembering also that timely disbursements to prepare for danger frequently prevent much greater disbursements to repel it; avoiding likewise the accumulation of debt, not only by shunning occasions of expense, but by vigorous exertions in time of peace to discharge the debts which unavoidable wars may have occasioned, not ungenerously throwing upon posterity the burden which we ourselves ought to bear.—Farewell Address. (1796)

FREEDOM, Washington's Love of.—Born, sir, in a land of liberty, having early learned its value, having engaged in a perilous conflict to defend it, having, in a word, devoted the best years of my life to secure its permanent establishment in my own country, my anxious recollections, my sympathetic feelings, and my best wishes are irresistibly excited whensoever, in any country, I see an oppressed nation unfurl the banners of freedom.—To the French minister. (1796)

GOD, Washington's Life Preserved by.—By the miraculous care of Providence, that protected me beyond all human expectation, I had four bullets through my coat and two horses shot under me, and yet escaped unhurt.—To John Augustine Washington. (1755)

GOD, Washington's Gratitude to.—Providence has a . . . claim to my humble and grateful thanks for its protection and direction of me through the many difficult and intricate scenes which this contest has produced, and for the constant interposition in our behalf when the clouds were heaviest and seemed ready to burst upon us.—To Landon Carter. (1778)

I am . . . grateful to that Providence which has directed my steps, and shielded me through the various changes and chances through which I have passed, from my youth to the present moment.—To the Reverend William Gordon. (1797)

GOD, Intervention of, in Establishing America.—It having pleased the Almighty Ruler of the Universe propitiously to defend the cause of the united American states, and finally, by raising us up a powerful friend among the princes of the earth [i.e., France], to establish our liberty and independence [upon] lasting foundations, it becomes us to set apart a day for gratefully acknowledging the divine goodness and celebrating the important event which we owe to his benign interposition.—General Orders. (1778)

The hand of Providence has been so conspicuous in all this that he must be worse than an infidel that lacks faith, and more than wicked that has not gratitude enough to acknowledge his obligations.—To Thomas Nelson. (1778)

When I contemplate the interposition of Providence, as it was manifested in guiding us through the revolution, in preparing us for the reception of a general government, and in conciliating the good will of the people of America towards one another after its adoption, I feel myself . . . almost overwhelmed with a sense of the divine munificence.—To the mayor, recorder, aldermen, and common council of Philadelphia. (1789)

No people can be bound to acknowledge and adore the invisible hand, which conducts the affairs of men, more than the people of the United States. Every step by which they have advanced to the character of an independent nation seems to have been distinguished by some token of providential agency.—First Inaugural Address. (1789)

The success which has hitherto attended our united efforts we owe to the gracious interposition of Heaven, and to that interposition let us gratefully ascribe the praise of victory and the blessings of peace.—To the Executive of New Hampshire. (1789)

I am sure there never was a people who had more reason to acknowledge a divine interposition in their affairs than those of the United States; and I should be pained to believe that they have forgotten that agency which was so often manifested during our revolution, or that they failed to consider the omnipotence of that God who is alone able to protect them.—To John Armstrong. (1792)

Without the beneficent interposition of the Supreme Ruler of the universe, we could not have reached the distinguished situation which we have attained with such unprecedented rapidity. To him, therefore, should we bow with gratitude and reverence, and endeavor to merit a continuance of his special favors.—To the General Assembly of Rhode Island. (1797)

GOD, All Nations Should Pay Homage to.—It is the duty of all nations to acknowledge the providence of Almighty God, to obey his will, to be grateful for his benefits, and humbly to implore his protection and favor.—Thanksgiving Proclamation. (1789)

GOD, The Author of All Good.—That great and glorious Being . . . is the beneficent Author of all the good that was, that is, or that will be.—Thanksgiving Proclamation. (1789)

HONESTY, And Common Sense, Needed for a Nation to Prosper.—It appears to me that little more than common sense and common honesty in the transactions of the community at large would be necessary to make us a great and a happy nation.—To the citizens of Baltimore. (1789)

LIBERTY, Future of, Depends on American Experiment.—The preservation of the sacred fire of liberty and the destiny of the republican model of government are justly considered as deeply, perhaps as finally, staked on the experiment entrusted to the hands of the American people.—First Inaugural Address. (1789)

MONEY, Borrowing.—There is no practice more dangerous than that of borrowing money.—To Samuel Washington. (1797)

MORAL CHARACTER, Of Greatest Importance.—A good moral character is the first essential in a man. . . . It is therefore highly important that you should endeavor not only to be learned but virtuous.—To George Steptoe Washington. (1790)

PEACE, And Military Preparedness.—If we are wise, let us prepare for the worst; there is nothing which will so soon produce a speedy and honorable peace as a state of preparation for war.—To James McHenry. (1782)

POLITICAL PARTIES, A Threat to Liberty.—If we mean to support the liberty and independence which it has cost us so much blood and treasure to establish, we must drive far away the demon of party spirit and local reproach.—To Governor Arthur Fenner. (1790)

POLITICS, Washington's Guiding Principle in.—I have no object separated from the general welfare to promote. I have no predilections, no prejudices to gratify, no friends whose interests or views I wish to advance at the expense of propriety.—To James McHenry. (1799)

PRINCIPLE, Will Triumph.—In times of turbulence, when the passions are afloat, calm reason is swallowed up in the extremes to which measures are attempted to be carried; but when those subside and the empire of [reason] is resumed, the man who acts from principle, who pursues the paths of truth, moderation, and justice, will regain his influence.—To John Luzac. (1797)

RELIGIOUS TOLERATION, And Leaving Judgment to God.—Avoid all disrespect to or contempt of the religion of the country and its ceremonies. Prudence, policy, and a true Christian spirit will lead us to look with compassion upon their errors without insulting them. While we are contending for our own liberty, we should be very cautious of violating the fights of conscience in others, ever considering that God alone is the judge of the hearts of men, and to him only in this case they are answerable.—Instructions to Benedict Arnold. (1775)

REPUTATION, The Kind to Seek.—The good opinion of honest men, friends to freedom and well-wishers to mankind, wherever they may be born or happen to reside, is the only kind of reputation a wise man would ever desire.—To Edward Pemberton. (1788)

SHAYS'S REBELLION, Washington's Reaction to.—I am mortified beyond expression when I view the clouds that have spread over the brightest morn that ever dawned upon any country. . . . My humble opinion is that there is a call for decision. Know precisely what the insurgents aim at. If they have real grievances, redress them if possible, or acknowledge the justice of them and your inability to do it in the present moment. If they have not, employ the force of government against them at once. If this is inadequate, all will be convinced that the superstructure is bad, or wants support. To be more exposed in the eyes of the world, and more contemptible than we already are, is hardly possible.—To Henry Lee. (1786)

SLAVERY, Abolition of.—There is not a man living who wishes more sincerely than I do to see a plan adopted for the abolition of [slavery]; but there is only one proper and effectual mode by which it can be accomplished, and that is by legislative authority; and this, as far as my suffrage will go, shall never be wanting.—To Robert Morris. (1786)

SLAVES, Liberated in Washington's Will.—Upon the decease of my wife, it is my will and desire that all the slaves which I hold in my own right shall receive their freedom.—Last Will and Testament. (1799)

SLAVES, Old and Infirm, Provided for in Washington's Will.—And whereas, among those who will receive freedom according to this device, there may be some who from old age or bodily infirmities . . . will be unable to support themselves, it is my will and desire that all . . . shall be comfortably clothed and fed by my heirs while they live.—Last Will and Testament. (1799)

SLEEP, Rise Early from.—Rise early, that by habit it may become familiar, agreeable, healthy, and profitable. It may for a while be irksome to do this; but that will wear off, and the practice will produce a rich harvest forever thereafter, whether in public or private walks of life.—To George Washington Parke Custis. (1798)

VIRTUE, Public, Needed to Safeguard the Constitution.—The [federal] government . . . can never be in danger of degenerating into a monarchy, an oligarchy, an aristocracy, or any other despotic or oppressive form so long as there shall remain any virtue in the body of the people.—To the Marquis de Lafayette. (1788)

VIRTUE, And Happiness.—There is no truth more thoroughly established than that there exists, in the economy and course of nature, an indissoluble union between virtue and happiness, between duty and advantage, between the genuine maxims of an honest and magnanimous policy and the solid rewards of public prosperity and felicity.—First Inaugural Address. (1789)

WASHINGTON (George), Humility of.—I wish . . . it were more in my power than it is to answer the favorable opinion my friends have conceived of my abilities. Let them not be deceived; I am unequal to the task [of commanding Virginia's military forces], and do assure you it requires more experience than I am master of to conduct an affair of the importance that this is now arisen to.—To Charles Lewis. (1755)

When I contemplate the interposition of Providence, as it was manifested in guiding us through the revolution, in preparing us for the reception of a general government, and in conciliating the good will of the people of America towards one another after its adoption, I feel myself . . . almost overwhelmed with a sense of the divine munificence. I feel that nothing is due to my personal agency in all these complicated and wonderful events, except what can simply be attributed to the exertions of an honest zeal for the good of my country.—To the mayor, recorder, aldermen, and common council of Philadelphia. (1789)

WASHINGTON (George), His Devotion to Duty.—You ask how I am to be rewarded for all this? There is one reward that nothing can deprive me of, and that is the consciousness of having done my duty with the strictest rectitude and most scrupulous exactness; that if we should ultimately fail in the present contest, it is not owing to the want of exertion in me.—To Lund Washington. (1780)

WASHINGTON (George), **Too Modest to Write His Memoirs.**— Any memoirs of my life, distinct and unconnected with the general history of the war, would rather hurt my feelings than tickle my pride while I lived. I had rather glide gently down the stream of life, leaving it to posterity to think and say what they please of me, than by any act of mine to have vanity or ostentation imputed to me. . . . I do not think vanity is a trait of my character.—To Dr. James Craik. (1784)

WASHINGTON (George), **His Attitude Toward Death.**—Do not flatter me with vain hopes; I am not afraid to die, and therefore can bear the worst. . . . Whether tonight or twenty years hence makes no difference; I know that I am in the hands of a good Providence.—Spoken to Dr. Samuel Bard, attending surgeon. (1790)

**Stay in touch with Glenn as you continue on your
lifelong journey to being George Washington**

• Nightly *Glenn Beck* program,
available live and on-demand: www.gbtv.com

• Get Glenn's free daily newsletter: www.glennbeck.com

• Follow Glenn on Facebook: http://www.facebook.com/GlennBeck